Y

# YORKSHIRE

HARRY J. SCOTT

ILLUSTRATED
AND WITH MAP

ROBERT HALE · LONDON

© *Harry J. Scott 1965 and 1977*

First published 1965 as *Portrait of Yorkshire*. Reprinted 1965. Revised 1970 and 1973.

*This edition first published 1977*

ISBN 0 7091 6245 6 (*paperback*)
ISBN 0 7091 1842 2 (*hardcover*)

Robert Hale Limited
Clerkenwell House
Clerkenwell Green
London EC1

Printed in Great Britain by
Jarrold and Sons Ltd, Norwich

# Contents

| | | |
|---|---|---|
| I | THE MOSAIC OF YORKSHIRE | 9 |
| II | PENNINE COUNTRY | |
| | The Northern Dales | 23 |
| | The Southern Dales | 59 |
| III | TEESDALE | 89 |
| IV | THE MEN OF THE MOORS | 98 |
| V | THE COAST AND THE WOLDS | 123 |
| VI | YORK AND ITS PLAIN | 152 |
| VII | INDUSTRIAL YORKSHIRE | 172 |
| VIII | HULL AND THE HUMBER | 194 |
| IX | YORKSHIRE FOLK | 199 |
| | *Index* | 203 |

# ILLUSTRATIONS

1   Penyghent, showing limestone scars and drystone walls

*facing page* 48

2   Bare fells—Cautley Spout             49

3   Richmond in Swaledale             64

4   High Force, Teesdale             65

5   Bowes Museum, modelled on a French château     80

6   Looking across the York Plain from Sutton Bank    81

7   The market town of Pickering         96

8   Whitby, where the Esk joins the sea       97

9   The South Bay at Scarborough        112

10  Flamborough Lighthouse           113

11  York Minster viewed from the walls      128

12  Knaresborough on the Nidd         129

13  Old and new Bradford           144

14  An early woolcombing machine        145

15  Queen's Gardens, Hull—once a busy dock     160

16  The end of Yorkshire—Spurn Point      161

Map                        *pages* 12–13

ACKNOWLEDGEMENTS

The copyright photographs listed above were supplied
by the following: Nos. 1–10, 12–14 and 16, Mr. W. R.
Mitchell of Settle; No. 11, Mr. J. Edenbrow of Leeds;
No. 15, Mr. A. N. Jefferies of Clapham.

# I

## THE MOSAIC OF YORKSHIRE

SOME years ago in a field near Rudston in the East Riding of Yorkshire I looked upon a recently excavated Roman pavement, since removed entire to a Hull museum. It was made up of hundreds of tiny stone cubes, like sugar lumps of various colours, worked not only into a geometrical pattern but also into a lively picture of Venus at her Bath, complete with the apple given to her by Paris and a back-scratcher! In little heaps by this tessellated pavement were more stones sorted into colours for the improvement of the picture. From this raw material the mosaic had been built up stone by stone by its artist. As each piece was added the portrait of Venus sprang to life. It became a living whole.

In some such way a portrait of the vast county of Yorkshire, with close upon four million acres (as many as there are letters in the Bible, we are told) and some five million people (more than some Continental states), might come to life exhibiting a unity not otherwise visible in its immensity of separate parts. For in seeking to portray Yorkshire the artist has a double task. First to differentiate between the county as a whole and the rest of England, so that its individual character is made clear, and then to differentiate between the parts of this whole so that they may be seen as distinct from each other even though they form a single county.

To think of it in another medium, Yorkshire spreads a vast canvas which demands broad sweeping strokes to depict those broad acres which stretch from the east coast of England to within a mere twenty miles or so of the west coast, and from Mickle Fell and its offspring, the Tees, in the North to the broad Humber in the south. Yet it has a multiplicity of detail which gives tone and value to the picture. Physically it is a four-dimensional subject, for it has not only length and breadth and height, but it has, in its limestone underworld, depth also. Historically, it is a conspectus of man in Britain, with his evidences from the Bronze Age relics on its heather-clad moors to the present-day

9

early-warning station of the Radar Age at Fylingdale. Industrially, its basic livelihood comes from the great urban products of coal and steel and their rural counterpart, wool. Its farming, whether of sheep or of crops, is in general, on the extensive rather than the intensive scale. Yet it has a thousand other and ancillary trades, many of them of no mean size.

Unlike those counties which are small and neat and compact, containing much treasure in a limited area, Yorkshire is wide and sprawling and generous in its offerings, whether it be extensive moorland or broad dale, high unbounded fell-tops or rich lush plains which carry the eye to still more extensive hills. Yet every mile of this country has its own particular delights. Its rivers, like the fingers of an open hand, begin as tiny trickles in the hills but waste no time in swelling out, after much tumbling over falls, to sizeable streams and are soon broad full-bosomed rivers sweeping—as most of them do—into one great magnificent Humber which has about it something of the breadth of an American river highway.

Is it possible to think of this Yorkshire as possessing a distinctive unity setting it apart from other regions of Britain? Has it that "wholeness" which certain geographers have sought to find in some areas against other areas? There are parts of Britain, as in East Anglia, where landscape, the familiar physical scene and natural features, offers a satisfying unity. Elsewhere, as north of the Border, a territory is most clearly politically or historically defined even though there is no common factor in the physical landscape. Again, in the Welsh coalfields or in textile Lancashire, economic causes may create a regional uniformity which sets a county or a territory apart. Or it may be something more vague and undefinable, some hidden quality, which yet exhibits a united whole to the observer. In a region of the vastness of Yorkshire with its variety of landscape, its troubled historic past, its many-streamed economic life—which all point to diversity rather than unity—it seems to me that the concept of the mosaic in which, the dictionary tells us, "a picture is produced by joining together small pieces of glass or stone of different colours to make a whole", may help to emphasize the uniting factor in this diversity and to portray the features and character of this region in a way otherwise impossible.

The question comes, can the same method be applied to the other half of the task, to illuminate those differences which exist between one part of this great county and another and provide its fascinating variety? Perhaps it may. Sometimes the landscape points the difference, or the architecture, or the place names. More often it is the lesser things—the shapes and colour of buses, the local flora, the particular smell of the streets or the odour of a trade—which provides the label to the part. No such analysis can be wholly exact for there is much that is common to them all including an intense county loyalty which often blurs sharp distinctions. Yet Yorkshire, as you learn its secrets, does reveal its variety. If the soil under your feet is red and heavy and the roofs are pantiled and those you meet speak of "Thoo" and "Hoo" you may venture to guess you are in its north-east corner. If the speech is hard and gritty like the drab black-brown moors about you and there is the bitter-sweet tang of textiles everywhere, then you are probably in the Holmfirth district near Huddersfield or perhaps Halifax, in the West Riding. If you are sitting on a dry-stone wall and there are limestone crags as a framework to the landscape and the grass is a particularly green grass, you may be anywhere in the western dale country; only the breed of sheep grazing nearby or a subtle change in the tone of the limestone will tell you precisely where. These are the background tones of the mosaic.

The towns can offer more detailed distinctions. If the houses are of yellow brick and the great walls which surround them are creamy white and you encounter flocks of cyclists in every street, without doubt you are in York itself. But if you sit in a café where the waitress calls you "Loov", and over and around every table there are shopping baskets and their broad-bosomed owners, and the talk is of Women's Institute rallies or Methodist love-feasts, then it is fairly evident you are in one of the market towns of the Pennine country. Such distinctions in an impressionistic way I have tried to convey in these pages, always aware that every generalization is beset by exceptions. It is in the sum of these impressions set against the background of the land that I feel a portrait may emerge that is not too far from truth.

There was a time when the fragments which make up Yorkshire were more clearly distinct than they are now. Each village was once a self-contained community in which a stranger was a foreigner, an "off-comed un" to be distrusted if not ejected. Even today there is a protective jealousy between one borough and another and between one rural area and its neighbour—a jealousy born of pride in those very differences between them. In one sense we must be grateful that this spirit lives on to counter the dead hand of uniformity in modern development. In particular our northern towns and cities are undergoing transformation at a rate that will completely change their appear-

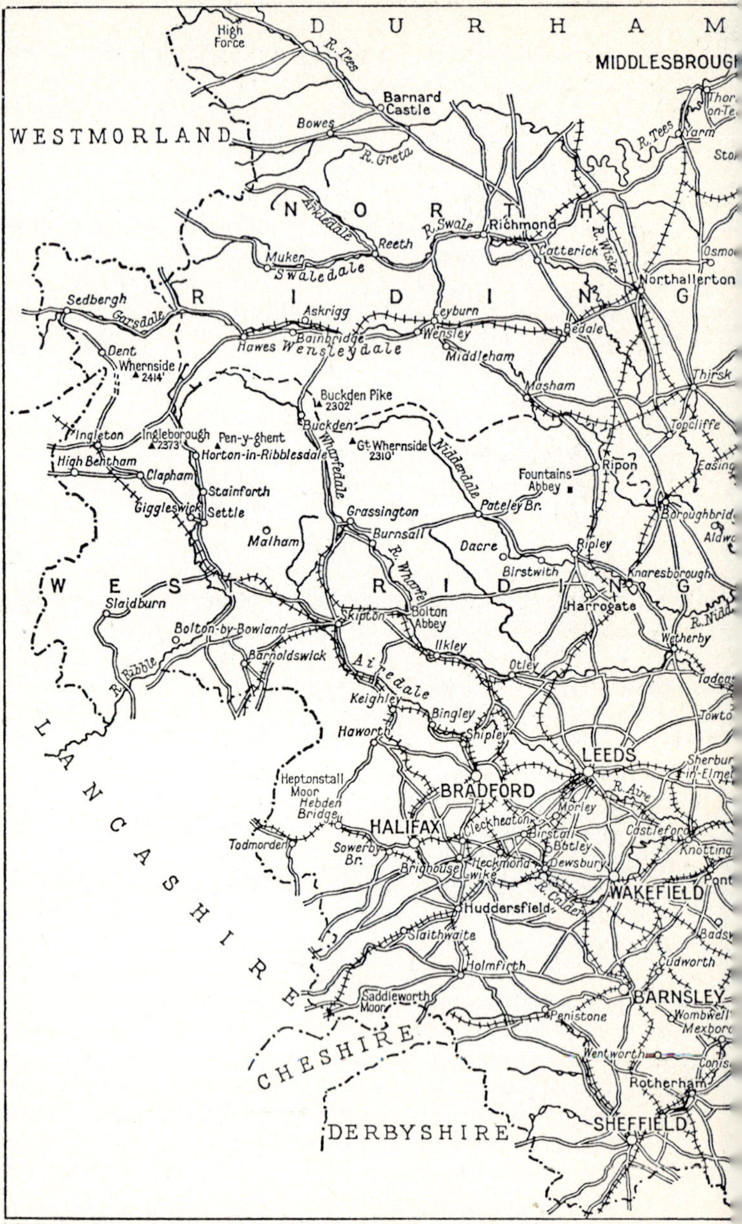

# YORKSHIRE

**NORTH SEA**

Redcar
Saltburn-by-the-Sea
Brotton
Loftus
Guisborough
Hinderwell
Whitby
Danby
Hawsker
Egton
Castleton
Robin Hood's Bay
Grosmont
Ravenscar
oughton
op Gate
Bilsdale
Goathland
NORTH
MOORS
R. Esk
R. Murindale
Clougton
Lastingham
Rosedale
Lockton
R. Severn
Kirkby
Moorside
Forge Valley
Scarborough
Rievaulx
Abbey
Pickering
Ayton
Helmsley
Thornton
le-Dale
Wykeham
Filey
pleforth
Hovingham
Wintringham
Castle
Howard
Malton
Weaverthorpe
Flamborough
Head
Norton
North Grimston
Langtoft
Bridlington
Kirkham
Abbey
Sledmere
BRIDLINGTON
Burton
Agnes
BAY
Fridaythorpe
Gt. Driffield
Barmston
Stamford Br.
Huggate
Skipsea
York
Millington
Warter
Atwick
Heslington
Pocklington
Middleton-in-
the-Wolds
Hornsea
Mere
Hornsea
EAST
Market
Weighton
R. Hull
Bishop
Burton
Beverley
RIDING
Skipwith
Skidby
Burton
Constable
Riccall
Osgodby
Selby
Howden
Brough
Hedon
Withernsea
Goole
Hessle
HULL
Paull
Patrington
R. Ouse
Easington
R. Aire
R. Trent
R. Humber
Sunk
Island
Kilnsea
Thorne
R. Don
LINCOLNSHIRE
Spurn
Point
Hatfield
ncaster
Bawtry

Scale

0    5    10    15 Mls.

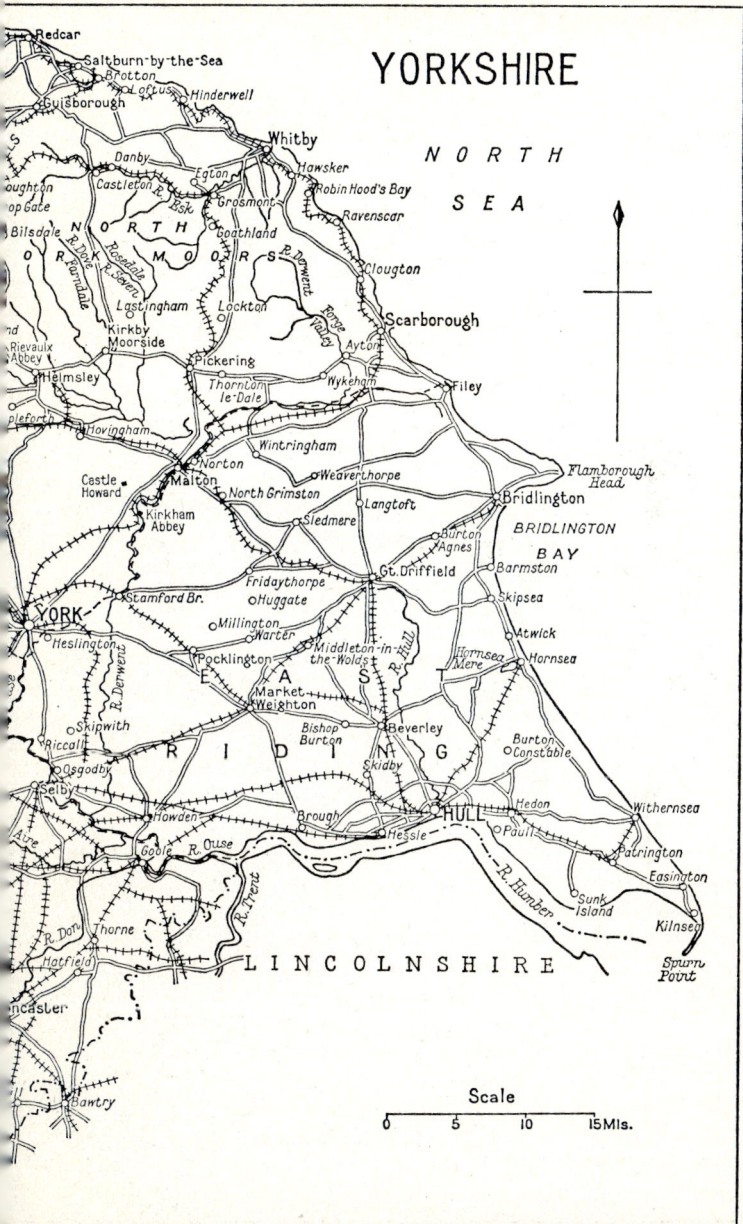

*Reproduced with permission from the Ordnance Survey*

ance and perhaps their character within the next half-century. Up to the middle twenties it was still possible to walk round Leeds, for example, with a copy of the old historian Ralph Thoresby's account of the city, written two hundred years before, and to find much still standing with which he would have been familiar. In my youth I have explored devious ways in that city with older enthusiasts for local history and have been shown links with the Knights Templars, the old cloth trades and the seventeenth-century theatre; not just fragments but whole buildings and streets. Very little of this now remains and every day another thread of history is snapped.

Lamentation serves no good purpose. Nothing can live for ever and we who have enjoyed the pleasures of an earlier age must be satisfied that we have known and loved them just as, in their time, the creators of that beauty must have looked back with nostalgia to an earlier golden age in Yorkshire. We are apt to regard the things we know, whether mountains or valleys, or towns or villages, as having reached their climax and their ripeness for us and our age. The places in which we played as children, the scenes we gazed upon in youth, the very trees we climbed or streams we fished in, we cannot visualize now as being different. We remember them as they were, and any change can only be for the worse. We had reached the summit; the future, we feel, can only be downhill. This is not so, of course, and the Yorkshire of tomorrow may be fairer, richer and more full of character than we have ever known it.

From the time of the saintly Alcuin, who was born at York, the county has not lacked those who would sing its praises, describe its beauties or derive inspiration from its broad acres. Spenser, in *The Faerie Queene*, summons six Yorkshire rivers, "Still Ure, Swift Wharfe, and Ouse, the most of might, high Swale, unquiet Nidd, and troublous Skell", to the marriage of Thames and Medway. And Michael Drayton, in the same century, honoured it as "the most renowned of Shires". That was generous praise indeed. Local poets and writers as well as travellers through the county have found much to commend, although here and there praise has been tempered by a word of criticism or correction. Andrew Marvell, Daniel Defoe, Wordsworth and Scott, the Brontë sisters, John Ruskin and Charles Dickens, have all found subject-matter in the county for their prose and poetry. In our own time we have had a host of Yorkshire writers some of whom have stayed to become regional novelists—William Riley, Halliwell Sutcliffe and Phyllis Bentley—others have moved to wider fields—J. S. Fletcher,

Winifred Holtby, Oliver Onions and J. B. Priestley—while still retaining their affection for the county. Some of the county's literature had an authorship lost in the mists of time. Who, for example, was the poet who wrote the haunting *Lyke-Wake Dirge*, with its warning of the dangers of the Whinny-moor, the Brig o' Dreead and the flames o' Hell, a poem now merely set down as "traditional"? And who penned the ballads of Robin Hood and the Curtal Friar of Fountains Abbey? There are many local rhymes and legends in each of the three Ridings whose originator is unknown, as well as a considerable body of dialect writing past and present to whose study the Yorkshire Dialect Society devotes vigorous enthusiasm.

Out of that dialect has grown a pungency of speech which has long been a characteristic of Yorkshire folk and is still to be encountered alike in a rural market town or in a Bradford bus. To say of a man that he is so well-off "he's bow-legged wi' brass" is a masterpiece of description; and you know immediately the type of person of whom it was said, "talk about hard-faced, ye could straighten nails on his". In the East Riding they say "a becalin (lowing) coo seean fergits its cawf", and in the North Riding you may hear a slow-coach spoken of as being "as nimmle as a stean (stone) pig-trough", while a traditional rebuke in most parts of the county to a too familiar friend is, "Don't thee thou me, thee thou them as thou's thee"—a phrase which dates to the older days of speech when "thou" was only used between families. Native proverbs have the same practical directness—"Onnybody can cure a kickin' hoss but them 'at hes yan", "There's t'most thrutchin' where there's t'least room", or "What's nowt (nothing) is nivver i' danger". A rich harvest awaits the collector of these "speyks" or sayings that are usually picturesque, often witty, and always apt.

A careful analysis of this folkspeech would, I think, reveal that it derives its quality largely from the diversity of occupation, of outlook and of character of those who live and work in the county. As we shall see, in the west and north are the dalesfolk, who wring their hard living from the Pennine fells and valleys with its bleak soil and grim weather; in the east on the tableland of moors which overlook the sea are the moorland men settled traditionally on their heather enclosed holdings where, up to a few years ago, turf fires which rarely went out and a simple existence were the common lot. There ancient superstitions lingered on to this century. Between these two, where the basin of the Ouse forms the palm of the hand of outstretched rivers, are the plainsmen of the vales of York and Mowbray, living in a flat fertile land.

In the rougher undulating lands of the Aire and Calder, where derelict farms look down on mill-thronged valleys, are the woolmen converting the fleeces, home and imported, into clothing; and further south upon and round the river Don are the men of coal and iron and steel in what was once a land of great houses and noble parklands but is now the "black country" of Yorkshire. All of these owe their existence to the river system of the county; only the men of the rolling wold country and of the coast owe no tribute to our rivers. But they, too, have their own character and forms of speech.

North and south through the centre of Yorkshire runs the unifying feature of the Great North Road, along which so much of our history has been carried. Even today amid the roar of motor traffic and the fumes of diesel oil and petrol, an atmosphere of coaching days still lingers round the towns along its course. Legends of highwaymen are still told of its heaths and inns. A multitude of famous travellers from John Leland in mid-Tudor times to Drunken Barnaby, whose journey was amorous and alcoholic, Lord Torrington, Celia Fiennes, who travelled on horseback, Defoe and Cobbett, who looked mainly at the crops in later centuries, have entered Yorkshire this way and have diverged from it in their itineraries. For a spell, in the railway days, grass grew in the streets of many of the old coaching towns and even on the Great North Road itself, but the motor-car has brought a new activity and a new prosperity. The old inns are now often road-houses or motels, the stables have become garages, village greens and market-places are parking grounds, and lorry drivers' all-night cafés are sprinkled along its edges. Whether the character of those who minister to travellers upon this highway has changed must be left to the travellers themselves. Lord Torrington, who travelled this way at the end of the eighteenth century, commented on one hostelry. "I longed to be able to kick the landlord"! Perhaps we may leave it at that as we set out on our travels to piece together the mosaic that is Yorkshire in the spirit which inspired Sir Walter Scott in his lines on *Rokeby*:

> Giving each rock its storied tale,
> Pouring a lay for every dale,
> Knitting, as with a moral band,
> Thy native legends with thy land.

## Long Long Ago

I once asked a young lady with a rucksack in York bus station if she was staying at the local youth hostel overnight. "Nay," she said, "I've got to get back to Castleford tonight. You see, my home's in Yorkshire." There seems little in common between a lonely fellside farm in Dentdale and a woolsorter's home in a rather drab street in a rather drab suburb of Bradford, or between a fisherman's cottage almost overhanging the sea at Robin Hood's Bay and an office-worker's newly built "semi" in a Wakefield housing estate, and still less between the airy sky-scraper flats now rising round all our industrial cities and a Wolds farm-worker's cottage in a village street. Yet, as I have suggested, each of these represents Yorkshire to someone; it is the mental picture of the county he or she would summon up if transported to a far land. The composite whole of this variety is the real Yorkshire with a form and face distinctive from any other county.

One way of discovering the whole is to take a cross-section that will reveal an underlying unity. We begin where the county is highest and oldest, among the hills of the west. Standing by the disorderly cairn which marks the summit of Ingleborough we are very close to the western boundary of the county. Some twenty-five miles away is the flat Lancashire coastline of Morecambe Bay with the glint of sun on the sea as it steals swiftly but silently over the sands which each year rise a little higher and spread a little further westwards. Once passenger vessels and coastal shipping carrying important freights worked up and down the Bay linking forgotten ports at Arnside and Milnthorpe with Ireland and the Isle of Man. Arnside then had its Customs House as Lancaster still has on its Luneside quay, but their activity has gone. I can remember as a boy seeing big ships lying alongside the stone pier at Morecambe, brought in for breaking up. And it seems but a short time ago that the old railway line from the pier crossed the promenade at Morecambe to the railway sidings close by the station. Road traffic was halted then to allow the transport of goods by rail. Now those lines have gone and even the railway station itself is threatened with dissolution.

The silting up of Morecambe Bay has stretched progressively southwards so that Milnthorpe is now an inland town noted not for its harbour, which no longer exists, but for its motor highway, the A.6. Arnside has its stumpy pier, but only rarely does the sea-water reach it, and then only at a depth for sailing dinghies. The only port on this part of the coast is now well south of Morecambe, at Heysham where there is a shipping link with Belfast and to which oil-tankers brought vital cargoes during the Second World War. As we shall see, the slow but steady silting up of this coast, separated from Yorkshire by only a narrow corridor of Lancashire, has its counterpart on the east coast, where Yorkshire is losing its coastline at the rate of inches a year.

From our vantage point on the summit of Ingleborough, we have a glimpse of the Lakeland fells to the north-west, but this is soon shut off by the great whale-back of Whernside which, with Penyghent, crouching like a lion to our right hand, and the mountain on which we stand, constitute the famous Three Peaks of Yorkshire, the circuit of which has in recent years challenged men of mettle to walk them, run them, ski up and down them, and even cycle over them—which involves as much carrying of cycles as riding—all within an ever-smaller number of hours. An old rhyme declared that

> Ingleborough, Pendle Hill and Penyghent
> Are the highest hills between Scotland and Trent

but the rhymester was wrong in that he forgot that Whernside, at 2,414 feet, is higher by a hundred feet than Ingleborough and by nearly two hundred feet than Penyghent, and he overlooked altogether Yorkshire's highest peak, Mickle Fell, which is 2,591 feet, and stands on that little spur of the county which separates Durham from Westmorland.

Long ages before man existed in these parts the peaks stood out as summits above the great ice sheets which covered much of the high lands of Scotland and most of the northern Pennines and extended eastwards to the moorlands on the edge of what is now the Plain of York. That Plain itself was filled with an enormous glacier which did much to shape the land between it and the Humber. One of the great ice sheets had pushed its way by the Solway gap into the valleys of the Tyne and the Eden; and from here over Stainmore past Brough and Barnard Castle into Teesdale where one arm continued into what is now the North Sea to link up with other icefields pushing down from Scandinavia and the Baltic. Another arm turned south, diverted by the great block of the Clevelands—which were never covered with ice— and became the Plain of York glacier, where it was joined by smaller glaciers coming down the valleys which are today the dales of Yorkshire—Swaledale, Wensleydale, Nidderdale, Wharfedale and Airedale —as well as into the Craven country and many lesser valleys. Where the ice did not penetrate it often had a permanent effect on the landscape by blocking up the outlets of streams and forming lakes.

It was this moving ice-sheet which picked up the great lumps of Shap granite which are found today in parts of Yorkshire far removed from Shap, as far in fact as the sea-coast at Whitby. One of these blocks, deposited near Dent, has most appropriately been set up in the town as a memorial to Adam Sedgwick, a native of the place who later became a great Cambridge geologist. On the hill called Norber, near Austwick in Craven, are great black boulders perched precariously on tiny pedestals of limestone, like circus elephants on their little stools. They were carried there by a glacier and dropped on to the limestone, which has weathered away leaving sheltered knobs on which the boulders stand.

That debris either as lateral moraines parallel to the hills or as terminal moraines which were its end product can be traced at intervals as part of the landscape from our vantage point of Ingleborough all the way across the county almost to the east coast. Where the glacier's recession was fast, instead of a moraine a floor of debris was deposited in the form of mud and stones that we call boulder clay, or as rounded hillocks called drumlins. We shall discover evidences of this ice-formed landscape in many places. But the greatest effect of the glaciers was in their planing action, removing rocks and boulders, using these as abrasives to scour deeper and wider the valleys down which they travelled, collecting them as debris from fallen cliffs along their edges and sweeping smaller debris before them, all of which would be deposited where it stood as evidence of the glacier's presence when the ice melted and the nose of the glacier retreated.

All this part of the country is in effect a great platform of limestone once laid down in a vast sea by the dying of countless millions of sea creatures whose skeletal shapes can still be seen every time you crack open a piece of rock. Over this flowed mud and sand and grit, which today gives those alternating beds in our Three Peaks of limestone, shale and sandstone, known to geologists as the Yoredale Series, capped at the summits with millstone grit and, once upon a time, still higher with coal measures which have been eroded on our mountains but which still exist elsewhere in Yorkshire deep below the surface. All this rests, almost horizontally, on the older folded Silurian rocks which are only exposed in a few places.

A series of great faults caused by earth movements cracked this limestone mass, so that what appears above sea-level on one side of the fault is deep below the surface on the other. A striking example can be seen by the motorist who travels from the Yorkshire border near Ingleton to the market town of Settle down the steep slope of Buckhaw Brow. This road runs under the very edge of the fault, so that he has

high limestone cliffs on his left and low clay-covered land, which once
held a small tarn, on his right. At Ingleton itself coal was mined until
a few years ago from comparatively shallow seams below ground. Yet
those seams were, millions of years ago, probably part of the coal
measures which rested on the top of Ingleborough. Below the worked
seams, if it were possible to penetrate deep into the earth, would be
found the same series of rocks which make up Ingleborough.

The high hills of Yorkshire, unlike those of the Lake District, do
not demand strenuous athletic prowess in their climbing. A long steady
pull up grassy slopes with here and there a shale pitch or some gritstone
boulders to negotiate will account for most of them. The primroses
and the wild thyme of the lower slopes give way to the feathery cotton
grass of the higher, boggier stretches, and if you are fortunate the last
rise to the summit may welcome you with mountain everlasting and
golden saxifrage.

In these western hills are potholes and caves by the hundred, with
strange names like Gaping Gill, Alum Pot, Jingle Hole, Yordas Cave,
and of varying size and complexity honeycombing the mountains.
They are typical of this limestone area of the Three Peaks and indeed
spread into the limestone stretches of Wharfedale and Nidderdale and
elsewhere. Usually they begin as swallow-holes or potholes on the fellside or in joints in the limestone "clints", and the action of acid-
laden water eating its way through the line of least resistance in the
underlying rock cuts out cave passages and considerable waterfalls
underground until it reaches an impervious layer that deflects it to the
nearest valley side where it debouches as a cave. The total depth of
the cave system depends on the distance between the point at which
the water disappears on the fell and the impervious layer of rock.
Exploration of the systems carried out by caving and potholing clubs
may be through the cave mouth but is more often down by way of
the initial pothole—a task requiring rope ladders, forms of illumination
and, to judge from the burdens borne by youthful potholers up the
mountain sides, an extraordinary amount of other tackle. Most of these
underground water systems are adorned by stalagmite formations,
some of which are of great beauty though lacking—because of the
absence of mineral ores—the colour that is often present in the other
limestone cave areas of Britain.

The visitor who climbs Ingleborough is usually told impressively
that if he gazes eastward there is no higher land between him and the
Ural mountains  Certainly so far as Yorkshire is concerned he is stand-

ing on its highest edge and the surface of the county slopes generally from where he stands to the eastern coastline and from north to south, as if a tabletop were tilted to one corner. In the north-east of the county is the next highest area, the tableland of the North Yorkshire moors, but compared with the Pennine backbone they are much lower. Their highest point, the bleak stretch of Urra Moor, reaches less than 1,500 feet above sea-level. Between the Pennines and the North Yorkshire moors lies the Plain of York where, by contrast, the land is little more than a hundred feet above sea-level and it falls along the Humber to fifty feet and less.

This tilt of the surface suggests what is in fact true, that the main flow of Yorkshire's rivers is east and south. They tend naturally to run to the lowest corner of the table to be gathered up into the Humber. Apart from the Tees, which forms the boundary line with the county of Durham and flows almost due east from Mickle Fell to the sea, the rest have their origins somewhere in the Pennines and by devious means flow to the south-east corner. Like the outstretched fingers of a giant hand they grasp the larger part of the North and West Ridings. The Swale and the Ure give birth to the Ouse, reinforced by the Nidd and the Aire. The Rye and the Derwent are the outstretched thumb. And in their grasp they contain most—but not quite all—of Yorkshire's life and industry. No other river system in Britain is comparable with this great gathering of tributaries by the Ouse and the Humber, for each of the tributaries are rivers in their own right, bearing on their banks cities and towns of no mean fame, and flowing, in their earlier reaches, through some of the wildest and grandest and loveliest country in England.

To the south of a line from Keighley to Leeds, along the foothills of the Pennines, appears the considerable area of the coal-measures—geologically above the millstone grit which here dips south below the surface—that creates the great Yorkshire coalfield and is the basis of Yorkshire's industrial development. Through this flows the southern river system draining the eastern slopes of the middle Pennines; the Calder, the Went, the Dearne and the Don which, with their tributaries, flow in a general north-easterly direction to empty themselves into the Humber into which the northern Pennine rivers have already poured.

We are not concerned here with the long geological history of this land, continuing processes of deposition in a great sea which received the scourings of still greater land masses to the north, the complicated land movements which squeezed and lifted and cracked the crust of the earth, raising this series of strata and twisting that, as if a great many-layered licorice all-sort had been bent and compressed between giant fingers. The general picture of the underlying rock floor that remains is as if that maltreated all-sort had been set down so that its layers were tilted roughly in the same direction as the surface of the land now tilts, but at a deeper angle, leaving the top edge of the sweet-meat to be planed away by the glaciers leaving a strip of each visible on the top. Thus moving eastwards from our mountain view-point, we leave the Silurian (which was the lowest layer of the all-sort) at Ingle-ton, and this is followed by the limestone layer, the millstone grit, and the coal measures, each of which was laid upon the previous strata at a later age. Then come the more recent layers, the clays and the chalk and the mud which take us to the east coast. Each exposed strip has its own particular vegetation and its own flora, it creates its own land-scape, and it has its own effect on the way of life of those who live upon it. The development of Yorkshire has been largely dictated by its geography.

## II

## PENNINE COUNTRY

It is a lonely road which stretches the sixteen miles from Ingleton lying snugly below Ingleborough on the western border of the county to Hawes at the head of Wensleydale. On either side after leaving the deep cleft of the Chapel-le-Dale valley is the bleak moorland of Widdale Fell and Cam Fell, partly heather-covered, partly clothed in grey-green bent grass. For many months of the year there is little colour, but in the late summer the grass turns a rich green and the heather seems to catch a purple fire over its surface. In the autumn sun-shine the play of light on the low hills and the chasing cloud shadows over the high fell-tops give a wonderful sense of spaciousness, with a northward view of range after range of hills. In winter gales, with snow blowing horizontally shutting out every view except a yard or so of road ahead, it can be grim in the extreme. You realize then the purpose of the snow posts and the black and white wooden fencing which marks off the road from the streams and gullies at the sides.

An even bleaker road enters Hawes from the west, linking it with Kirkby Stephen and Westmorland. There are many stories of stranded travellers at the isolated Moorcock Inn and of snow-bound trains on the near-by main line to Scotland. Almost within sight—on a fine day—is Garsdale, once called Hawes Junction—which is one of the remotest stations in Yorkshire where old railway men will tell you of an engine standing on a turntable that was blown round by the force of the wind. That turntable has now a protective wind-break of railway sleepers, as has much of the line itself between Garsdale and Dent where they also have snow-barriers. On occasion engines have been buried up to their funnels and the stationmaster at Dent has been unable to find the railway track, the platform and even the station buildings.

A third road, higher and yet bleaker, enters Hawes from the north over the famous Buttertubs pass from Swaledale. This road, which reaches a height of nearly 1,700 feet, provides on a fine summer day a romantic journey over the roof of the Pennines with Fossdale and Abbotside Common on one side, Stag Fell and Muker Common on the other, with an accompaniment of grouse calls, the bubbling cry of curlews, the bleating of sheep, and the occasional glimpse of a kestrel hovering over the fells.

Here on these lonely tops it is possible to appreciate visibly the physical structure of this part of England, to understand with more than topographic imagination what our schoolteachers meant when they talked vaguely of the Pennine Range, or with still greater obscurity of the "Pennine Chain", which more than one child mind has translated into something metallic made at the ironworks down the road. Here the modelling of the great hills can be seen as if on a relief map, their tops not jagged edges or craggy peaks as in the Lake District but vast expanses of rolling brown tablelands, often flat-topped, their valleys cut out like U-shaped troughs by glacial action into the long narrow parallel dales with stepped-up sides where the harder rock has remained firm and the softer layers have eroded away. Often these ridges of hard rock have remained in straight lines along the dale sides as if drawn with a ruler, while below, the screes have become grass covered and fall in a gentle slope to the valley bottom. The pattern of rock and grit and clay emerges in a curiously simple form so that what was a geology lesson becomes a visible reality; they become familiar as the remembered lines on a human face.

Each of these long stretches of tableland has its attendant dale alongside so that it is easy to see how most of the great rivers of Yorkshire rise in the high central Pennine mass, travel generally east and south down their respective dales, narrow and swift in their beginnings, then widening out as they move towards the broad flat Plain of York and eventually become swallowed up in the all-absorbing Ouse. The exception to this is the little valley of Dentdale, which as befits a border dale has an affinity with both the Lake District and with Yorkshire, and whose river ultimately joins the Lune and so acquires a Lancashire ending. The most northerly of the truly Yorkshire rivers is the Swale, rising in the heights above Keld, joined by the Arkle Beck at Reeth, and never really shaking off its accompanying moorland sides until it reaches Richmond and becomes a fat uninteresting river for the rest of its course. Over the high and deserted stretch of fell-land which begins as Abbotside Common and becomes Whitaside and Harkerside Moors is the next in order, the Yore or Ure—you spell it differently according to whether you are a native or a visitor—which rises near the Westmorland border and flows down a bleak valley through Hawes and then becomes the ever more pastoral Wensleydale as it flows east. At Aysgarth it goes gay over a rocky three miles of waterfalls or "forces" and then settles down to a comfortable middle-age spread as it reaches Masham and Ripon, and joins the Swale to become the Ouse. South again, a more complicated system of moorland gives rise, between Great and Little Whernside, to the Nidd, trapped early in its life by a series of reservoirs, and never seeming to recover its first childlike abandon as it continues through Pateley Bridge and Knaresborough, its banks becoming more and more residential and industrialized until it eventually joins the newly created Ouse at Nun Monkton, its last few miles being rewardingly pastoral. It twists and turns among the meadows and cornfields as if anxious to make the most of what remains of its existence.

The Wharfe begins still deeper in the Pennines on the remote slopes of Cam Fell a few yards only from the rising of the Ribble—which for only half its course is a Yorkshire river and then passes into Lancashire, a fate it earns for flowing almost due south instead of eastwards like the rest of the Yorkshire streams. More than one observer has commented that a shower of rain over that little boggy patch of land on Cam Fell may by a freak of wind be carried into the Ribble or the Wharfe, in one case to end in the Irish Sea, in the other to flow into the North Sea. The Wharfe is a romantic river, beginning life in the wild hills, having its gay moments as it passes through the narrow gorges of the Strid, flowing peacefully through the parklands round Bolton Abbey and on through the Victorian health resort of Ilkley with a mere touch of industrialism at Otley and a curtsey to royalty at Harewood, finally joining the Ouse at historic Cawood.

Last of our Pennine rivers is the Aire with its own sad story of dirt and demoralization. It begins brightly enough as a stream with a mysterious origin, rising on the high tableland of Malham, disappearing into the limestone and vanishing from sight only to appear some miles later at a pleasant sleepy valley whence after some remarkable convolutions it flows past Skipton where its troubles begin. What was a clear limestone stream becomes more and more polluted with every mile through the manufacturing regions round Keighley and on to Leeds, by which time it has become a dirty scum-covered and lethargic river eventually to pour its industrial scourings into the now swollen Ouse near Goole, the dishonoured one of the great family of Pennine rivers.

## Dentdale

If we look first into the far north-west of Yorkshire there is a curiously remote and "lost" corner of the West Riding which, peaceful and charming in itself, is the cause of much controversy from time to time. In shape it is not unlike a garden trowel. The "handle" is Widdale Fell some 2,200 feet high and its shaft continues into the centre of the trowel as Rise Hill, some 400 feet lower. The outer edges of the trowel are on one side Baugh Fell, also about 2,200 feet and shutting off Yorkshire from the north and, on the other, Whernside (2,400 feet) and Gregareth (2,200 feet). Between these two edges and on either side of the long central shaft of Rise Hill run two streams, rising near the handle and meeting at the point of the trowel where they join a third stream, the Rawthey, at Sedbergh.

These two mountain streams, in summer often no more than tinkling trickles of water but in winter noisy roaring torrents, are the Dee and the Clough, the first running down Dentdale and the other down Garsdale, which are thus different from other Pennine dales which usually take their names from their rivers. This is truly wild mountain country physically isolated from the rest of Yorkshire by its remoteness and inaccessibility. There is a touch of irony in this isolation, for express trains linking London and Scotland roar across viaducts over the stripling Dee and Clough, and passengers in these trains have views in quick succession first down the length of Dentdale then—after burrowing through the tunnel which runs through Rise Hill—down Garsdale. Yet few trains nowadays ever stop at Dent or Garsdale stations. Sedbergh at the other end once had a railway link with the rest of the world, but no passenger service is now available. All that is left is a tenuous and limited bus service up and down each dale and a few high mountain roads often impassable in winter because of snow.

It is this "lost" character of the area which is the cause of recurring argument, accentuated by the activities of a Local Government Commission seeking to eliminate many of the boundary anomalies of our counties. Should this outlying corner of Yorkshire, jutting "like a sore thumb" into the neighbouring counties of Lancashire and Westmorland, be transferred administratively to the Lake District to which in a geographical sense it can be held to belong? Sedbergh is only some eleven miles from Kendal in Westmorland and twenty-seven miles from Lancaster. The Moorcock Inn, near Garsdale station, is on the main road to Kirkby Stephen in Westmorland. Yet the county affairs of the twin dales are controlled from Wakefield, the administrative capital of the West Riding, some eighty miles away. The boundary reformers have a strong case on all rational grounds. Yet traditional county loyalty is strong. Those who live in these dales regard themselves as Yorkshire folk, with Yorkshire associations going back over the centuries and with close links, however difficult, with the rest of the Dales country of Yorkshire. As one farmer from these parts declared not long ago when asked for his opinion on the proposed redrawing of boundaries, "What, move us into Lancashire? Nay, I couldn't stand the climate!"

It is curious that two poets, Robert Southey in his miscellany *The Doctor* and William Howitt in his *Rural Life of England*, did more than anyone to picture this part of the Yorkshire as a place of perpetual knitters. Southey told this story in his dialect account of two children sent from Lakeland to Dentdale to learn to knit, and in it he coined the now well-known phrase "the terrible knitters i' Dent". Howitt and his wife lived for some time at Gibbs Hall on the lower slopes of Rise Hill and one of the fruits of his residence was a delightful essay in which he described this craft which came only second to farming as a means of livelihood in the dale.

"Men, women and children all knit. Formerly you might have met the wagoners knitting as they went along with their teams; but this is now rare, for the greater influx of visitors and their wonder expressed at this and other practices, has made them rather ashamed of some of them, and shy of strangers observing them. But the men still knit a great deal; and the women knit incessantly. They have knitting schools, where the children are taught and where they sing knitting songs, some of which appear as childish as the nursery stories of the last generation. Yet all have some reference to this employment and mode of life; and the chorus, which maintains regularity of action, and keeps up the attention, is more important than the words.

"These songs are sung not only by the children in the schools but also by the people at their sittings, which are social assemblies of the neighbourhood, not for eating and drinking, but merely for society. As soon as it becomes dark, and the usual business of the day is over, and the young children are put to bed, they rake or put out the fire, take their cloaks and lanterns, and set out with their knitting to the house of the neighbour where the sitting falls in rotation, for it is a regularly circulating assembly from house to house through the particular neighbourhood. The whole troop of neighbours being collected, they sit and knit, sing knitting songs and tell knitting stories. Here they often get so excited that they say, 'Neighbours, we'll not part tonight,' that is, till after twelve o'clock.

"All this time the knitting goes on with unremitting speed. They sit rocking to and fro like so many weird wizards. They burn no candle, but knit by the light of the peat fire. And this rocking motion is connected with a mode of knitting peculiar to the place, called swarving, which is difficult to describe. Ordinary knitting is performed by a variety of little motions but this is a single uniform tossing motion of both the hands at once, and the body often accompanying it with a sort of sympathetic action. The knitting produced is just the same as by the ordinary method. They knit with crooked pins called pricks, and use a knitting sheath, consisting commonly of a hollow piece of wood, as large as the sheath of a dagger, curved to the side, and fixed in a belt called the cowband. The women of the north, in fact, often sport very curious knitting sheaths. We have seen a wisp of straw tied up pretty tightly, into which they stick their needles, and sometimes a bunch of quills of at least half a hundred in number. These sheaths and cowbands are often presents from their lovers to the young women. Upon the band there is a hook, upon which the long end of the knitting is suspended that it may not dangle. In this manner they knit for the Kendal market stocking, jackets, nightcaps and a kind of cap worn by the Negroes, called bumpcaps. These are made of very coarse worsted and knit a yard in length, one half of which is turned into the other, before it has the appearance of a cap."

These knitting sheaths to which Howitt refers are now highly prized. They vary considerably in the variety of decoration. I possess one which was probably whittled in his spare time by a farm lad, perhaps for presentation to his lady love. Some others were probably bought at a fair and are more elaborately worked. In the museum at Whitby on the Yorkshire coast are some curved types, while later specimens are much more highly ornamented and, in fact, were probably more for ornament than use. The whole subject of hand-knitting in the Yorkshire dales has been explored at length in a book by Marie Hartley and Joan Ingilby, which suggests that this domestic craft had considerable ramifications.

The only group of houses larger than a hamlet in this lost corner of Yorkshire is Dent itself, occasionally referred to as Dent Town to distinguish it from the dale. It is a child's playbox sort of village, with cobbled streets, a church, two inns, some tiny shops, an old bridge over the stream and a village green which is curiously hidden away behind the village. The church is large for the size of the place and can scarcely have been filled even when the dale was more populated than today. It once had a three-decker pulpit, but only the top portion now remains in use.

It was the son of the vicar of this church who was for over fifty years Woodwardian Professor of Geology at Cambridge. Professor Adam Sedgwick was very much the local boy who made good and the village is as proud of him today as he was proud of his village. A memorial tablet in the church declares: "His University claimed his life's labour; but though removed for the greater part of his life from his beloved birth-dale, his love for it was always fresh, and he ever revisited it with increasing affection." Near the church is a large slab of Shap granite converted into a fountain to commemorate him. Sedgwick's own thank-offering to his birthplace was, rather oddly, a record of the place as he recalled it and as his father had remembered it compiled as a "Memorial" for presentation to Queen Victoria in support of his case in a dispute over a local church matter. He won his case and the "Memorial" became a widely read and quoted history of Dent.

There is a charming story told of William Howitt's meeting with Adam Sedgwick. The Howitts were walking one day down a lane in the dale when they observed a rough-looking countryman slashing a hedge. After talking to him about the dale, William Howitt gave him half-a-crown which was received with thanks. Some months later, in London, at a scientific gathering, William Howitt was approached by one of the most distinguished guests, Professor Adam Sedgwick, who greeted him by saying that he had much enjoyed the conversation in Dentdale and the gift of the half-crown.

The valleys down which the Dee and the Clough converge are today charming pastoral settings for small sheep farms with no suggestion of industry and to a casual glance with no activity at all on the almost deserted hillsides. At one time and another both coal and black "marble", which was not marble at all but a very dark limestone, was worked in these dales, and up to recent years black marble fireplaces were to be found in many houses in the district. Like Whitby jet they had their period of popularity but I do not know of many now giving a kind of funeral atmosphere to dales drawing-rooms, although my own house once had one. Cheese making was also widely carried on as a farmhouse industry.

It is in this part of the country that you will still see hay-sledges in use in the late summer. The use of hay-sledges is perhaps of less note to a Yorkshireman than it would be to a southerner. In few other parts of England is the device still existing as a farm implement. It still has great uses on the awkward fell slopes, and to watch it in use is to see one of the last survivals of a more primitive agriculture. It is on record that Turner, the artist, in one of his Yorkshire journeys, came across a hay-sledge at work on a farm near Rievaulx Abbey and sketched it in his notebook. When the sketch came into the possession of the National Gallery none of the authorities knew what it represented. Eventually in a catalogue it appeared as "a dismounted cart". That was a century ago, so that even then the hay-sledge must have ceased to be a common object of our countryside.

Dentdale and Garsdale meet at Sedbergh, where the Dee joins the Rawthey, a lively little town of one single main street which, according to the time of your visit, you may find either completely deserted or packed solid with traffic. For in the summer months of the year this narrow street becomes the direct route for coach traffic travelling from Newcastle and the north-east to Blackpool, returning each weekend with sun-browned holiday-makers whose seaside days are ended. In recent years this main street has been by-passed to allow one-way traffic, but the huddle of stone-built houses is not easily disturbed even for modern traffic. One of the oldest buildings, apart from the church which is of Norman origin, is the grammar school founded in the early sixteenth century by Roger Lupton and which has now become part of the great public school for which Sedbergh is famous. The school is set in magnificent surroundings amid the foothills of the Howgill fells and with a beautiful school hall. It has had many distinguished pupils.

Down a by-road a mile or so outside Sedbergh is the charming Quaker meeting house of Brigflatts, almost unchanged from the time it was built. George Fox, the founder of the Quaker faith, has recorded that he preached outside the church at Sedbergh and was roughly handled by the townsfolk. He also preached in the open on the nearby Firbank fell.

Dentdale attracts many holiday visitors mainly because of its seclusion. Here a man may find that unbroken peace which is now so rare. There is something about the dale of the still tranquillity of an early steel engraving. In summer you could wander here all day, listening to the larks that still sing in the empty air as they did in the days of the Norsemen, and you might never meet another soul. In winter on the high tops which surround the dale you could lose your way and wander for hours in miles of grass and bog and cold rock, and risk death from exposure.

## Swaledale

The airy road over the Buttertubs Pass provides a tempting first sight of the valley of the Swale before it descends rapidly into Muker as if to escape from the winds which can roar over these heights like an express train. It is the beauty of this "prospect", as older writers called it, which is the reason why so many motorists pause for a while by the Buttertubs to gaze down on the view before them. Once the Buttertubs, deep fern-lined fluted shafts in the limestone close to the roadside, were regarded as one of the minor wonders of Yorkshire, things of menace and danger capable of creating those enjoyable shudders which older travellers looked for in strange lands. It is on record that a lady visitor once asked a shepherd resting beside them how deep they were. "Very deep, mum," he said. "Ah'm told some of 'em's bottomless and some's deeper than that."

Nowadays they are very small beer compared with the greater pot-holes of the Craven country, and the creation of a modern motor road by them has removed any danger of the unwary traveller straying into their depths. The slopes on which they are found do, however, provide a vista of valley and moorland which is probably unrivalled. North-wards is the rounded isolated mass of Kisdon with the little hamlets of Thwaite and Muker at its foot, a strange hill almost encircled by the infant Swale and its tributary, Muker Beck. Indeed if the little tributary started a few hundred yards earlier it would link up with the main river before it had scarcely begun and Kisdon would then be, in effect, a 1,600-foot island in the Swale. Beyond Kisdon are the high Stones-dale Moors with Birkdale Common out of which the river and its collection of tributory streams rise. It is a lonely and apparently desolate country of blue-grey hills and narrow ravines where every few miles reveal new delights in tiny mountain streams, sudden little waterfalls, hidden glens and not a single empty cigarette packet to remind you of humanity. Place names like Raven Seat and Bleaberry Head bring to mind the rarer bird and plant life in these hills.

There is scarcely a fence and never a hedge to be seen. Territories are divided one from another by dry stone walls, some, close to the villages, dating back to the first days of the habitation of these dales, others far-flung over the green fells like a grey network of intricate design are modern in that they are no older than the great enclosures of the late eighteenth and early nineteenth centuries. Dr. Arthur Raistrick, in a little book on *The Story of the Pennine Walls* has described the manner of their building as set down under the Enclosure Act for the guidance of the Commissioners, who usually took the lion's share of the pastures enclosed:

> "We do hereby Order and Award that the same shall be done by good stone walls, in all places made 34 inches broad in the Bottom and 6 feet high, under a stone not exceeding 4 inches in thickness, which shall be laid upon and cover the Tops of the walls in every part, that there shall be laid in a workmanlike manner 21 good Throughs in every rood of fence, the first 12 to be laid on at a height of 2 feet from the ground, and the wall batter or decrease gradually from the Bottom to the Tops which shall not be less anywhere than 16 inches broad under the uppermost stone."

Traditional methods of wall building have changed little down the years. "The wall," says Dr. Raistrick, "is built in two faces, the best stones being picked from the heap and laid to make a continuous course as near the same height as possible right along the run of the wall. The space between their inside ends and the middle of the wall is packed with 'fillings'. Now the rough broken stone used as filling is not thrown in but a first class waller will put it in, dropping or placing each bit carefully, so as to leave no space unfilled and so that the fillings grip and tighten on one another as the wall grows."

At the time of the enclosure a good waller, with the help of a boy to place fillings, would build a rood, of seven yards, in a day. "Old wallers working on a fell side would, on arriving at the wall in the morning, throw their heaviest hammer some way up the hillside and declare that as the length to be walled that day." It was a custom, too, at the end of the day's work to take a running kick at the wall, pressing the foot hard on the middle courses to discover if there were any loose walling stones or any rattle of shifting fillers. If not, it was a good job well done.

Another feature of this dale countryside are the small gaunt stone-built outbarns scattered over the fellsides. Windowless, lacking chimneys, and isolated even from roads, they appear forlorn and purpose-less, yet they have a double use; below as a shelter for cattle or farm machines and above as a store for the hay gathered from the meadow in which the barn stands. Where the making of roads up these steep fells would be almost impossible and where the farmhouses are many miles away it is a simple and ancient solution to a difficult problem, just as the wayfarer on foot in these parts will find vast ingenuity in the devising of stiles and sheep ways over or through the stone walls to facilitate passing from one field to another in a district where wood for gates is an expensive luxury. In Ireland I was once told that when stock was to be moved from field to field it was the custom to pull down a bit of stone-walling and then rebuild it. Here man has devised such means as the "cripple-hole"—a square gap in the lower part of a dry-stone wall with a flag or flat stone to roll in front of it to close it— or the self-closing stile which has two large flat stones on either side, so balanced that they fall together when not in use. Old bedsteads or even discarded television aerials are modern substitutes for gates.

The road over the Pass arrives in Swaledale between the hamlet of Thwaite and the village of Muker, if such a fine distinction of status can be made. Thwaite is famous as the birthplace of the Kearton brothers, Richard and Cherry, pioneer photographers of wild life long before the days of precision cameras and electronic flash apparatus. They were the sons of a shepherd and they received what education that they had at the little school at Muker and on the moors and fells around them where they knew every bird and nest and crag. After finding work at a publisher's office in London they began taking photographs of nests with an ancient box camera, making "hides" of sheep skins and using camouflaged suits. Richard wrote the books and his brother produced the photographs, and between them they could claim to have started the present-day intensive study of natural history.

Muker is the "capital" of this end of the dale, with an annual "tup" sale each October bringing in the dalesmen from all the outlying area between Richmond and Ravenstonedale and from Hawes to Barnard Castle. The rams which are disposed of at these sales with no more than a nod or the lifting of a finger to the auctioneer are the aristocrats of their world and bear rolling names like "Bumper" and "Moorcock Inn" and "Stonedale" in the pedigree book. Their good and bad points, the prices they reached and the achievement of their owners provides the staple of conversation in the dale for many weeks after the sale. You cannot speak more highly of a Swaledale farmer than to call him "a terrible sheep man". From the days of the great monasteries, and probably long before, the prosperity of the valley has depended on sheep. It has produced its own special breed, the grey-and-black headed curly-horned sheep adapted by centuries of hard living to the grim fell weather. Annual sales of this breed are still held at the remote Tan Hill Inn which stands some 1,700 feet above sea-level in the midst of the high moors. The nearest village is Keld, eight miles away, once a Viking settlement and now noted for its youth hostel, one of many on the Pennine Way. There are places on these hills where you can feel something of the loneliness of the sea, where the great fells sweep up and dip down in great frozen waves and involuntarily our eyes, like those of a sailor, search the great expanses of mile upon mile of tumbling moorland, straw-brown in colour, for a glimpse of humanity; a lone farmer with his dog, a curl of smoke from a fellside farm, a tiny car moving along a distant road, or even a few cows on a low pasture. The only sounds are the bleating of sheep, the tinkling of a mountain stream, or perhaps the drumming of a snipe near a moorland tarn. This is solitude.

Yet West Stonesdale, Gunnerside, Arkle Town and a dozen other little hamlets tucked into the hills were once considerable centres of population when the lead mining industry was flourishing. When the slump came much of that population scattered in search of work to the industrial towns of East Lancashire and to America. From time to time I receive letters from "exiles" and their descendants asking for news of the "homeland" and wondering if the dale has changed in their absence. In this age of "progress" it is comforting to them to be told that the dale remains almost unchanged and undeveloped.

Ten miles down the dale is Reeth, "capital" of the middle stretch, perched on a green shelf or plateau along which are ranged its shops and its hostelries which appear to be perpetually gazing with an air of surprise at the broadening vistas as the valley sides spread out and the once narrow dale becomes more cultivated and wooded. Probably Reeth is still dreaming of those prosperous days when it was truly the capital of the mining industry which from very early times honeycombed the moors with shafts and tunnels and whose spoil heaps can still be seen along the sides of Arkengarthdale, the valley of the Arkle Beck which joins the Swale at Reeth. Lead-mining was a thriving industry in most of these dales until the import of cheaper supplies from abroad brought about its end at the close of last century. It had its widespread workings, its smelt mills and chimneys appearing unexpectedly in isolated ravines and valleys and it had an immense ramification of customs and traditions. All the way from Teesdale to the Grassington moors above Wharfedale evidences of this industry can be found. Here and there an old working can still be broken into from some hillside to reveal tools and equipment, as it was when the last miner left. The total crude ore produced during the best years of the mines was over 300,000 tons, of which Swaledale produced more than half.

Travelling up Arkengarthdale itself a good moorland road gives excellent views of the old mine workings on the slopes of Hurst Moor. The road divides near Langthwaite, the left fork curling back to Tan Hill and the head of Swaledale and the other on the right leading over the watershed to Barnard Castle and the Tees. A collector of curious place names could gather a good harvest in this dale with such oddities as Whaw, Wham, Windegg, Booze and Eskeleth; names full of hill thunder and the rattle of Viking armour.

Facing Reeth and looking up-dale a mile or two further on is Grinton, now almost forgotten but still holding tight to its claim to be one of the largest parishes in Yorkshire. This stretched all the way from Keld almost to Richmond, including more than twenty miles of the dale, and justified a larger than usual parish church at Grinton. On the hill slope above is a curious castellated tree-ringed building that was once an ornate shooting lodge. Now it is a highly popular youth hostel with a breath-taking view of the dale from a terrace in front. A painter would require an extensive palette to capture even a fraction of one day's colour from this vantage point. I have seen it change in a matter of minutes from a scene done in slightly faded water-colours, blurred at the edges, to the boldest of strong oils in which every detail stood out. Yet it has been strangely neglected by artists.

After Grinton the dale changes character from the hard, austere, stone-dominated upper dale to the increasingly well-wooded and softer country of the middle dale which continues through Marrick and Marske to Richmond. There were once notable priories along this stretch of the river, at Marrick on one side and at Ellerton on the other. Broad valley pastures now take the place of the walled fell-farm lands and give a foretaste of the future course of the Swale to its meeting with the Ouse, in which the river enjoys a placid, scarcely broken middle and old age, first through meadows and then through the cornfields of the arable plain. You can follow the valley or from the quiet village of Marske there is a pleasant road which crosses the top of the village and which will take you to Richmond along the same way which Leland once travelled. As you top the climb up Clapgate Pass there is a footpath with the sign "To Willance's Leap" which leads to the edge of a steep cliff. If you inquire the fate of this bold character you will learn that Robert Willance was a worthy citizen of Richmond in the early seventeenth century who was hunting on horse-back on these tops when a mist came down. He hastened to get home but missed his way and spurred his horse over the cliff edge and both horse and rider plunged into the valley 200 feet below. The horse was killed but surprisingly its rider survived although he lost a leg as a result, and the worthy Willance lived to become an Alderman of Richmond. If you have a sneaking suspicion that you have heard this story before you will not be wrong as similar legends can be found elsewhere in the county; there is one, for example, concerning Robin Proctor's Scar, near Austwick in Craven. But in any event it will have led you to a delightful view back up Swaledale.

Richmond is dominated by its castle as it has probably been ever since people lived there, which means since 1071 when the first Earl Alan of Richmond, known as Alan the Red, received from the Conqueror the considerable possessions of the Saxon Earl Edwin as a reward for his services in subduing the north. Here on an ideal site the new Earl began building, with skilled workmen brought from France to instruct such local labour as could be pressed into service. Steep cliffs down to the river provided defence as well as an outlook across the Vale of Mowbray to the east. Strong high curtain walls and a great stone keep, 100 feet from foot to battlements, protected what is now the town side. Within was a vast courtyard that could contain men, stores and provisions on a siege-worthy scale. The castle was regarded then as impregnable and even today its commanding position is impressive. Yet history apparently produced no one willing to test it— perhaps because it protected little except itself and stood isolated from the beaten track. Only a few minor assaults by Scottish raiders offered a feeble threat to its strength. Indeed for long periods of its history it was sadly neglected and Leland on his travels described it as "a mere ruin". It has been left to a modern Ministry of Works to put it back into something like order as a showplace and a view-point rather than as a place of strength.

It is a pleasant thing to sit and muse under these old walls and watch the gracious cloud shadows dappling the open plain before you. Behind is the great courtyard which once echoed with the song of minstrels, the rough discourse of soldiers, the soft laughter of women, and occasionally the clang of arms. At your feet, but a long way down, is the river which partly encircles the castle. Eastwards only distance encloses the view and you realize that however far you look that way there is more, much more, to come until you reach the sea. Filling the intervening miles there are villages, and towns and cities and vast broad acres over which the pageant of Yorkshire's history has been played. There are churches and abbeys by the score each with their story. There are rivers and roads and castles around which battles have been fought for religion, for possessions, for politics and often, it seems, just for the joy of fighting. Men have fought for or against their kin or each other according to their mood or passion. Often their struggles have left no more trace than a passing breeze on this summer day. Sometimes their conflicts have shaped the course of our history. To see Yorkshire whole we shall have to come down from our outpost and wander across these acres from castle to castle, by abbey and farmstead, through towns and villages until we reach the sea.

As we muse thus we may be conscious of a figure coming along the terrace towards us. It comes slowly, perhaps stealthily, pausing now and then, and in an absent-minded way we wonder if some phantom of all this buried past has come upon us. But it is only an old man out with his dog and he tells us a more recent legend of the castle by which we sit. Many years ago some soldiers quartered in Richmond resolved to test the truth of an old tale that an underground passage ran from the castle to Easby Abbey. But they did not like the thought of making the journey through such a long, dark tunnel, with its precarious roof and foul air; instead they got hold of a little drummer boy, filled his head with the tales of the treasure and sent him off alone. Away he went through the dark passage, playing boldly on his drum; while the soldiers, listening to its muffled rolling, followed above ground through the streets of the town. The sound of the drum became fainter and fainter until, when they reached the spot now occupied by Richmond Grammar School, it ceased altogether. And as that was the last that anyone ever saw of the little drummer boy, no one knows whether he found the treasure. But on a quiet night you can still hear, very faint and distant, the long rolling of a drum underground. Or so the old man said.

There is another legend of Richmond which concerns a potter named Thompson who once lived in the town. He was afflicted with a nagging wife and to escape her tongue one day he came to this very crag where we now are. From here he espied an opening in the rock and probably with the idea of escape still strong in his mind, soon found himself in a subterranean passage, and finally in a huge cavern. Around the walls hung shields and arms. On the floor lay a number of armoured knights, and in the centre, on a raised dais, lay a regal bearded figure grasping a huge sword. Thompson, with Yorkshire curiosity, touched the monster sword. Instantly all the sleepers stirred. So he, with Yorkshire caution, withdrew his hand. The sleepers became immovable once more. Thompson decided to go and tell his wife about it. He found his way outside again. He told his wife and she told a man who recognized, from his description of the shields, the arms of Arthur and the Knights of the Round Table. Unfortunately the entrance to the cave could not be found again, so Potter Thompson had the honour of being the only man who ever entered the legendary dormitory of the great British king and his knights. Since then even ubiquitous servants of the Ministry of Works have failed to find King Arthur's apartment.

I shall not take you inside the castle as it would take a book to describe its Great Hall, one of the oldest of its kind in Britain, and its dignified Great Tower (and such a book can be bought at the entrance), but it is worth while to walk down the steep and narrow street into the thoroughfares of the town, many of which are still there scarcely changed over the centuries and along which the mailed knights on their short powerful horses would ride. For the town grew up to serve the castle, and was in fact its outer ward. It had its own outer wall pierced by three main gates, all of which have gone and only fragments of the wall remain.

In the centre of the cobbled market-place is the church with its curfew bell still rung to warn the townsfolk to cover their fires at night—a necessary precaution in the days when many of the houses were built of wood. So much besides the old bars and gates has been destroyed including two ancient crosses which, from all accounts, were of great beauty, that it is a pleasure to record that at least one ancient building, the old Georgian theatre, has been rediscovered, restored to its original condition and brought back to use. This theatre was first opened in 1788, was performed in by the brothers Kean, then forgotten, to become an auction room, a corn chandler's store, a furniture repository, and a depot for wartime salvage. Then it was reopened a few years ago with a gala night in which Dame Sybil Thorndike and Dame Edith Evans took part and a galaxy of distinguished people sat in the ancient boxes. One old custom has also been revived. Fifteenth-century halberds are placed on one side of the Mayor's doorway every Saturday to mark his position as Clerk of the Market. Modern troops now spend some of their leisure in the streets down which the men of the castle once rode, for not far away is the great training camp at Catterick established by Lord Kitchener during the First World War, expanded greatly during the Second, and still a considerable military establishment.

On the north side of the town outside the line of the old walls the tower of the Grey Friars still stands and looks across at the castle without shame, for its building was a last flourish before the dissolution of the monasteries dispersed the Franciscan friars with their plans for a new church which might have had the glory of Fountains or Rievaulx. Perhaps the ghosts of Robert Sanderson, the Prior, and his little group of brethren still haunt the lovely tower. Another monastery close by was also brought to ruin by the dissolution, that of Easby, although that had been established long enough to have its abbey church, its domestic buildings and its guest rooms. Little is known of its origin, although it appears to have been the burial place of many of the great Scrope family of the dales. Its gate-house has been preserved and just a little of its fabric was transferred to the church at Wensley before the rest was destroyed on the orders of Henry VIII. The best of its glories can only be traced in the outlines which remain near the riverside.

One of Yorkshire's oddest customs is observed not very far away at Kirkby Hill, when new wardens are elected to administer the Dakyn Trust which provides for each inmate of the almshouses of the Hospital of St. John the Baptist and also makes educational grants. The Trust was founded in the mid-sixteenth century by Dr. John Dakyn, rector of the parish, and is known locally as Kirkby Hill Races, though nobody quite knows why. The procedure laid down by the old rector is still carefully observed.

Six candidates for the two positions are first chosen from the "gravest and honestest men of the said parish". On election day the vicar proceeds to the Common Hall or the school, writes each name on a slip of white paper, and then, before all those assembled, folds each slip with a brown paper covering. Next, a cobbler who comes over from a neighbouring village for the purpose, encloses each brown-paper pellet in cobbler's wax and throws the lot into an earthenware pot filled with water. From this the vicar has to pick out two "as chance shall offer them". This done, the two pellets are opened and the enclosed names read out as those of the appointed men. The remaining pellets are left in the pot and locked away securely, for in the event of a warden's death during his term of office, a successor is chosen by another pellet being withdrawn from the pot. The documents referring to the Dakyn Trust are written in ink on vellum, and the calligraphy is superb. Until recently this was chained in the church, but it has had to be removed to the vestry for further safety. The Trust is still a valuable one, deriving most of its funds from farm lands round Richmond, East Cowton, Sleagill, and Northallerton.

Incidentally, there is a curious historical link between the Yorkshire Richmond and Richmond, Surrey, and the link is in the name. Henry VII bore as one of his titles Earl of Richmond, this being the Yorkshire Richmond. He also rebuilt the famous Palace of Sheen on the Thames. He was so proud of his achievement and so anxious to commemorate his own part in it that he changed the name of Sheen to Richmond, and so began the confusion which so often arises, particularly over the original "Lass of Richmond Hill". Local records show without much doubt that she was a "Yorkshire lass".

Beyond Richmond the Swale turns south through a tortuous course passing under Catterick Bridge and then through miles of pastoral country, from time to time doubling back upon itself as if anxious to delay its meeting with the Ure. It is possible to linger at many places along this peaceful stretch. It was at Catterick, according to Bede, that Paulinus baptized converts in the river; at Bolton-on-Swale there is a monument to Old Jenkins, who was reputed to have lived to the age of 169 years. The river passes through the grounds of two great halls, Kiplin and Langton, and finally under the bridge at Topcliffe, near to the modern military aircraft station at Dishforth.

Topcliffe-on-Swale has a certain claim to distinction in that, according to legend, it was the village in which a king was ransomed. After Charles I had surrendered himself to the Scots at Newark they took him as far as Topcliffe where they camped. While they were there an English Commissioner arrived to negotiate for the release of their royal prisoner and there was much hard bargaining. Eventually a sum of £100,000 was agreed upon, but before half the sum had been paid the Scots tired of waiting and handed over their prisoner to the representatives of the English Parliament and retired to the north. A more doubtful claim to fame is that the village was the birthplace of one of Yorkshire's odder characters, John Mealy-Face, who had a reputation for being close-fisted and over-thrifty. On one occasion, according to Baring-Gould, he discovered that his wife was baking bread during his absence to satisfy the hunger which his meanness imposed. To check this extravagance he therefore made it his habit to press his face into the flour-bin before leaving home, so that any change in the impression would be obvious on his return. It was this ingenious scheme which earned him his nickname but it did not prevent him having three wives before he died. An ancient market cross and some pre-Norman remains in the church suggest that what is now a pleasant little village has had a long history and may have once been a place of considerable importance.

More twists and turns, two more great houses, and the river which began on the wild roof of Yorkshire reluctantly joins the Ure at Myton.

## *Wensleydale*

Almost unnoticed on the left of the road from Kirkby Stephen to Hawes is the little valley of Cotterdale running deep into Abbotside Common. Up this valley three centuries ago travelled the indomitable Lady Anne Clifford in her journeys from Skipton to her castle at Pendragon under Wild Boar Fell. Among the high fells over which she went is the source of the Yore, or Ure, the river of Wensleydale. In winter Cotterdale is a bleak and desolate place, but on a hot summer day with golden plovers, larks and sandpipers in full song and with the warmth thrown back from the hilly pastures it is a sheltered and delightful retreat from the world. Even on a Bank Holiday when Wensleydale is invaded by holidaymakers in their hundreds it is possible to find yourself the only person in the valley. Once it was a thriving place with a coal trade of its own and populated by three notable families, the Halls, the Kirks and the Kings. Hence an old rhyme which described the dale: "Three halls, two kirks and a king; the same road out as goes in." That road remains, but it is ignored by motorists hurrying by to the better-known Hardraw.

Coal was mined in Cotterdale from the seams lying under Great Shunner Fell by means of galleries driven into the hillside up to 500 yards and more. Beyond that the coal getters sweated and toiled in tunnels of the same dimensions as the seam, little more than three feet high and wide. The coal was put into bogeys and pushed out to the galleries where it was loaded into larger wagons. The hauling was reminiscent of the grim pictures of the worst days of coal mining with half-naked men tugging at the load with chains between their legs. Their only illumination was candlelight and in winter they only saw daylight on Sundays, as they started and finished work each day in the dark. Eight hundredweight of coal at the pit mouth cost about 3s. 6d.; but carting it away doubled the price. The pits closed just before the First World War.

There are not many waterfalls in the country which have to be approached through an inn door. Hardraw Force is the exception for it lies at the head of a little glen that is reached by a footpath starting at the backdoor of the "Green Dragon" at Hardraw. You pay a few coppers, pause perhaps to listen to an ancient musical clock which stands on the stairs, and then walk through the inn to the fall which has its origins in a stream which descends the south side of the Butter-tubs Pass. Over a lip of rock nearly a hundred feet high the water trickles or roars according to the weather and season in a straight drop to the boulders beneath. Trees round the edge of the glen shut out much of the light, but if you are fortunate in your timing a beam of sunlight can give dramatic lighting to the falling water. In very severe winters the stream freezes as it falls and I have been shown many remarkable photographs of immense piles of ice reaching almost from the foot of the fall to the top. On a level patch by the pathside where the glen opens are the remains of a bandstand, looking as oddly out of place in this isolated corner of Yorkshire as would a herd of cows in Piccadilly. It was once a popular custom to hold band and choir contests at Hardraw and competing teams came from many West Riding towns and cities. Special excursions were run, and many towns-folk had their first taste of the dales on these trips. I know of one man who enjoyed his visit so much that he decided to remain in Wensley-dale. He found lodgings and work at a village a few miles down the dale, married his landlady's daughter, and still lives there.

Great numbers of sheep run on the moorlands above Cotterdale and Hardraw—some seven thousand sheep "gaits", or rights of pastur-age for one sheep, are officially recognized, and the owners of these sheep rights meet each February in Hawes to appoint shepherds to look after the stock. Hawes itself is a long grey town which serves as a market-place at the meeting-point of many dales. You will be told that it is the highest market town in the country, but as most roads leading into it appear to drop down to the town from a height, the claim is not obvious. Its most considerable industry is cheese-making, at one time carried on in an old mill near the bridge over Gayle Beck but now transferred to new premises behind the town. Started largely as a way of utilizing the surplus milk from the farms at this end of the dale, the making of Wensleydale cheese has now become a large-scale undertaking, drawing its milk from a wide area and selling its products to a national market.

Wensleydale cheese, according to Mr. Morton Shand, is "the premier cheese of England and one of the world's classic cheeses". Yet oddly it may have had a French origin, for it was the monks of Jervaulx Abbey, the original site of which was close to Hawes, who introduced the method they brought with them from France at the time of the Norman Conquest. After the dissolution of the monasteries, which probably brought about the scattering of the monastic flocks, cow's milk was substituted for ewe's milk and this has continued, the old recipe still being used and passed on from generation to generation. I remember when the making of this cheese was still a cottage or a farm craft and it was a common sight on every main road in these parts to see crudely painted notices offering "Home-made Wensleydale" for sale to passing travellers.

The setting up of small cheese factories at Hawes and other towns in the dale saved "Wensleydale" from complete disappearance, for the home-made cheese has almost vanished. There are many who will tell you that those who only know the cheese of today know not the real Wensleydale, which was allowed to ripen for many weeks, was turned at regular intervals, and acquired a savour which the paler, more urgently produced varieties today lack. But we must be thankful for the smaller mercy that "Wensleydale" lives on, even though as a pale shadow of its former exquisite self. And, tell it not in Cheddar or Cheshire, there are rumours that pioneers are at work on a "Blue Wensleydale" that will reach higher realms of glory. Certain it is that the ideal place to eat Wensleydale cheese is in a Wensleydale inn as the final course to a hearty meal, with the sunlight gleaming through the room lighting up the willow-pattern on the ancient sideboard and with the rich green of the Wensleydale fell pastures visible through the windows. There on the pastures, like Noah's Ark animals, are the cows which most probably provided the richness of the cheese you have eaten, for only animals fed on this limestone herbage can produce the milk which gives the true flavour of "Wensleydale".

In his illustrated volume on *The Costume of Yorkshire*, written by George Walker in 1814, and now a valuable rarity, the author gives a vivid description of one feature of life in this dale.

"Simplicity and industry," he declares, "characterize the manners and occupations of the various humble inhabitants of Wensley Dale. Their wants, it is true, are few; but to supply these, almost constant labour is required. In any business where the assistance of the hands is not necessary, they universally resort to knitting. Young and old, male and female, are all adepts to this art. Shepherds attending their flocks, men driving cattle, women going to market are all thus industrially and doubly employed. A woman of the name of Slinger, who lived in Cotterdale, was accustomed regularly to walk to the market at Hawes, a distance of three miles, with the weekly knitting of herself and family packed in a bag upon her head, knitting all the way. She continued her knitting while she staid at Hawes, purchasing the little necessaries for her family, with the addition of worsted for the work of the ensuing week; all of which she placed upon her head, returning occupied with her needles as before. She was so expeditious and expert that the produce of the day's labour was generally a complete pair of men's stockings.''

Overlooking Hawes from the south is the great hill of Wether Fell over which runs the Roman road from Bainbridge to Ribblehead, a road which continued in use until the Richmond to Lancaster road was made. Less than ten miles to the east is another distinctive hill, Addlebrough, flat-topped and sharp-edged. Between the two lies Semerwater, the lake with a legend. The story, almost too well-known to need retelling, is of a weary traveller benighted in these hills who came upon a city where he begged for food and shelter. He was turned away at every door except one, where a poor couple helped him. The next morning he cursed the inhospitable city and declared it should be drowned under the waters of the lake. At which the waters gushed down the hillsides and the lake was formed. This legend may have some link with truth in that there could once have been a lake settlement there, but this is as speculative as the legend.

Semerwater is an almost perfect example of the effects of the glacial action mentioned earlier in these pages. The ice sheet which carved out Yoredale scraped the sides of Wether Fell and of Addlebrough and blocked the outlet of the valley between them holding back the drainage from what are now Fleet Moss and Stake Moss. The lateral moraine from the scrapings was deposited across the mouth of the valley when the ice receded, with the water banked up behind it forming the lake of Semerwater. As the pressure increased a channel was broken through to the Yore and the result was the River Bain, some two miles long and the shortest river in England.

It is perhaps easier in this remote valley, cut off by its moraine from the main dale and scarcely visited by other than local folk—and not even by many of them—until less than a century ago, to picture our early Scandinavian settlers than anywhere else in Yorkshire. Here they would find country not too unlike their native lands, with low country for their stock in the winter and the *seters*, similar to those at home, providing hill grazing in the summer. Hence the place names they left behind, Appersett, Burtersett, Countersett, and Marsett. Addlebrough may well be the burial place of the old Norse chief after whom it was named—a skeleton is reputed to have been found beneath a cairn on its summit. All the roads into this lost world end as green tracks which climb out of the great bowl in which the lake lies, blue and still on a hot summer day, steely grey and whipped into waves on a wild winter's afternoon and, as I once saw it in moonlight on an autumn evening, coldly silver and eerie against a black silhouette.

Until, in the past ten years, Semerwater was discovered as a playground for sailing dinghies and, even worse, for noisy motor-boats, the whole dale was a sanctuary for bird-life with rare hawks on the hillsides, dippers and wagtails on the streams, and whooper and other swans on the lake as well as grebe and a great variety of ducks. An osprey was once recorded there and the polecat was probably quite common.

Wether Fell, Addlebrough and Penhill dominate the southern side of Wensleydale and through the seasons of the year exhibit a vast range of colour from the fresh white of newly fallen snow to the deep indigo shadows of a summer evening when the sun has just gone down. Greys, greens and browns in infinite variety are the familiar tones of everyday wear, but when the hills put on their "Sunday best" there seems to be no colour in the paint-box they do not use for adornment. The colours are matched by the rounded shapes and contours of the hills in no less variety, so that to see a straight line on a map of these parts is unexpected, for there are more twists and turns to every inch of Ordnance Survey—as every motorist knows—than anywhere else in England. Yet there it is on the slopes of Wether Fell, a line as straight as a taut rope, starting at Bainbridge, where the Romans had a fort, and running south-west by Dodd Fell to Ribblehead and the Chapel-le-dale valley, passing on the way that boggy moss on the great watershed of the Pennines where the Wharfe and Ribble rise, one to flow into the Ouse and so to the North Sea, and the other to break through the Lancashire coast to the Irish Sea.

Bainbridge is a village with a green, its most important feature if you ignore the rounded knoll of Brough Hill, which the Romans regarded as significant enough to adopt as their fort. The village has a hornblower, too, whose task it is to sound a tocsin each night between September and February for the benefit of wayward travellers. There is also an old Quaker meeting house, one of many evidences of the former strength of Quakerism in the dales, for there are old meeting houses at Countersett and Carperby and one existed at Hawes until a new road scheme swept it away a few years ago.

At Bainbridge the road down the dale from Hawes to Leyburn divides, one to take in the villages on the southern side of the river and the other to follow, although at a higher level, the northern bank. So the bus service also has to divide itself to meet the needs of villages that face each other across the dale. Each of these villages has its own history, often visible in its stones or its customs or in its place name, linking it with the earliest settlers in these days as we have noticed with the villages having Scandinavian place names higher up the valley. As we move down the dale there are fewer Scandinavian names and more evidence of Anglian settlement with their three dominant endings, "ham" a farmstead or homestead, "ley" a clearing in woodland, and "ton" an enclosure with a hedge or fence or perhaps a wall. These are often linked with some feature as with a tree in the many Thorntons, or sheep as in Skipton or Shipley, or horses in Studley or Studfold. Sometimes they are joined to a family name indicating ownership.

Askrigg, on the north side of the river, no doubt originally denoted a ridge of ash trees, although it might well have become Askley as it was apparently one of the last clearings up the dale made by the Angles before they reached the Norsemen's territory. It was one of the half-dozen chartered market towns in the dale, Wensley—the original market, hence the name of the dale—Carperby, East Witton, Leyburn and Hawes being the others. A delightful book, *Yorkshire Village*, by Marie Hartley and Joan Ingilby, tells the story of the place and its people, its fame as a clock-making centre, its rise and fall with the coming and the passing of the railway, and its link with Nappa Hall down dale from Askrigg.

At one time Askrigg possessed one of the most delightful houses in the dale, with gables and mullioned windows, nail-studded doors, old fireplaces and timber beams. It was built by one, William Thornton, in 1678 and had a balcony across the front joining the two wings, erected it is said so that those who lived there could have a good view of the bull-baiting in the market-place in front of the house. In later years it became a hostelry and then, alas, was burnt down.

Behind Askrigg, just before you reach Nappa Hall, a road climbs north almost straight up the steep hillside and becomes a mountainous pass over Swaledale and, like all these "over the tops" roads, offers almost unbelievable views of the dales on either side with line after line of hills on every horizon vanishing into misty distances until you would think that Yorkshire consisted solely of wild moorlands broken only by great plateaus like those of Addleburgh and Ingleborough.

It is often said that the Metcalfe family originated at Nappa Hall, but as long ago as the thirteenth century there were Metcalfes in

Wensleydale. Nappa Hall was built by a Metcalfe who was Chancellor of the Duchy of Lancaster about 1450 and it was lived in by members of the family for many centuries afterwards. Lady Anne Clifford, of Skipton, would call there to see her cousin Thomas Metcalfe as she journeyed in her wooden-wheeled carriage to her castle in Westmorland. In 1663 she recorded in her diary her thankfulness at coming safely out of "those dangerous places" through which she travelled, and a modern traveller might well do the same. Nappa Hall is now a farmhouse, but much of the original building remains though put to other uses. Askrigg Church has many memorials to departed Metcalfes.

The roads on each side of the river are linked by a cross-road at Aysgarth falls. The road begins near Carperby on the north side, a village which has earned local fame as one of the "best-kept" in the dale, and leads steeply down to the river level and sharply up the other side to Aysgarth perched high on the southern slope of the dale. The river is crossed by a bridge which gives a magnificent view of the first of three great falls which interrupt its placid course. The falls are one of the "sights" of Wensleydale and in high summer the road is packed with the cars of sightseers. I came here once on an afternoon in spring when the river was still high after rain. At the upper fall it came smoothly from under the trees and then found its level way interrupted by a ledge of rock, fell abruptly, then gathered itself together again in a broad pool to flow under the bridge. The wooded background was dark and sombre, but the fresh green of the young grass banks had a brightness upon it which was in contrast to the dark brown of the river's body.

A few miles downstream, after scrambling through the scrubby hazel woods, I came upon it again at the lower falls where it tumbles over a longer, broader flight of stony ledges. Now it was white with the imprisoned air and bursting foam bubbles. Along its side were high rock walls through which down the years it had cut its way and against which, even now, after great thunderstorms on the high hills or in a time of melting snows, it tears and rages as if to give itself more room to expand. Ash and birch and willow in a company of mingled greens give it a frame of foliage. From a placid brown stream between quiet pastures the Yore is transformed for a short stretch or four miles to a fierce, noisy and, at times, foaming torrent. Then, its wildness abandoned, it settles down to become a serene and stately river for the rest of its course through the grounds of Bolton Hall, under the bridge at Wensley and on to Masham.

Two side valleys enter Wensleydale near Aysgarth, one is Bishopdale which rises over Kidstones Pass to link this dale with Wharfedale, and the other is the lonely Waldendale, a self-contained, almost forgotten valley with a stream, the Walden beck, running down it and a few isolated farms on its fell sides. Looming over these two dales stands the great lump of Penhill, flat-topped and dominating on its other side the valley of the river Cover. Penhill was a beacon hill in the time of the Napoleonic War, and it has a legend of a giant who lived upon it and long ago ravaged the whole countryside. Directly facing it across the dale is the great stronghold of the Scropes, Bolton Castle.

There are places one visits which call for an intimate and detailed historical knowledge to ensure their full appreciation. There are others where the old associations of the place need only be kept pleasantly vague in the mind without concern about the details, like "the murmur of innumerable bees". One such is Bolton Castle, where one remembers that Mary Queen of Scots spent many months of imprisonment, and the Scrope family played their part in the history of the north, but where for most of its time the ordinary life of the castle was carried on. Something of all this was re-created during the Festival of Britain celebrations when the folk of the village which takes its name from the castle dressed themselves up as castle retainers, men-at-arms, bowmen, and nobles, and for a week the castle became colourfully alive. The story of the imprisoned Queen was played out again in the very rooms she had used, and after the spectacle you could go out and refresh yourself with mead and watch the archers at the butts. Fortunately, although much of the castle has been ravaged by time and weather, enough remains to enable the twentieth century to recapture something of the spirit of the days of chivalry and hard living.

It is curious that the place which gave all this dale its name—and it is the only major dale which does not take its name from its river— should be so quiet and unobtrusive a place. Wensley is apt to be merely another village on the way to the dale. It is overshadowed by the nearby market town of Leyburn. It does not flaunt its beauty. Yet it is a charming, tidy little place, with a market charter which dates from very early in the fourteenth century, a church which was founded still earlier, and rather oddly the burial place of Peter Goldsmith, who was the surgeon who attended the dying Nelson on board the *Victory* at the battle of Trafalgar. The place had its importance as the market for the dale, but Middleham, Leyburn, Askrigg and Hawes all stole

*Penyghent, showing limestone scars and drystone walls*

its glory and its importance. Out of Wensley's main street leads the entrance to Bolton Hall, with its lovely parkland and extensive woods. It is linked with the great Scrope family in that the Hall was built by a Duke of Bolton who married Mary, the only surviving child of the last Lord Scrope of Bolton Castle, in the seventeenth century. The Duke was an eccentric in that he disliked the daylight hours, preferring to roam the woods and hunt with his hounds at night. He also insisted that guests at his dinner table should not rise until he was ready to leave—and as he sometimes did not leave the table for some twelve hours at a time the ordeal was a grim one. It may have been this unusual nobleman who inspired the Ingoldsby Legend, "The Lay of St. Cuthbert", concerning the Scrope of Bolton who prepared a great feast but lacked guests, although the author rather strangely confuses this Wensleydale Bolton with the Wharfedale Bolton and its Abbey.

Far removed from Ingoldsby nonsense is the very down-to-earth market town of Leyburn with a broad airy square, thriving shops, an important auction mart, and, more recent development, a large milk collecting and processing factory. Although its market charter was granted long after that of Wensley—in the reign of Charles II—it captured the trade of this end of the dale and a wide area around. Much of its importance arises because it is the meeting place of many roads, and today of many bus routes. A road sign at the top of the market square points the ways to Bedale and Northallerton, to Masham and Ripon, to Reeth and Richmond, and to Middleham and Hawes, and there are many minor by-ways.

Along the roadsides in and out of Middleham are notices "Beware Racehorses". They are a reminder of Yorkshire's long tradition of horse breeding and racing, and horse selling; to which some would add horse stealing. Camden tells us of a race in the Forest of Galtres at which the winner was awarded a golden bell and he commented on the great number of people who attended and the considerable amount of betting which took place. The Catterick racecourse is said to be the oldest in England. The St. Leger race at Doncaster which carries the name of Colonel St. Leger was first run in 1776. Defoe said of Bedale that "the country round as indeed the whole of the county is full of jockies and dealers in horses". Middleham itself once had a racecourse which was in use until last century.

Someone once declared his belief that there has always been some kind of horse-racing here from the earliest moment at which there were two horses and two Yorkshiremen. That this characteristic has

*Bare fells—Cautley Spout*

continued is clear from the existence today not only of the major meetings at York and Doncaster, but of a number of smaller but highly popular local events through the flat-racing season at Ripon, Thirsk, Redcar and elsewhere. Up to recent times there were regular horse fairs in each of the Ridings when inn yards would be overflowing with animals and the hotels crammed with their owners. There was a considerable export trade to the Continent of Yorkshire horses, including particular local breeds like the well-known Cleveland Bays and the other lesser-known Holderness breed. When Rider Haggard made one of his tours of agricultural areas he noted that "when two Yorkshiremen in any way connected with the land meet together it is strange if within five minutes their conversation has not drifted on to the subject of that noble animal, the horse. That this should be so assists the county in many ways. Thus a great many of the farmers add to their incomes by breeding and making hunters which they sell to dealers for anything up to £250."

"Shake a bridle over a Yorkshireman's grave and he'll rise up and steal your horse" is a traditional saying in the county. It was more politely expressed, but no less pungently, by George Borrow when in *Romany Rye* he said, "By no means allow a Yorkshireman to get up into the saddle, for if you do it is three to one that he rides off with your horse. He can't help it. Trust a cat amongst cream, but never trust a Yorkshireman in the saddle of a good horse." Perhaps we may take some credit from the emphasis on the quality of the horse, for it is true today that most Yorkshire country folk know a good horse, just as a Bradford man knows a good cloth or a Sheffield man a fine piece of steel. Incidentally, it is worth noting that the old description of a Yorkshireman as a "tyke" can be applied equally to his dog or to his sporting qualities, or even to his horse provided that there is the necessary element of shrewdness in each. What shrewdness means in this connection is illustrated in the words of the man returning from a horsefair at Howden in the East Riding. Asked if he had had a good day he replied, "Aye, I set off this morning wi' two horses, sold four and brought three home."

As a background to the horses at Middleham is the rather heavy and ponderous castle, built in the thirteenth century close to the site of an earlier castle built by a nephew of William the Conqueror. It later passed to the Neville family of Raby Castle, who enlarged it and made it one of the strongest fortresses in the north and the Nevilles presided over its fortunes as the Scropes did at Bolton. The most famous of the family was Richard Neville, Earl of Warwick, whom history knows as "the king-maker". Here he entertained Edward IV, and here it is said his daughter and heiress, the Lady Anne Neville, was wooed and won by the crook-backed man who became Richard III and whose only son, Edward, was born and died here. It was at this time that Middleham had its spell of historical greatness for it became the centre of government in the north. Hence Shakespeare's setting of Middleham as the scene for much of *Henry VI*. Still earlier than all this it had been an Anglian settlement and an important place in the control of the forest of Wensleydale, as well as the scene of a great annual fair.

## Nidderdale

No other dales river has so unpredictable an early life as the Nidd, which gives its name to the dale but is otherwise a modest and long-suffering stream. It begins on the fells of Great Whernside, which lie between Wharfedale and Wensleydale and must not be confused with the other Whernside of the Three Peaks territory. It joins the Ouse at Nun Monkton fifty-five miles away. For long ages a multitude of little tributaries trickled out of the fellside and joined as one to make the river. Then came the thirsty Corporation of Bradford, seeking water supplies for a growing city forty miles away, and gathered up the head-waters into the Angram and Scar House reservoirs. Not all the river was thus absorbed, and what was left set off down the dale again only to plunge underground on its own account at Goyden Pot, a vast labyrinth of underground passages. For two miles it flows out of sight except to venturesome potholers and then surfaces again near Loft-house, to provide a pleasant setting to the attractive village of Rams-gill, a tourist magnet for Harrogate's visitors.

At this point one might think of it as a typical Yorkshire dales river over which old men can lean on the bridge and in which youngsters can tickle the trout under its banks. Yet in a mile or so it is recaptured again, this time in the great length of the Gowthwaite reservoir, a compensation reservoir which it must be admitted has something of the beauty of a Scottish loch, steely grey under a cold sky, whipped into breakers by a boisterous day, and coolly attractive on a hot summer's afternoon. To build this it was necessary to demolish the pleasantly mullioned Gowthwaite Hall, one of the homes of the Yorke family who owned much of this dale as far back as Elizabethan times.

A member of this Catholic family was accused of harbouring at the Hall a conspirator in the Gunpowder Plot and the story is told in the dale that the family was heavily fined for allowing a Catholic play to be performed in the house. It is also said that when the reservoir was built the then tenants refused to move until the water was actually lapping at the door, but this scarcely agrees with the fact that, with true Yorkshire carefulness, much of the old Hall was dismantled and used to build another house which can be seen on the up-dale road to Ramsgill.

Once free from the reservoir the Nidd begins a more peaceful career by flowing through the small gritstone town of Pateley Bridge. Few small dales towns have had so chequered a career—in which it follows the pattern of its river. The original settlement began on the hillside above the Nidd, over which there was a ford or bridge crossing from earliest times. The town expanded downhill to the bridge. As a link between Fountains Abbey and Bolton Priory and later a lead mining centre, it must have seen much traffic as a network of roads spread out from the town. The traffic declined with the closing down of the mines and Pateley lost prominence until the railway link with Harrogate was created in 1862. The building of Bradford's reservoirs at the head of the dale, for which a light railway was constructed from Pateley, created a boom lasting several years, the years of its prosperity. Then once more came a decline and Nidderdale began to think of itself as a forgotten dale, accentuated in the early 1950s by the closing down of its passenger rail link with Harrogate. Of late years there has been a fresh stirring of activity, but lacking outside stimulus there is no immediate prospect of any substantial prosperity. As there is no through road running up the dale it suffers the general malaise of a cul-de-sac. On the skyline overlooking the town and valley stands "Yorke's Folly", or what remains of it, built to provide work when there was little employment in the district in one of its lean times.

Beyond Smelthouses, so named because here the monks of Fountains Abbey smelted the lead-ore mined on the desolate moorland between the Nidd and the Wharfe, and beyond the pleasingly-named twin villages of Summerbridge and Dacre Banks, the river is overlooked by more stonework, this time not man made. These are the fantastic Brimham Rocks to which the imaginative have given names like the Pulpit, the Dancing Bear, and the Oyster Shell. Wind and rain have eroded an outcrop of millstone grit into these weird shapes on the skyline to which visitors come with their cameras.

Beyond Glasshouses the dale broadens out, the hills decline and the river cuts its way through what was once a glacial lake. In consequence the pastoral hillsides of the upper dale are replaced by flatter arable fields and the surrounding lands become more and more a built-up dormitory area for Harrogate. Yet in its short journey from Pateley Bridge this now humdrum Nidd has provided power for a corn mill, several twine mills and a saw mill. Once there were forty mills on this stretch of the river from Ramsgill and the dale was famous for its linen, woven and bleached, first in the cottages then in the mills. Some of its products were used in the royal household. From its birth in the fells the river has flowed down flowery mountain gills, fed great reservoirs, journeyed mysteriously through underground caverns, and become a useful if ordinary river. It ends its varied career by cutting its way through a deep gorge of magnesian limestone at Knaresborough and flowing out into the open plain.

To visit Knaresborough is at once to be reminded of the most famous witch in England, Mother Shipton, who lived in a cave near the Dropping Well from which she issued her remarkable prophecies:

> Carriages without horses shall go,
> And accidents fill the world with woe:
> Around the world thoughts shall fly
> In the twinkling of an eye.
>
> Under water men shall walk
> Shall ride, shall sleep, shall talk.
> In the air men shall be seen
> In white, in black, in green.
>
> Iron in the water shall float
> As easily as a wooden boat.
> Gold shall be found and shown.
> In a land that's not now known.

Unfortunately for her reputation she slipped badly in her final forecast that "The world to an end shall come, in eighteen-hundred-and-eighty-one."

What to me is the most remarkable thing about Mother Shipton is that she died in her bed instead of at the stake or in some other uncomfortable way, which was the fate of almost every other witch of her time. She had been threatened with a burning by, among others, the great Cardinal Wolsey, for when she heard that he was on his way to York she recklessly declared that he might see the city but would certainly never enter it. A more placid man than Wolsey might well have been upset by this and he sent three of his staff, including the youthful Lord Henry Algernon Percy, heir to the fifth Earl of Northumberland, to warn Mother Shipton that he would burn her as soon as he entered York. Curiously he sent them disguised so that she would not know from whom they came.

With her witch's cunning she saw through their pretence, greeted them all by name and was so little disturbed by their threat that she fed them on cakes and ale and then told them to be gone. It was not long afterwards that Wolsey reached Cawood, some eight miles from York, where the gatehouse of the castle in which he lodged still remains though now converted into a farm, and stayed there before proceeding to York. But he never did reach the city for he was arrested for treason at Cawood by the same Lord Percy and died soon afterwards at Leicester where he made the famous declaration which every schoolboy learns: "If I had served my God as faithfully as I have served my King He would not have left me in this plight."

Having visited Mother Shipton's Cave and the Dropping Well, in which objects suspended under the dripping water become petrified, and the Hermit's Chapel hewn out of the rock, in which one of Yorkshire's most famous murderers hid his victim, and perhaps the castle dungeon, of which gruesome tales are told, most of us having supped full of horrors turn with relief to the town itself which clings to the rocky hill. From the green patch around the castle ruins the deep view of the gorge of the Nidd is attractive and behind it the town has still some pleasant old-world corners and some unusually good shop and house fronts. Unfortunately many have vanished under modernization and others are threatened. The castle itself was founded in the eleventh century by another of the Conqueror's Norman knights, one Serlo de Burgh, but its most famous occupant was Queen Philippa, wife of Edward III, who earned her niche in history by pleading for the lives of the burghers of Calais in 1347. This goes some way to atone for the unpleasantness of most of the castle's history. Its end came in 1646 when the Parliamentary forces starved the Royalist garrison into surrender and most of the place was destroyed. Knaresborough and its neighbour, Harrogate, make comfortable springboards from which to visit a region of lovely country houses, the noble ruin of Fountains Abbey or the grouse moors of Blubberhouses which stand between the Wharfe and the Nidd.

Although Harrogate never achieved the fame as a spa of Bath or Cheltenham, or the popularity of Scarborough as a holiday resort, it rose from a place reputed to be wild and desolate and out-of-the-world to be a fashionable retreat for the nobility and gentry to which at the height of the season nineteen coaches ran daily from all parts of the country. These brought the general run of wealthy visitors. The still wealthier came in their own coaches and "chaises", the beginning perhaps of that later distinction between bus travellers and "car folk". At first it was the Yorkshire gentry who came to "take the waters", but as its fame spread Harrogate attracted a wider clientele—and perhaps Betty Lupton had something to do with it.

Betty Lupton is a legendary figure in the history of Harrogate, so much so that she acquired the title of "Queen of the Wells". For over fifty years, until her death in 1845, she dispensed the waters which came from the original spring, dipping into the spring with a long-handled horn spoon, and distributing the sulphurous evil-smelling drink to the regulars who rose early, quaffed dutifully, and then walked the medicine off by promenading the Bogs Fields, now renamed the Valley Gardens. She lost her occupation when the spring became part of the Royal Pump Room, but her stool and ladle are still preserved in the town. It would have been still more interesting if it had been possible to preserve some of the "quips and quodlibets" which she dispensed with the waters.

Harrogate is a light-hearted town compared with most of its northern neighbours. The passing of years gives an air of frivolity to older buildings like those which form a circle round the war memorial, and the local authority keeps the gaiety by illuminating the main streets and gardens with fairy lights all the year round. There is an enchanting air about Harrogate in mid-winter when the multi-coloured lights twinkle in the frosty atmosphere and are reflected back from rainbow-coloured snow. And as befits a resort there is a wide choice of hotels and restaurants, although woe betide you if you seek food after mid-evening.

Today Harrogate is in the throes of a revolution from health resort to conference centre. No longer does it attract the long lists of distinguished and wealthy visitors who stayed at the hydros and took the waters, were pushed about in bath chairs by elderly "chairmen", and had their names dutifully recorded each week in the local "Lists of Visitors" or even the national papers. The bath chairs have almost all gone. The horse carriages and landaus are no more. Many of the hydros have become offices. And the morning parade for the "waters" is a vanished custom. The last war brought government offices and civil servants. Industrial concerns set up laboratories and even factories. What were rose gardens became exhibition rooms and conference halls for industry. Even the green belt which circled the inner town and known as The Stray is threatened and great blocks of flats now overlook the walks where our grandparents sauntered between meals.

"French Weeks" and similar attractions still draw some visitors. Glorious gardens inside the town and outside at Harlow, the "Wisley of the North", and elegant shops, give the place an air of cultured ease. But the conference is the thing and where the seekers of health once strolled near the chalybeate springs, white-labelled delegates now stride briskly from meeting to meeting.

Roads from Knaresborough and Harrogate meet at Ripley which at first glance is no more than a pleasantly built wayside village. Yet the place was once a market town, mentioned in Domesday Book, and its name suggests it was originally a clearing in the forest. Hidden in trees behind the houses is Ripley Castle, one of those quieter jewels in the treasury of Yorkshire castles. It rises gently out of land that is level for miles around, it hides itself in its trees, and outwardly sleeps. Seen from a distance its castellated roof line, which is all that appears to the passer-by, catches the sun and its light-gilded turrets suggest something enchanting beneath. The family line of descent has continued unbroken here down six-hundred years and the present Sir Joslan Ingilby is the twenty-second in that line. Big events in history have passed it by; it has retained a domestic existence into which plotting and conspiracy came as an interruption of normal life. To Ripley for lodging came Oliver Cromwell after the battle at Marston Moor in which, most awkwardly, the Sir William Ingilby of the time fought with the Royalists. His reception from Sir William's wife was, naturally, cool. She received him into the house, but would only allow him to rest on a sofa, while she sat on a chair with a pair of pistols on a table before her. The all-night vigil must have been uncomfortable for both parties. Legend adds that when this Yorkshire wife was asked why she had two pistols she replied, "I might have missed with the first."

Rudding Park, some three miles from Harrogate, is a mansion that is an upstart by comparison. Amid lawns, gardens and woods, this attractive Regency house makes up for its youthfulness by the richness of its furnishings and the unusual quality of its collection of pictures, tapestries and curios. A century older is Newby Hall, not very far away, a Robert Adam masterpiece, similarly secluded and with gardens running down to the river Ure. It, too, has wonderful ceilings, paintings, furnishings and an Italian marble bath, with a lid, which required over 200 gallons of water to fill it.

In the peaceful green parklands of Studley Royal, amid broad sweeping lawns with a sprinkling of tiny classic temples reflected in ornamental waters, stands the lovely Abbey of Fountains. On a summer day, against the green of the lawns and a background of great trees, the grey stones of the ruins appear to sparkle. In the autumn when the trees are tawny and gold the abbey seems even more richly brilliant. And in a few weeks of floodlighting each year the place acquires an ethereal glory which cannot easily be matched. The illuminated abbey ruins give the impression of having been discovered in an inward-dreaming sleep from which at any moment they might awaken.

There must be much for it to dream about in the more than eight hundred years of its existence. It began in poverty, as befitted its origin as a revolt against the ease and slackness which had crept into those who followed the Rule of St. Benedict. It achieved vast possessions and wealth, only to suffer the fate of other religious houses at the Dissolution and see its brethren, its wealth and even its stones scattered. In 1098 the Abbot Robert, of Molesme, in Burgundy, with a small following, founded a new order at Citeaux, or Cistercium. Here came the Englishman Stephen Harding, the great St. Bernard, who two years later founded the abbey of Clairvaux. The work of colonizing in England followed quickly. In 1128 the first abbey was built at Waverley, in Sussex; the second abbey was Rievaulx in 1129; and Fountains, built in 1132, was the third. This abbey grew, like the one at Citeaux, from a desire for a better and stricter monastic life. Some monks who shared this view left the Benedictine Abbey of St. Mary's at York; they had no means and no shelter until the Archbishop Thurstan helped them, and they settled in Skelldale, beside the river which is a tributary of the Ure.

"How beautiful a site they chose. Those early monks must have had a good eye for a site!" The exclamation comes naturally at Rievaulx, at Bolton Priory, even at Kirkstall in Airedale if you can disregard the black industrialism which has crept up to the very gates of the Abbey. At Fountains it is inevitable. Yet these dozen monks from York who first saw the site in the valley of the Skell described it as "a place of thorns and rocks, a better dwelling for wild beasts than for men". They made a clearing and in its midst erected a thatched hut round the trunk of a great elm. They named their new crude monastery De Fontibus, from the springs which abounded in the valley. And they chose one of their number, Richard, to be their prior. Before long they began to realize their ambition to raise a monastery in stone.

Enough remains today of the structure of the buildings to recall their grandeur as they rose under the direction of that same Geoffrey of Clairvaux whom St. Bernard had sent to instruct the monks at their entrance into the order. The stone was to hand in the valley itself. The great church was built on the north side of the cloister, the chapter house and dormitory on the east, the refectory and kitchen on the south, and the storehouse and the living-place of the lay brethren on the west. Thus the monastery had a great central group of buildings, in which all the main activities were carried on, around the cloister. Later two guest houses were added; then, under three abbots, all called John, in the thirteenth century, there were important additions. Under John of York the number of monks greatly increased and the church was enlarged eastwards. The second, John of Ely, and the third, John of Kent, completed this work, probably with the eastern transept—the chapel of the nine altars as it was called from the nine chapels within it. John of Kent also reconstructed the cloister and the infirmary. The River Skell was made to pass through four tunnels and the infirmary was built above them. In the next century the chapel and kitchen attached to the infirmary were built; and in the fifteenth century abbot Marmaduke Huby built at the end of the north transept the tower which today stands among the ruins.

Within twenty years of its foundation Fountains was sending out colonies of monks, and had formed eight daughter houses with their own abbots. Gradually, too, the abbey bought extensive lands in Yorkshire, and held some in other counties; and the monks carried on a widespread trade in lead and wool. At the time of the Dissolution the abbey had an income of about a thousand pounds a year.

Probably its remote situation, like that of Rievaulx, saved it from greater destruction in the suppression. The abbot was hanged, the monks were driven out, the abbey roofs were removed and the lead melted down, the wood from stalls, screen, and altars was burnt, and the ornaments and vessels were taken away. Yet of the actual stone-work of the buildings much was left standing, so much indeed that there was a suggestion a few years ago that the abbey might be rebuilt in its original form. Sir Stephen Procter, in 1579, pulled down some out-buildings to construct Fountains Hall, a lovely building which stands in the grounds of the abbey.

As it remains today, with deer feeding in the grounds of Studley Royal, with water-fowl on the ornamental ponds, with great trees lining the walks, and with the great abbey dominating the scene, it is one of the most peaceful places in Yorkshire.

From Knaresborough to the Ouse the Nidd runs through that soft pastoral country which distinguishes the central plain of Yorkshire and is more historically than scenically inviting. There is a cluster of small castles and notable houses: Spofforth Castle, a fourteenth-century fortified manor house of the Percies now in ruins; Ribston Hall, where in the gardens the Ribson Pippin originated; Goldsborough Hall, an Elizabethan house in which the late Princess Royal spent some of her early married life. An earlier glimpse of history is to be found in the Saxon church at Kirk Hammerton and, still earlier, at Cattal is the site of the Roman road between Isurium (Aldborough) and Tadcaster.

Nature itself makes a contribution to history just here for deserted and forlorn in a field of cows is the famous Cowthorpe Oak whose age may be anything from six hundred to two thousand years, according to your credulity. Like an aged man bent double with the stress of time, it has sticks to support it and appears to be more gnarled and wizened at each visit. I am told now that it is dead, but this has been said many times before and lo! a new twig will appear or an old branch bear leaves. In its lifetime the tree has sheltered a hundred people at a time and, according to local reminiscence, a dance was once held beneath it, which is not unbelievable if you accept the general belief that its branches formerly covered half an acre.

A few miles more and the Nidd joins the Ouse near the isolated village of Nun Monkton, a chocolate-box-cover of a village with red-roofed cottages round a broad green, with a duck pond in which cattle cool their feet and around which the geese gather noisily—a fitting conclusion to the wanderings of this gentle vagrant river.

## THE SOUTHERN DALES

### Ribblesdale

Yorkshire is not generous with its rivers. It does not share them with its neighbours unless it can use them to define its borders or carry its wares. The exceptions to this are all in the north-west of the county where the Ribble begins as a Yorkshire river and runs out on the Lancashire coast below Blackpool, and where a few smaller streams contribute to the Lune, which reaches the Irish Sea through Lancaster. The Ribble, from which the dale takes its name, is born on the Yorkshire Pennines and its childhood and youth are spent in the county. Only when it develops middle-age spread does Ribble slip quietly into Red Rose territory just before reaching Clitheroe.

In searching for the source of the river it is natural to go to Ribblehead. The place is there on the map and the notion is logical. But you will find that already at this point the river is a sizeable one, and if you go after heavy rains or when the snow is melting it will be almost uncrossable. The choice before you is that of seeking out the longest of the many small contributory streams, which will take you several miles further on to Wold Fell, or the highest, which is in a marshy patch on the lonely Cam Fell. Once the river really acquires an identity its one idea would seem a desire to escape as quickly as possible from those fells. In little more than ten miles of almost straight course it has shaken them off, but not before it has enjoyed a mixed experience of life, among potholes, past lime quarries, by caves and under many ancient bridges. Before by-passing the old market-town of Settle it achieves the distinction of becoming a salmon river. Once free of the hills the Ribble takes a leisurely and even aristocratic course through pastoral lowlands.

The three great peaks of Whernside, Ingleborough and Penyghent attend the stripling and it is here, as we have seen, that potholes and caves abound. Most of them contribute to the growing river, though often by tortuous means. Alum Pot, near Selside, for example, is a huge gash in the limestone, nearly 300 feet deep. It can be entered by rope ladders directly down the shaft or by a natural diagonal passage through the limestone known as Long Churn. This begins on the moorland some distance away and gives access to the main shaft at a point about 100 feet from the top. Oddly, however, the stream which flows out of Alum Pot goes underground, flows under the river, and bubbles up on the other side in a small circular pool known as Turn Dub, from which it then condescends to join the Ribble from the side opposite its source. On the Peny-ghent slope is a comparatively small "pot" known as Calf Holes, only some thirty feet deep but with a considerable underground stream system which ultimately feeds the river. I can recall a Sunday morning expedition with a group of potholers some years ago to rescue a drake called Donald which was missing from a nearby farm and was believed to have fallen down this hole into the stream. It was not a hazardous enterprise like many of the more recent rescues of humans who have had mishaps in pot-holes. But it was very tedious. For the missing bird could have swum either up or down stream underground and the length of the system is 1,500 feet. After some hours the bird was located on the downstream side—and "he" had laid an egg!

Also on the Penyghent side of the dale is Hull Pot, a vast open cavern whose roof long ago caved in and which now looks like excavations for the foundation of some giant building. It is roughly rectangular, some 300 feet long and about 60 feet deep, and has a small stream fall-ing into it at one end (again eventually feeding the Ribble). On at least one occasion when a cloudburst broke over Penyghent and left the sides streaked with gullies, the water poured into Hull Pot and filled it to the top—a useful swimming pool for the giant who was once supposed to live on the slopes of the mountain, and whose burial place is known as the Giant's Grave on the other side of Penyghent.

Old pack-horse tracks enter and leave this dale in all directions. Some of them have a Roman origin like that we have already met in Wensleydale, which runs from near Ribblehead over Cam Fell to Bainbridge, at an altitude of nearly 2,000 feet in places. Others lead into North Craven, to Malhamdale, to Wharfedale and to Dent, and were made during monastic times when much of this land served as sheep runs for the abbeys of Fountains, Sawley, Bolton and even Furness. Sheep and wool were carried along them then, and in later days salt and clothing and much other traffic. After all, they were the only roads, something it is difficult to realize in these days when even the remote Cam Houses on the heights of Cam Fell has its road link with motor traffic. Some of them are today little more than a line of dots on a map, as you will find if you attempt to walk them. Others are in reasonable evidence if not reasonable condition. They must have been a rigorous test of stamina for both men and beasts in their heyday. Yet along them until some 150 years ago went the pack trains of galloway ponies (or "galls" as they were called), some twelve to twenty animals in single file, with a bell horse as leader. This got its name from the bells on its harness, presumably to give warning of the train's approach—although it was scarcely likely that passing traffic would be frequent enough to warrant this. Perhaps it was to keep the rest in good spirits, just as walking parties sing to help them over the last miles. At any rate I remember country children playing "bell horses", which must have been derived from this. The speed of such a train, in the charge of one man at the head and a boy at the rear, must have been dependent on both the weather and the state of the track, and it is surprising that so much was transported by such primitive means.

The straggly village of Horton near the head of Ribblesdale houses only an isolated little community yet there has been a village there since the Domesday Survey. It has achieved some fame because of the slate by which it is surrounded. These slate beds, often on edge, appearing in the limestone, puzzled early geologists, and although the problem has now been cleared up by blaming it all on the great faulting which occurred in these parts, "Horton Slates" usually appear with the Norber boulders as illustrations in geological textbooks. Meanwhile the good folk of the dale turned the slate to practical use by quarrying it and using it in great slabs for the paving of cottage floors, the making of immense rain-water tanks, and even for tombstones. I write this with my feet on one of those slate-paved floors. Only a few years ago we removed a century-old slate tank from behind my house. And as for a slate tombstone, who knows?

Horton has a sturdy little stone church dating back to Norman times, and like a number of villages in this part of Yorkshire it had a school in the churchyard. This is now a cottage. The modern age is represented not very far away from the church by an oak sign which marks "The Pennine Way"—that long-distance walking track which begins in Derbyshire and runs to the Scottish border.

If Ribblesdale were all river, mountains, caves and grey stone villages it would be one of the most attractive of the Yorkshire dales. But alas the very substance of the mountains attracts the quarrying industry, and a good deal of upper Ribblesdale is scarred by limestone working and the kilns and smoke and noise which goes with it. Long before modern mechanization, dales farmers used limestone, burning it in small kilns which still can be found among the hills, and spreading it on their land. They used a great deal of local timber for firing the kilns. But lime for spreading on land is only one of the many uses for which limestone is quarried today. Whole hillsides, once green and white, disappear to meet the ever-growing demand. The scars which remain are grey and dirty and unnatural, and the surrounding countryside wears a veil of dust while the smoke from the kilns frequently blots out the entire landscape.

Below Horton the river and road down the dale keep close company, passing some attractive old halls and through a number of tiny grey hamlets. It also passes under one of the few properties of the National Trust in the Yorkshire dales, the old pack-horse bridge at Stainforth, built in the seventeenth century to give access to Knight Stainforth Hall, which once had the reputation of being ghost haunted. The river does not actually pass through Settle; indeed it divides the ancient parish of Giggleswick with its old grammar school now a famous public school and its ebbing and flowing well, from the newer parish of Settle. And at this point it leaves the hills for the open country.

Settle has existed at least since Saxon times. Roger de Poictou owned it in the time of Domesday. It has a market charter going back to 1248 and has been granted many fairs down the centuries. It still has an old world look about its market-place, backed by a great limestone knoll appropriately called Castleberg, and with a two-tiered Shambles, with houses on the top floor and shops beneath, as well as a fairy-tale Town Hall which might have come out of "Toytown". Settle was the home town of George Birkbeck who, after qualifying as a physician and taking up a professorship at Glasgow, discovered an intense interest in craftsmanship among those who made the apparatus for his lectures. He founded classes for these mechanics and was almost overwhelmed by the attendance. On moving to London, his enthusiasm for the idea burgeoned into the London Mechanics Institution which he founded in 1823 and in the following years mechanics institutes sprang up all over the country and continued until the development of national schools and technical education replaced them. Birkbeck College associated with London University perpetuates his name. Settle also produced Benjamin Waugh who was the originator of what is now the National Society for the Prevention of Cruelty to Children.

Southwards from Settle the Ribble makes wayward twists and turns, as if rejoicing in its freedom from the constricting fells. It ambles by Rathmell, where the first Nonconformist College in England was established in the seventeenth century but is now only a name. It passes through the former territory of the once powerful Hammerton family, who claimed they could ride from here to York without leaving their own land. Beyond Hellifield, which thousands of travellers recollect as one of the bleakest railway junctions in the north, the river finishes its last few miles of Yorkshire life in the parkland which once belonged to the Lords Ribblesdale. There were only three of them with this title which became extinct in 1925, but in their time this family of Lister lived in great state at Gisburn Hall, surrounded by woods and parkland in which deer and wild white cattle roamed, a fat, comfortable territory unusual in this part of the county. The river's farewell to Yorkshire was bestowed at the Cistercian Abbey of Sawley, founded in the twelfth century, and built round a magnificent abbey church nearly 200 feet long. Little of any of it remains but it is a pleasant place at which to take leave of a river which has spent the most interesting portion of its life in Yorkshire.

Yet we cannot leave Ribblesdale without a glance at one of its most remarkable features and one which has nothing to do with its river or its roads or, directly, its hills. This is the Settle to Carlisle railway which will shortly achieve its centenary, if "British Rail" allows it to live so long. Nearly £4 million were spent in laying the track up the valley of the Ribble to the vale of Eden, across hard, resentful country. When Mr. James Allport, the indomitable general manager, retired in 1880 he said: "If I had one work in my life that gave me more anxiety than another, it was the Settle–Carlisle line." In the background of a portrait presented to him was an illustration of Blea Moor and its famous tunnel under Whernside.

The railway grew out of frustration and annoyance. The Midland company, which was growing fast, had no outlet for its Scottish traffic. The company had leased the "Little North Western" line and could run trains from the south as far as Ingleton, but here the trade had to be handed over to a bitter rival, the London and North Western, who were competing with the Midland in almost every large town in England and were therefore not anxious to co-operate. When Mr. Allport travelled to Carlisle he was turned out of his carriage twice during the journey, at Ingleton and Tebay, where different ownership meant changing to other trains. "I have been by a fast train from Derby to Ingleton, and then been attached to a train with six or eight coal trucks to be carried on to Tebay," he exclaimed at one company meeting. No satisfactory agreement could be reached for running Midland trains direct to Carlisle by way of Shap Fell, so the company looked for an alternative route. The year was 1865. A sharp-eyed official noticed that a Bill was being introduced into Parliament for the construction of a line from Settle to Hawes. It was to be called the North of England Union Railway and would cost around £500,000. When the House of Commons had given its approval, and the Bill was ready for the House of Lords, the Midland intervened, came to an agreement with the promoters, and reintroduced it in the session of 1866 as a line through to Carlisle, with a branch to Hawes.

*Richmond in Swaledale*

In 1868, a young Tasmanian, Sharland by name, walked from Carlisle to Settle in ten days, planning the route the metals should take —and buttoning up his jacket against some of the worst weather the Pennines could provide. He needed tremendous optimism, with no little engineering skill, to undertake the job, for a certain Mr. Locke, whose reputation as an engineer was high, had said that such a railway was impossible. Sharland must have enjoyed the walk down Edenvale, but when he came to the tawny hills, home only of sheep and grouse, with a few scattered farmsteads, he no doubt shivered from apprehension as well as from the climate. On Blea Moor a furious blizzard was encountered, and he was marooned with his half-dozen men in a lonely inn with the landlord and his family for three weeks. He must have thought much in those three weeks about rivers, bogs, gradients, and the uncertainties of life in these parts.

In November of the following year the first sod was cut and the construction of the railway began. It was a battle against fearful odds of weather, lack of supplies and problems of manpower. This last was overcome by establishing shanty towns on the fells around Ribblehead. The tunnel under Blea Moor, some 2,600 yards long, was made by sinking seven shafts through the moorland, and the building of it took four years. Then Batty Moss at the head of the dale had to be spanned by a viaduct of twenty-four arches. There were other bridges, viaducts and tunnels in Dentdale. Finally, when the line was complete, forty horses drew the first engine from Ingleton to Ribblehead, along the green floor of Chapel-le-Dale. Half-way up this valley lies the tiny church of St. Leonard, almost lost among trees and just away from the road. Here a marble slab commemorates those who lost their lives in the construction of this remarkable stretch of railway. The line was opened to passenger traffic in May 1876.

## Wharfedale

It is difficult upon first entering Wharfedale from its wild beginnings in Langstrothdale to realize that this was once an important hunting chase, granted by the king to the Percy family, with a forester's lodge where the village of Buckden now stands, and probably many more people living in it than dwell there today. As there were assistant foresters as well as bowkeepers living in other lodges in the dale it suggests that this was once a well-wooded area. Indeed, in some early documents it is referred to as a forest, which would imply a royal

*High Force, Teesdale*

hunting ground. It is unlikely, however, that it was ever used as such, and today you have to travel several miles from the watershed down the stony dale before you reach trees and woods. Buckden itself is not mentioned in the Domesday survey as by then a village had not grown up around the forester's lodge, but Hubberholme (then spelt Huburgham) is noted as part of the manor of Kettlewell. Yet there must have been habitation in the dale long before the Norman survey, for there is a Bronze Age stone circle at Yockenthwaite, still preserved, and a number of Iron Age remains. Walking between the gaunt and lonely fells today it is easier to imagine neolithic man living there than to picture the hunting nobles and their restrictive laws for the preservation of game.

Upper Wharfedale's most interesting association, however, is through the evidence of its Norse settlement, evidence which comes mainly from wonderful place names like Yockenthwaite, which is probably derived from "Eogan's clearing". Cray, Beckermonds and Deepdale are others of Norse origin, as is Hubberholme, derived from the personal names of the owner, with "holme" from the Norse "holmi", meaning flat land near a river—and it is the only flat stretch in this part of the dale. Kettlewell, the first large village a few miles further on was once spelt Chetelewell, again from a Norse personal name.

We noted in upper Wensleydale that Scandinavian place names are frequent. So in many parts of upper Wharfedale, invasion by the Norsemen, not up the dale from the east, but by way of the Lancashire and Cumberland coasts and over the Pennine ridges, brought a strong element of Norse—mixed with Irish, for they had set up a kingdom in Dublin before they reached us—which they left at the heads of these dales. It is doubtful whether they found many people living in these parts when they arrived, for the earlier Anglian and Danish invaders from the east were not accustomed to mountainous lands and I can imagine them, as good pastoral men, turning up their noses at the uninviting territory and turning back to the flatter and more congenial lands in the eastern part from which they had come. This is borne out by the frequency of "gills", "ergs", "scales" and "setts" in the names of places where the Norsemen established their sheep-walks in upland country not too unlike their own, and by a similar frequency of the Anglo-Danish elements in place names, such as "kirby", "thorp" and "by", which we shall find as we move into the East and North Ridings.

Before we travel down the dale, however, we must pause to recall a local story and a local custom. The story is of the Rev. Thomas Lindley, who held the living of Halton Gill in Littondale and who as part of his duties had also to conduct a service each Sunday at Hubberholme Church. The journey over the Horse Head Pass involved a climb of something like 1,800 feet on each trip and a total journey of some six miles which sometimes he performed on foot and often on a white pony. It was told to me that the good folk of Hubberholme would wait to see his white pony appear over the ridge of the hill, and then the bell would be tolled for the service. The custom is the annual "land-letting" ceremony still held each new year in the George Inn at Hubberholme, at which bids are made for a year's use of a pasture. The bids, made by the "Commons" in the bar, are considered by the "Lords" (the Vicar and his Churchwardens) in the parlour, and the rent of the successful bidder goes to the poor of the parish. From recollections of several attendances at this ceremony I can vouch that parliamentary dignity does not overawe the assembly. It is regarded as a social occasion and even bids are forgotten for the first hour or two until the landlord remembers his customary obligation to provide food for the company. Then, after a silence that comes from concentration on eating, the bids begin, and there is sometimes keen competition. When the final bid is accepted a sing-song follows and the traditional "Song of Wharfedale" is heard in which, in earlier years, it was customary to work in the names of local characters and their idiosyncracies.

Buckden is now a highly popular tourist centre with little evidence of its ancient hunting background or of Scandinavian influence, but it has another claim to fame in that it is situated on that Roman road which, like the one already encountered in Wensleydale, began at the fort at Bainbridge, this time setting out not for Ribblesdale but for Ilkley, another Roman centre. From Bainbridge it climbed by Semerwater, over Stake Moss to the Kidstone pass, which links Wensleydale and Wharfedale and now has a motor road over it. The Roman road then descended sharply to Buckden and on to the village of Starbotton before continuing down the dale. Yet in Starbotton we jump quickly over many centuries, for this is a charming seventeenth-century village, with many houses built then still standing, some of them with great inglenook fireplaces inside and pleasant lines outside. A great flood at the end of the century swept many of them away, but a modern road through the village has not spoilt its peaceful air.

Down the dale under the shoulder of Great Whernside is Kettlewell, dating back to Domesday times and beyond, linked later with the Neville families, and always a self-contained and busy community. From fourteenth-century Poll Tax returns we get a picture of a village with a mill, a bakehouse, two tailors and a blacksmith as well as an official who supplied beasts to the monasteries and to Skipton market. There would, of course, be shepherds and cowherds to provide the stock and probably stewards and officials of Coverham Abbey which owned much of the land of the village. A very steep and twisting road behind the village leads rather secretively into Coverdale, of which it is said that "only a Yorkshireman knows it exists and he cannot find it". Actually, that obscure dale has a place in history as the birthplace of Miles Coverdale who gave us one of the earliest translations of the Bible.

Almost opposite Kettlewell is the great limestone crag of Kilnsey which is nearly 200 feet high in parts and which has a remarkable overhang providing sport for climbers. This is a fine example of the undercutting of the Great Scar Limestone by the glacier which came down Wharfedale. The extensive fell of which it is part is, like Ingleborough and the other limestone heights, honeycombed with potholes and caves, many of which have only recently been opened out and many of which without doubt still remain to be discovered.

An old chronicle says that the Wharfe here "meeteth with a rill coming from Haltongill Chappell, by Arncliffe, and joining with all north east of Kilneseie Crag". This "rill" is the river Skirfare which travels from the same Three Peaks watershed and flows down the secluded Littondale, which Wordsworth poetically named "Amerdale". At the far end of the dale, which runs roughly parallel to the Wharfe until it breaks through an old moraine into the larger river, is the little hamlet of Halton Gill from which Parson Lindley climbed and the beautiful village and church of Arncliffe, where once the monks of Fountains Abbey had a grange. Many knowledgeable summer visitors to these parts turn into this dale, leaving behind the clamour of traffic along the main Wharfedale road. It is only a little dale but it is completely typical of the whole of this western dale country of Yorkshire, with its U-shape, the result of glacial action, and its limestone cliffs which are part of the great platform of limestone of the Three Peaks country.

On a day when the sky was full of sunlight and fleecy clouds cast blue shadows on the fells, I walked up Littondale along a road verged by dry-stone walls and listened to the tinkle of the water on the pebbles. The Skirfare was in kindly mood. Often, when there has been heavy rain on the tops, it roars down its old bed and threatens to wreck every bridge along its course, but on this mild day in spring it was free from the brown stain of peat, and the bright heads of dandelions tossed in the breeze which swept low over the fields. Colour is not too apparent in these limestone dales. Unless you look for it you would come away with the impression that all was green and grey, but artists know Littondale well, and they can choose freely from the soft colours and tones. Farming folk living and working in these parts would be lost without their dogs, but there was one old man who used to live in Littondale and once dispensed with the services of his dog. He rounded up 140 sheep from 1,000 acres of rough ground near Halton Gill and took them by road to Foxup, half a mile away, penning them without assistance.

A farmer I watched during my visit had gone to the other extreme. As I plodded steadily on towards Cosh (an historic little hamlet with a terse Yorkshire name which lies at the very head of the valley) I saw a car stop near a field gate. A farmer stepped out. A sheep-dog followed him. The farmer opened the gate and admitted the dog to the field. The wiry animal moved stealthily round a flock of sheep and drove them to the road. When the farmer had set the sheep off down the road and closed the gate again he clambered into his car and drove after the departing flock, his dog racing along at the side ready to obey his commands. I wondered when the procession had passed how the dog could hear the whistles of its master above the din of the car engine! I have seen men working in the fields of Littondale nearly every hour of the day and certainly every day of the week, and wondered if they had leisure moments. But dalesfolk play as hard as they work. Years ago it was not unusual for dances at Halton Gill to continue right through the night until the farm labourers had only sufficient time to don their working dress before starting another day. Near the little village of Hawkswick you can see the lynchets of the old system of strip cultivation used by our forefathers in the earliest days of agriculture.

The Wharfe valley where the Skirfare joins it is flat and broad, with grey-white limestone terraces on either side over which and down into the valley run a maze of dry-stone walls. They can be seen by every traveller on the road through the dale but are at their most impressive as I have seen them on a hot summer day from the summit of Kilnsey

Crag. Then they seem to gleam in the sunlight against the intense green of the grass rather, as one visitor to the dale put it to me, "like a fine piece of embroidery done with silken threads on a beautiful green cloth".

At the end of this stretch of ancient glacial lake is the village—almost a little town—of Grassington, noted for its cobbled square (although this is a frequent subject of contention among the residents), its old customs like clock-dressing and the notable "Gerston Feast", and its passion a century ago for the stage. There was a barn theatre here in the early years of last century in which Edmund Kean and other notable "stars" performed as well as some rather eccentric local actors. It has always had an eye for the popular appeal and was so favoured a place that for some years it had its own short railway line to bring visitors from Skipton. Of late it has been the centre for a stirring of interest in country dancing.

I have read somewhere that it was once a Maytime custom for young girls to carry broomsticks on the top of which were shrouded garlands. They demanded a penny from the onlookers and would then uncover their garland. It sounds a pleasant custom but I suppose that if it were revived today sixpence would be demanded and the garland would be made of plastic flowers. The old dancing and festivity of Maytime is no more and such celebrations as are held are revivals rather than survivals of the old custom. Yet attempts have been made in many parts of the county to capture the old dances before they disappear entirely. From the dale country to the east coast, stiff old farmers and trembling old ladies have been persuaded to demonstrate to younger dancers what they could recall of the old steps. Miss L. M. Douglas, of Settle, was an enthusiastic collector of dances with picturesque names like "Buttered Peas", "Meeting Six", "Brass Nuts", "Turn off Six" and "Huntsman's Chorus". All of these come from Wharfedale villages and hamlets except "Brass Nuts", which was a Ribblesdale tune. She had a novel way of inducing the retiring dalesfolk to rediscover the old steps. She would take a party of young people dancing through the dales each Whitsuntide and they would perform on village greens to the music of an accordion. Before long residents would appear at their doors to protest that these were not the dances they remembered.

"That was just what I wanted," Miss Douglas told me, "for it was easy to persuade them to demonstrate a few steps and perhaps hum a tune. Our dancers would watch and listen and begin to dance, and quite soon an elderly lady or an old man with a stick would be out on the green showing us all how it should be done."

Before her death Miss Douglas had gathered up enough dances to make into several slim books.

On the Yorkshire coast the Flamborough sword dance, with its intricate figures and final triumphant interweaving of the uplifted swords with its symbolism of comedy, conflict and victory, was brought back to life on the verge of oblivion, and the Goathland Plough Stots, which included both dance and ritual, was revived and continued for some years after the Second World War. Others still heard of from time to time are the Kirkby Malzeard sword dance, the Loftus sword dance which is a mid-winter ritual dance of Cleveland, an old traditional dance at Ampleforth, and the Grenoside dance performed by the inhabitants of a small mining village near Sheffield.

I watched a company of Morris Men from Leeds dance their way on the village green of Malham from scornful apathy on the part of the spectators to almost wild enthusiasm. A holiday background of parked cars and busy noisy traffic round the green did not conduce to an old-world atmosphere. Hikers in slacks and jeans, and with bulging rucksacks, refreshing themselves with potato crisps and "pop", were at the outset a more than unsympathetic audience. Yet some age-old magic in the music and the steps of the dancers caught the interest and then the appreciation of the onlookers, as perhaps it did in days when earlier onlookers were mead-filled yokels. Before long the rucksacks were dumped on the green and nailed-booted hikers and their girl friends were trying the same dances with rather elephantine steps.

Down the dale from Grassington there is a confused maze of roads leading through delightfully quiet little villages with well-kept greens and ancient churches; Thorpe, hidden in a fold of the hills; Burnsall, with a maypole on its green; Appletreewick, with three old Halls; Barden, where there was a hunting lodge when this part of the dale was a royal forest. This lodge later became the Barden Tower of the Cliffords.

The most attractive stretch of the Wharfe, with a welcome footpath beside it, runs all the way from Barden to Bolton Priory, with deep woods and attractive river beaches. Not far from Barden itself is the narrow stone cleft known as the Strid through which the Wharfe is squeezed to become a fierce mill-race in normal weather and an almost frightening torrent after a storm. Actually the Strid itself, if studied carefully, can be seen to be part of a line of collapsed potholes which have

been ground by swirling pebbles out of the millstone grit. On the platform of rocks above the Strid are more potholes with pebbles in them
which in time of flood will grind the holes still larger. The valley here,
like the river, is deep and narrow. Yet a mile or two further on the
Wharfe is once more a placid stream in a broad valley although, like all
these mountain-born rivers, liable to rise swiftly and even dangerously
after heavy rain on the fells along their course.

Appropriately, the loveliest stretch of the river is that in which it
curves gracefully round the ruined Bolton Priory, built on the site of
the manor of a Saxon earl in 1154 by Augustinian Canons who earlier
had established themselves at Embsay, a few miles away. After the
death of the earl the remains of his manor were given to the Canons,
who apparently took their time over the building of the new Priory
as it was still unfinished at the dissolution of the monasteries 400 years
later. They were probably too greatly occupied, once they had established themselves, in the maintenance of great flocks of sheep on the
surrounding fells and the production of wool as well as with a good
deal of general trading to concern themselves with the completion of
their abbey. Certainly the reports of the King's Commissioners showed
that they had acquired great wealth, even though they had raised many
loans by pledging their wool as security.

At the dissolution all the buildings except the nave of the church
had their roofs removed and much of the stone was used in the building of Bolton Hall for the Earl of Cumberland, to whom the property
was sold, thus linking it again with Skipton, for it was Cecily de
Romille of Skipton Castle who gave the land and endowments for the
original foundation at Embsay, and her daughter, Adeliza, who gave
the canons "the whole manor of Bolton".

Geologists find it worth while to walk the short stretch of road to
the railway station—once the arrival place at holiday times of hundreds
of visitors, who were met by carriages and horse-drawn vehicles of
all kinds, their drivers jostling to be first in the queue to convey the
excursionists to the Priory ruins, the river banks, and the Strid. Behind
the station is a remarkable example of a fault line with strata upon
strata of twisted rock like an illustration in a textbook (indeed photographs of this appear in many geological studies). The line of the fault
runs close to the Abbey and accounts on its southern side for the glacial
gravels and sands which result in the level grassy land.

At Bolton Bridge there is a choice of three roads, to the left over
Blubberhouses Moor to Harrogate, to the right along the southern

edge of Embsay Moor to Skipton, and straight ahead down the Wharfe Valley to Ilkley. The river valley is here quite broad with the gritstone heights of Rombalds Moor on one side and Beamsley Beacon on the other. We are here in heather country and in the autumn these high moorlands are purple, with colourful arable farms in the valley, broken here and there by the brown woodlands of the great parklands of Weston and Farnley.

Whether our earliest ancestors had an eye for scenery or whether some other attraction led them to this place, the stretch of country in which Ilkley now stands has been occupied since the start of the Bronze Age, which means about 2000 B.C. On these moors are many stone circles and rocks with the mysterious cup and ring markings which have puzzled archaeologists down the years. Every kind of explanation, possible and impossible, has been given for them. Similar markings have been found on stones in many parts of the world, but the mystery remains. Other and later relics suggest that sites were continuously occupied until the Romans arrived and found a Brigantian settlement here. In their turn the Romans set up a fort near the river, and called it Olicana and linked it by the road up the dale and over the Stake Pass with Bainbridge. The Roman occupation lasted probably three centuries and what remained of it was in due course taken over by Anglian invaders, who gave it the present name by adding "ley" (for clearing) to the Roman name and shortening the result. It was, however, no more than a large village by the time of the Domesday Survey, and probably remained so until, in the seventeenth century, there was a spate of building in stone throughout the dale country and a number of Halls were built in and around the town, as well as a grammar school.

Doubtless this "new-fangled" building was looked at askance by the older inhabitants in their primitive homes, but there is no evidence that the next building rash, which arose out of the discovery of springs of medicinal waters, was anything but welcomed, particularly in Victorian times when hydropathic establishments sprang up and the growing town became famous as a health resort. Regular coach services ran from Leeds and Bradford, to be followed by a railway with day excursionists, who still find the moors and the river an attractive escape from industrialism.

Although it never rose to the popular heights of Ilkley as a health resort, Otley, the next town in Wharfedale, has many claims to fame. It was the birthplace of Thomas Chippendale, whose furniture gave its name to a style that is now world famous. It has a grammar school founded in the reign of James I and the only school during his reign to be named after his eldest son, Henry, who died five years after the granting of the charter. The town is forever linked with the artist J. M. W. Turner who frequently stayed with his friend Walter Fawkes at the nearby Farnley Hall and did much of his best painting in Wharfedale. Chippendale's workshop is no more. The Grammar School is now housed in a new building—although the old school still stands in the Manor Square as the headquarters of the local Arts Club. And the collection of Turner paintings once housed at Farnley Hall has been dispersed. Yet Otley maintains its status as the market town for this part of the dale and an extensive area of country around.

It is also curiously industrialized for a country town: printing machinery, paper-making, leather manufacture, candles, timber, worsted spinning, all of them are represented, many of them with long histories and many of considerable size. The motive power of the river has probably been the strongest attraction although the distribution of the goods when made to such centres of population as Leeds and Bradford, involving steep hills out of the Wharfe valley, can have been no easy task in the days before motor transport. Strangely, too, the railway link to Otley seems to have played no very great part in its industrial story.

From the steep hill of the Chevin behind the town there is a hawk's eye view of a great length of the Wharfe valley, with the river winding like a dull silver thread through the meadows and crops and pastures of this arable country, by ancient farms and close under the high walls of Harewood House and Park with its royal associations, now open to the public. The gardens of Harewood House were designed by Capability Brown whose ambition it was to make shrubberies grow where none had grown before and who was employed for this purpose and for the creation of gardens by many great Yorkshire houses. This is quietly beautiful country, unspoiled (except near Otley by gravel workings on the river banks), dignified and lush in comparison with the earlier stretches of the river. Beyond Harewood the Wharfe winds and meanders close to pleasant little villages like East Keswick, Collingham and Linton, which in recent years have become dormitory communities for Leeds and Harrogate.

Some of these mid-Wharfedale communities are changing as the old rural life becomes submerged in the urban spread from the West Riding towns. Wetherby, once a market town for the middle dale, has now a plural character in which the two combine. In the winter months it is still very much a country market; in the summer thousands of holiday visitors pour in for boating and riverside walks and it becomes a suburban resort. Despite modern incursions it is still in many ways an old-fashioned town reminiscent of stage-coach days and posting horses, an impression which is strengthened as you look on its attractive colonnaded market hall, its high street climbing up from the river and its largely unspoiled old inns with their sporting prints and portraits of jockeys and trainers—a reminder of Wetherby's place in the racing calendar. They still talk with pride of the Wetherby-trained horse which won fourteen races and of stallions sold to the Argentine, and on race days the town is crowded almost beyond endurance, but the traffic problem which once threatened to choke the place has been mercifully removed by the creation of a by-pass and the town is in process of discovering itself again.

Medicinal waters once promised to make Boston Spa another Ilkley, but nothing came of it although it still holds the character of a resort. Thorp Arch, nearby, is the home of a great new national reference library of science into which books and periodicals in every language pour each day, to be consulted or borrowed by scientific workers throughout the country. Perhaps it is appropriate that the thirst for knowledge should be slaked so near to Tadcaster, with its enormous breweries, engaged almost entirely in slaking the physical thirsts of a great area of the West Riding.

The Wharfe completes its romantic course by joining the Ouse at Cawood, where all that remains of the castle at which Cardinal Wolsey stayed and at which he was arrested on his last journey is now only a gatehouse used by a farmer. It was once a noble place where kings and queens rested on their journeys to the north, where great feasts were given, and where both Parliamentarians and Royalists found themselves besieged by the other. But the glory of the place has departed.

## Malhamdale

Malhamdale is the name given to the upper valley of the river Aire, from its mysterious cavernous sources almost to the point at which it makes a first contact with that industrial life which later converts it from the purest of mountain streams to the most polluted river in England. It is, in its beginnings, a "romantic" dale in the scenic sense beloved of old writers, with tremendous rocky cliffs and deep gorges and peaty streams which appear and disappear—presumably they would have written "at the whims of Mother Nature". The valley shares with all the western dale country the cross-gartering of grey limestone walls with here and there a solitary outbarn.

A less sophisticated, simpler lady than her northern sisters, Malhamdale has no great castles, little fluttering of historic skirts, few fineries of "pretty corners". Nor has she the distinction, once proudly held by the more populous Wensleydale—until reorganisation ordered otherwise—of having had a railway along her to bring her admirers; she can boast only a twisting secondary road. This is a sister of quieter charms, not touched up for show, yet with a particular quality of lightness which none of the other dales can claim. You are immediately aware of that lightness in this green and white dale. The white of the limestone cliffs and outcrops sparkles against the green of the rich fine turf which clothes the fells. It is a botanist's paradise in that, although small in area, it is crossed by two of those great geological upheavals already referred to, the Mid-Craven and the North Craven Faults. These have had the effect of providing moors favourable to heather and bracken and bilberry, and limestone screes where the mealy primrose, wild thyme and the mountain pansy flourish. It is possible to find that hedge-lover and limestone-hater the foxglove, and mountain everlasting, a rare flower of limestone heights, almost within sight of each other. Somewhere on the boggy land in between, where the older impervious slate has been uplifted, there will be the silky-topped cotton grass, butterwort and sundew. Botanists who know this valley well have their secret places wherein can be found the rarer orchids, the blue Jacob's ladder and the cloudberry.

This dale has one remarkable characteristic. Its greatest attractions are not historic, but belong to prehistory. They are geologic rather than human. What we most enjoy in the dale today is there because of what happened to this part of the earth a million or more years ago.

That mighty landslide which travelled east and west across this part of Yorkshire tearing apart the strata left great cliffs marking the lines of the faults. One of these cliffs is visible to every motorist travelling between Ingleton and Settle as it provides the gigantic wall of Giggleswick Scar to the road on which he travels. Another appears in Malhamdale as a gigantic barrier across the head of the valley. The great Cove of Malham, which is a showplace of the dale, is an immense bastion of torn rock some 300 feet high, from the base of which a stream appears. A mile or so to the east is Gordale Scar, an even more remarkable sight, for here a moorland stream has cut its way through the limestone cliff, forming a vast gorge, with towering masses of rock on either side some 400 feet high, often overhanging. You can test unbounded imagination here, for the geologists will tell you that this vast chasm was once a pothole and cave, worn away by the action of water, a cave which long ago collapsed leaving what was a great underground chamber open and roofless. The stream still bounces down the chasm in great leaps, and it is possible with care to struggle up the water-worn and tumbled rocks by its side to moorland at the top. Deposits of limestone carried down by the stream can be seen lower down its course in the form of tufa—lime-saturated moss—covering a small waterfall known as Janet's Foss. Janet was the queen of the local fairies and in a cave behind the fall, according to legend, was her home. More mundane minds will tell you it was used as a shelter by miners from ore workings nearby.

There are many evidences of the effect of the Ice Age on the landscape of this dale, particularly in the Dry Valley above the Cove. This was once an outlet for the melting ice from the higher lands, cut deep by its torrents, fed by many side streams and broken by great falls. Although it carried a great weight of meltwater, deep below its course the river bed was itself still frozen hard as a result of long periods of intense cold. But as the Ice Age ended and the climate became warmer, the ground thawed, and the joints in the limestone bed of the river opened. Centuries of water erosion acting on the soluble limestone widened the joints and the water disappeared through them to follow underground courses. Some say that deep below ground there may be a yet undiscovered cavern perhaps of the size of Gordale. Now you can walk or scramble at some risk to ankle and dignity down the dry and desolate valley that was once a river.

The source of this now vanished river is Malham Tarn, half a mile in diameter and the largest lake in the West Riding. This tarn, like so much else, owes its existence to the uplifting of strata by the North Craven Fault, for it is supported on a block of Silurian slate brought up by the displacement of the land and is retained by a glacial moraine. The tarn is a happy hunting ground for students of fresh-water biology and modern anglers enjoy fishing it as did the monks of Fountains Abbey five centuries ago. The sturdy-looking Tarn House which overlooks it was a mansion built by the millionaire Walter Morrison and has had many famous visitors from John Ruskin to Charles Kingsley. It now houses students of the Field Study Centre who can find the raw materials for their work—everything from geology to art—practically on their doorstep. The overflow from this glacier-formed tarn was the river which poured down the Dry Valley and over the face of Malham Cove into the green valley below. As the water disappeared at the shamble of boulders and gravel now called Water Sinks, the waterfall over the Cove face became dry. The water which thus vanishes into the earth at Water Sinks reappears several miles further down Malhamdale at Aire Head Springs—an almost insignificant bubbling up of water which later becomes one of Yorkshire's big rivers. The stream which appears from a narrow opening beneath the Cove comes from another source on Malham Moor, and although this ultimately joins the river Aire is not its true source stream, although it was generally believed for many years to be so. Many chemical tests were necessary to prove that water which disappeared on the top of a cliff was not that which appeared at its base but made an underground journey of several miles before it saw the light again.

The physical forces which created these changing river beds and underground watercourses are continually at work. Between the Cove and the Scar there is a cone-shaped hill named Cawden which on occasion bursts its side and floods the village street. It is believed that inside the hill there is an undiscovered lake which from time to time overflows. In recent years the "bursts" have been fewer and it is possible that the lake may drain and become a considerable underground cavern, perhaps in its turn to collapse. Much of the landscape will doubtless change still more in future centuries.

This background of scenery, then, is a living thing handed down from the dark backward of time linking our own age and its geological origins with a sense of immediacy that cannot be conveyed in words. One wonders what prehistoric man must have thought of this strange lost world when he first wandered into it. He certainly did come, for he left evidences of settlement in quite a few places in the dale. There is no evidence, however, that the Romans ever discovered Malhamdale. Perhaps this territory was too uncouth for them. It was left to the invading Anglo-Saxons in the sixth century to find and colonize the lower lands, probably following up the river Aire from the east. Where they settled they left their place names as visiting cards: Airton, Calton, Hanlith, and the village of Malham itself. They were followed, probably in the ninth century, by the Danes who left their mark in the place names of "thorpe" or "by" where the Angles used "tun" or "ham". Thus Kirkby, where there was a church, and perhaps Scothorpe (now Scosthrop) where there was a settlement near a wood. A third invasion came when the Norsemen arrived a century later and in turn settled in and around the dale. They brought a stranger outlandish speech and left names like Thorogill, Stanggill and Trenhouse. When men from different lands come together there is usually barter between them, if not of goods then of words and ideas. Until quite recent times the isolation of this dale retained within itself the characteristics of these three waves of invaders with a distinctive dialect and way of life.

Malham, the "capital" of the dale, lies at the far end of that twisting road which begins at Skipton in Airedale and meanders through quiet pastoral country before the hills close in at the head of the valley. Beyond Malham the road becomes a mountain highway which only a few years ago was a rough track and which still requires good brakes (or adequate lung power) for its negotiation. On the way to Malham is the little village of Airton, where there was an ancient mill worked in monastic times or probably before. There is still a mill on the site. Nearby is an early eighteenth-century Quaker Meeting House and a seventeenth-century squatter's cottage on the village green. A mile or so further on is Kirkby Malham which gives its name to the large parish which embraces the dale. It has probably had a church for a thousand years and the parish registers of Kirkby Malham have provided the starting-point for one of those controversies which historians love. The name of Oliver Cromwell, signed in full and followed by "regd", presumably an abbreviation of "registered", appears twice in the registers—on January 17th and July 25th, 1655, as witness to marriages at the church. Are the signatures authentic? Were they forged for any ulterior reason? Or were they the work of an unknown practical joker?

In support of the genuine character of the signatures is the fact that General Lambert, who lived at Calton Hall nearby, was one of Cromwell's trusted officers. It could well be that the Protector visited the General in that year and stayed at Calton Hall, and it would not be beyond possibility that the register, which had to be "subscribed" by a Justice of the Peace, would be taken by the parish clerk to the nearest "big house" for the purpose at a convenient time for both marriages to be so "witnessed". I have known rural council documents and many committee minutes similarly dealt with in the twentieth century. Various authorities have declared the signatures to be genuine and not the work of practical jokers.

Against this Thomas Carlyle, whose opinion was sought on the matter and who, after all, was the author of a life of Cromwell, declared that there was no resemblance between the entries in the register and the genuine signature and that it was ridiculous that a statesman of Cromwell's standing should witness a village wedding. It has also been pointed out that the Protector's usual signature was "Oliver, P," and not the full name. Evidence in the Public Record Office shows that the great man was present at Councils of State in London on July 24th and 26th of that year. It is unlikely that he would travel to a remote dale in Yorkshire in the middle of winter. So there could be little possibility that he was actually at the marriage ceremonies. And would not the parish clerk have made some note in his register if the man who was shaking all England at the time had put his hand to it?

The village of Malham itself was formerly a famous centre for the buying and selling of sheep and cattle, dating back to the days when both Fountains Abbey and Bolton Priory had granges there. In the eighteenth century, according to a contemporary historian, as many as 5,000 head of Scotch cattle were pastured nearby for sale and there was an annual Sheep Fair where upwards of 100,000 sheep were shown at one time.

Nowadays visitors have replaced sheep as a source of Malham's prosperity. They come to this dale from many parts of the West Riding at weekends and on public holidays. The green at Malham on a hot Sunday afternoon in summer resembles a seaside beach with fancy-dressed visitors, picnic parties, impromptu dances to the ever-present transistor, family games of cricket, sun-bathers, some earnest elderly walkers who disdain hiking regalia and many pseudo-potholers who carry enough equipment to descend a hundred potholes but who rarely move from the green. As a background to all this, instead of the fisherman's nets of seaside resorts there is a fringe of bicycles, scooters, up-to-the-minute motor cycles and ancient cars, for modern youth must be mobile and these weekend visitations are, save for the few elderly earnest walkers, mainly youthful—and noisy. By evening the crowds begin to move away, for they have to return to Leeds, Bradford, Keighley, York. The noise dies down and apart from the late roar of a group of motor cycles or a late-dawdling car changing gear on one of the hilly roads home, somewhere around midnight peace descends upon the dale, the caterers "side away" the last plates and dishes, local residents come to their doors for a reassurance that peace

*Bowes Museum, modelled on a French château*

has returned to the dale and probably shake their heads over the day's litter deposit. Somewhere an owl hoots in the stillness. In a moment the ancient dale slips back a thousand years almost unchanged.

As a place over-abundantly provided with the natural wonders that early travellers and celebrities enjoyed, Malhamdale always had a flow of distinguished visitors. The poet Thomas Gray noted that the village was locally spoken of as "Maum", but described it as "a village in the bosom of the mountains seated in a wild and dreary valley". J. M. W. Turner, the artist, visited it from Farnley Hall and used the limestone cliffs as a subject to his own liking. Charles Kingsley used the same, crags as a setting for a part of *The Water Babies*, and John Ruskin who stayed at the Buck Inn in Malham village—and characteristically presented it with a mosaic pavement—wrote of Malham Cove, in *Prosperina*, that "the stones of the brook were softer with moss than any silken pillow; the crowded oxalis leaves yielded to pressure of the hand and were not felt; the cloven leaves of the herb Robert and robed clusters of its companion overflowed every rent in the rude crags with living balm".

So Malhamdale has her softness after all, and they are the better for being found in a region which in past ages has been torn by mighty cataclysms and is the depository of so many stony riddles. There can be few places so quiet and peaceful with its warm hills and pleasant streams.

*Airedale*

It would probably be wrong to carry the simile too far, but the gentle sister of the Dales family which is Malhamdale changes her looks and character with a vengeance when she changes her name to Airedale. So little similarity is there between the turgid, grimy river upon which you gaze over Leeds bridge and the soft and sparkling river which we left at Malham that you would immediately deny relationship between them. The romantic sister has become a harridan through bad treatment and it is Yorkshire's misfortune that there is no firm authority to step in to right the wrong. Aire is a tamed and much abused river and the dale suffers.

Trouble begins for the river soon after it passes Skipton. Before this it runs through warm pastoral country, meandering round great ox-bows, amid trees and soft hedges which here begin to replace the stone walls of the upper dale. In the distance is Pendle Hill and the Lancashire

*Looking across the York Plain from Sutton Bank*

border, with the parklands of Gisburn and the edge of the Forest of Bowland in between. Skipton itself, the sheep town of history and still a big sheep market, has a pleasant high street sloping gently down from the church and the castle, both closely linked with the Cliffords, and through the most famous of them, the Lady Anne Clifford— Countess of Dorset, Pembroke, and Montgomery—with a great slice of England's history.

There is a "truly rural" air about the town, particularly on market days when food stalls line the High Street, farm tools and colourful implements jut on to the pavements, every shop is crowded with basket-carrying housewives, and buses in from the nearby villages feel their way down the bustling road like liners edging into dock. While their wives shop, farmer-husbands gather at the cattle market or prop themselves on their sticks while talking of sheep, pigs, poultry and cattle. More than their womenfolk they show something of the lean, tall and gaunt-faced hill-country stock, compound of Saxon, Dane and Viking, which is noticeable everywhere in the Dales. On market days Skipton is a gathering ground for a large area nebulously known as Craven, which includes not only the fringes of Malhamdale but all the country lying on either side of the Keighley-Kendal highway running north-west to the boundary of Yorkshire near Bentham. Along that road are Ingleton, Clapham, Settle, Long Preston and Gargrave, some of them having their own market days for good measure. South-west lies the pastoral country around Gisburn as well as the semi-industrial region of West Craven along the Lancashire border where forests of chimneys mark the cotton towns of Barnoldswick (locally called "Barlick") and Earby. Few Yorkshire towns knew the rigours of the inter-war textile depression as much as these two centres. The war brought diversity to their industry, with Barnoldswick turning out jet engines, mattresses and a host of other products, and Earby having a plastics firm, a branch of a tractor organization, and a textile mill of a special type geared to the surgical dressings industry.

These border-line Yorkshire communities are subject to the tug of county loyalties. Feelings are sometimes so strong that prospective fathers insist on their wives going into maternity hospitals at Yorkshire Skipton or Lancashire Colne, depending on which county cricket team is supported. Their mills and factories are ringed by fields and although Barnoldswick has a brand-new church of modern design it still cherishes its ancient parish church whose furnishings include a splendid three-decker pulpit and pews of old oak. To enter the main door you walk on gravestones which date back to the seventeenth century. The old villages of Thornton, the two Martons, Gisburn and Sawley testify to the pre-Industrial age. Sawley clings to the pathetic remains of a Cistercian Abbey, close to the river. It is one of the few controlled by the Ministry of Works for which no charge is made for admission. Agriculturally this is predominantly sheep country, and on every road you will meet double-decked cattle-wagons packed as likely as not with sheep and leaving behind them a pungent acrid tang. On cattle market days in Skipton the air is full of sheep smells, sheep-noises and the herding cries of drovers rounding up errant strays.

As a background to all this activity of a country market town, yet here without incongruity, are the giant thread-spinning mills and the beginnings of that industry which lies along the banks of the Aire for the rest of its course. Southwards from Skipton the chimneys sprout even more thickly. Here and there among them you will find a link with the past, as at Kildwick with its ancient "Lang Kirk of Craven", or behind Keighley where Haworth and its moors recall the gifted Brontë sisters and attract visitors from the far end of the earth to the grim parsonage where Emily and Charlotte and Anne lived and wrote. These gritstone moorlands are greyer and more sombre than the green moors of the limestone dale country. They at least have not changed since the Brontë sisters knew them 100 years ago. They sweep through vast silences only broken by the sound of the wind over untenanted miles away to Blackstone Edge, with few roads, little evidence of humanity, and only an occasional stream and the wild bird life to offer movement or ease their monotony. Here and there a ruined building strikes a chord of remembrance. Then you recall that this was the original of a hall or house recreated in the minds of one or other of the sisters. Here is the true shrine of Charlotte and Emily rather than the grey churchyard at Haworth in which they are buried.

At Keighley you meet the textile industry in full force, for here is made much of its machinery, and wherever you look now it will not be at limestone scars or green fells but at mills perched on hillsides as well as in the valleys, drab chimneys and gigantic power stations. Here and there you glimpse the Yorkshire stretch of the Leeds and Liverpool canal which was begun by the engineer Brindley in 1770 and completed in the year of Waterloo. As the result of nearly 150 miles of arduous engineering, this linked the Lancashire shipping port with the industrial West Riding. At Bingley in the Aire Valley are the remarkable five-rise locks which, with others, raises the canal level some 120 feet along a hillside. Elsewhere there are aqueducts, cuttings, and superimposed road and water ways. Yet presumably these difficulties stimulated rather than daunted their builders, for this was the beginning of an era of canal-building which gave industrial Yorkshire a network of water-ways, linking rivers, creating inland docks, and stimulating the exports and imports that were its life-blood.

Half a century or so later came the railway into this dale when three companies, amalgamated into the Midland Railway, developed the line from Leeds to Bradford and later extended it to Keighley, Skipton, Hellifield and Ingleton, where it linked with the London and North-Western system through Sedbergh to Scotland. Later, as we have seen, the Midland Company drove its own line up the "Long Drag" from Hellifield through North Ribblesdale and over the wild Pennines to Carlisle, thus linking London and Scotland directly through the centre of England. From this line up the dale as far as Hellifield there were branch lines linking it with Guiseley and Ilkley, the Worth Valley, West Craven and the Lancashire-Yorkshire boundary. And here and there along the lineside still remain the sidings which carried goods to and from the actual mills and workshops.

The water-ways, like the adjacent railways, have come upon lean times, and there are continuing threats of closure. Great new roads run alongside them filled with a faster, more insistent traffic. Across them sweep monster arches carrying strange tankers, articulated vehicles and many-wheeled vehicles which you imagine look scornfully down upon the older and less mobile means of transport they have supplanted. Elderly gentlemen wrote to the papers a hundred years ago lamenting the decline of the roads and falling into ruin of the wayside inns because of the coming of the new modes of travel. They still write to the newspapers lamenting the decline of the canals and the passing of the railways. A century hence what will they write about? Perhaps that airports serving Leeds and Bradford and elsewhere are once more causing the roads and motel and transport cafés to be deserted.

There is considerable civic pride in the West Riding. Although Leeds, Bradford and Pudsey are separated by less than a dozen miles and would be no more than adjacent boroughs in Greater London with a common allegiance to the whole, here they have a fierce local patriotism which a few years ago might have been expressed in physical violence and today is marked by expansionist rivalry. So, too, of a dozen smaller towns within a twenty-mile radius. It is an extension of this local loyalty to the whole Riding which has played so large a part in stimulating the development of the University of Leeds into the largest single institution of its kind in England. A vast area almost to the city centre is being cleared to provide room for a university which by the end of the present decade will house and provide facilities for some ten thousand students. Bradford's College of Technology is similarly expanding to university status and there are demands for other universities in the Riding to meet growing needs.

The river Aire never seems to me to belong to Leeds as it should. It flows through the city but is not part of its life. No one walks beside it; those who cross it do so hurriedly without giving it more than a glance; they never venture on it. Leeds in fact takes the Aire for granted, if it thinks of the river at all. If it led anywhere it might be more popular, but it is only in its upper reaches that the river is attractive and they are too far away. The days when the Cistercians built one of their most beautiful abbeys upon its banks at Kirkstall, and when men and boys bathed in it and even fished in it have long gone by. Still further away are the days when the old rhyme was true that:

> Castleford maids must needs be fair
> For they wash in Calder and rinse in Aire.

Ask anyone in Leeds today the way to the river and you will be looked at askance. It is unknown alike to its University and to suburbia on the north bank and to its industrial area on the south. Motor highways—its links with the A.1 and the M.1, its ring-roads, and traffic ways to the rest of the West Riding—these are what matter to a city of a hundred trades from clothing to engineering, from food-canning to printing.

There long remained an outpost of the old Celtic people in the kingdom of Elmet which existed round the lower reaches of the Aire and Wharfe. Loidis (Leeds) was within that kingdom, and local pride still insists on the full titles for the villages of Barwick-in-Elmet and Sherburn-in-Elmet. Centuries later Penda of Mercia brought back paganism to a land which had become a Christian community under King Edwin whom Paulinus had baptized at York. Edwin was defeated and killed at the battle of Hatfield but Penda himself was defeated in conflict at Whinmoor near Leeds, a fact which the city has rather oddly marked by naming some of its streets after the pagan Mercian ruler.

Up to the beginning of last century Leeds was almost entirely a market town, mainly concerned with the merchandise of cloth. The town grew out of such a purpose and the market was held regularly on Tuesdays and Saturdays for many hundreds of years. Originally the market was held on Leeds Bridge but later in the seventeenth century it was moved to Briggate where it remained for fifty years until the first Cloth Hall was built in Kirkgate on the site of the first Leeds hospital. This hall was succeeded by the Coloured Cloth Hall at the junction of Park Row and Wellington Street and the White Cloth Hall and New Assembly Rooms in the Calls, this last being removed to King Street when the North Eastern Railway was constructed and occupying the site where the Hotel Metropole now stands.

It was the coming of the railway which gave impetus to the growing town. The first line opened to Leeds was the Marsh Lane to Selby line just over a century ago. One regular train a day ran to meet the steam packet from Hull. The Midland Railway was opened in 1842 and was followed in the same decade by the Leeds and Bradford line, the Leeds, Dewsbury and Manchester line and the Great Northern Railway. This with the increasing use of steam power ended the old farmer-clothier tradition of the textile trade. Enterprising citizens like the Marshalls and Gotts opened mills and warehouses, and the buying and selling of cloth by the piece on sight gave way to the work of travellers with samples, the new mills created a demand for coal and machinery and gradually pits were sunk and furnace chimneys appeared as Leeds became an engineering centre.

At Castleford the river Calder joins the Aire—and makes it no cleaner even though the tributary has its source in the hills on the Lancashire border. Along it and its own tributary, the Colne, are more mills, more factories and some coal mines. Its chief ornament is the county town of the West Riding, Wakefield, administering a region which runs from the Pennine fells on the border of Westmorland to the southern extremity of Yorkshire and which has an annual budget as large as many European states. This has given it a fine range of administrative buildings which, although somewhat besmirched by industrialism, still have a dignity and impressiveness that recent town-planning has enhanced. Yet even so, no unwarned traveller would regard it as a cathedral city. It can claim no likeness to Anthony

Trollope's portrayal of quiet cloisters and hushed precincts and no comparison with Ripon or York or Beverley. Yet although the bishopric only dates back to 1888, the cathedral stands on a site which has religious links with Saxon times and is itself a noble building with one of the loftiest spires in the county. Nearby, on a bridge over the Calder, is a chantry chapel which in its original form dates back to the fourteenth century. When Defoe visited it in the early eighteenth century he noted it down as "a large, handsome, rich clothing town, full of people and full of trade." I wonder what he would say of it today. To me it always seems to have a lost, irresolute air as if uncertain of its situation in life.

Nearer the source of the Calder is Hebden Bridge—originally "Hepton Brig", with Heptonstall above it—an oddly toy-like town with rows of houses built into the hillside in such a way that you enter the top half of the house from a street on one level, and the other half from a lower level. The hillside is itself a promontory jutting into the place at which two valleys meet. Somehow, you feel that there should be a fairy castle at the top to make it like an illustration from a child's picture book. Yet there are mills in the valley, and an ancient humped bridge over which loads of cloth have been carried for centuries. And it all exists among miles of rolling brown moors in which are notable beauty spots like Hardcastle Crags and Crimsworth Dean.

In the Colne Valley is Huddersfield, the centre of a crowded tangle of houses, mills and factories from which the dale runs to Slaithwaite (pronounced "Slough-it"), with its giant wireless masts on the hill above and the Standedge Tunnel carrying both railway and canal traffic through the hills below. Local football teams in these parts are handicapped by an almost complete lack of any flat areas on which to create a pitch. When visiting teams complain at being expected to play on boggy sloping hillsides they are told to "show us a better place". All around are bleak barren moors, with grim gnarled trees, deep "cloughs" or "gulleys", sprinkled with gaunt gritstone boulders among the bogs—an unfriendly land when the mists descend into the valleys, as they often do.

After seventy miles of journeying from its romantic limestone origins, the now unlovely Aire joins the Ouse at Boothferry Bridge. Here it is a black tidal river flowing between mudbanks. One of the oddest characters of Yorkshire once lived hereabouts at Rawcliffe on the Aire bank. He was Jimmy Hurst (or Hirst) who drove about the countryside attired in a gigantic lambskin hat, an otter-skin coat, striped stockings and buckled shoes. His carriage was drawn by Andalusian mules. And his pride and joy was a glass-sided coffin with sliding doors in which he was eventually taken for burial, the bearers being twelve old maids led by a Scots piper.

# III

## TEESDALE

From the top of Mickle Fell to the Scottish border is less than fifty miles, which may be the reason why the inhabitants of these parts often claim to add the virtues of the Scots to their qualities as York-shire folk. Certainly there is a difference of character and temperament between those who live in Teesdale and those of the other Pennine dales, and it is probably due to both physical geography and historical development that there should be an affinity between the folk of this region and those further north. And there may be an added reason in the very nature of the country.

If I am correct in suggesting that the further north you go the wilder and lonelier become our Yorkshire rivers, Teesdale in its upper reaches amply confirms the notion. Of all our rivers—and Yorkshire shares the Tees as the boundary line with the county of Durham—this has the bleakest and most remote of origins in the moorland fastnesses of Cross Fell, Milburn Forest and Dufton Fell. Here is a world of wild open "tops", bare windswept fell-sides, swampy valleys, and sudden waterfalls leaping down cliff faces. On a wet cold day with the mists swirling overhead it can be the dreariest place on earth with the whine of the wind the only sound and trickling streams the only landmarks, a sodden world deserted by man where only the mountain sheep roam. Yet on a bright spring day I have wandered along Langdon Beck to Cauldron Snout when this 200-foot waterfall was no more than a gentle trickle from ledge to ledge, when this land of Mickle Fell and the lonely Pennine Way seemed temptingly soft and quiet, when from every ridge golden plover kept up their lovely plaintive piping and round your feet were spring gentian, globe flowers (whose nickname is dumplings), mountain pansies and blue violets like a gaily patterned carpet.

This is the land of dark basaltic cliffs where, in some primeval cataclysm, igneous rock was forced up in white heat through cracks in the limestone, changing the character of the surrounding rock by its intensity of temperature and then cooled down leaving this intruding Whin Sill of columnar basalt. Where the Tees breaks through a gorge in this basalt barrier it forms the expressively named Cauldron Snout, and it flows down the gully of basalt, with many rapids, to leap finally some eighteen miles from its source over the great fall of High Force into a deep fearsome rock basin. The Force itself is split into two by an enormous central bastion of rock and the river may fall as a single eighty-foot stream on the Yorkshire side or round either side of the bastion as a double stream, or in times of high flood in a tremendous overpowering torrent over the bastion itself, filling the whole rock basin with spray and thundering sound.

Much of the gathering ground of all this water has now been transformed—despite the protests of conservationists and naturalists—into a reservoir for Teesdale's industry. But it is possible to ignore this sign of "progress" and still enjoy the fall.

When the river is in full spate it appears churned as white as milk until you are close upon it, then it has the tint of rich cream with coffee-coloured streaks. Of the fall itself there is often nothing to be seen except a great curtain of spray rising out of the ravine eighty feet into the air and drenching everything in a fine mist, often with a rainbow on its fringe. Away behind the mist is the heavy sinister roar of invisible waters. You feel like shouting with the exhilaration of it all.

Of no less geological interest than the Force is the fact that this stretch of country was largely shaped by glacial ice which swept over gaps from the Lake District and the Eden Valley, carrying Borrowdale lava, Shap granite, and even rocks from the south of Scotland, eventually pressing eastwards and southwards to what is now the mouth of the Tees, down the Yorkshire coast to Robin Hood's Bay, and through the vales of Mowbray and York. A trail of boulders is evidence of the glaciers' travels. In their study of the geology of Yorkshire, Kendal and Wroot refer to a tract of sea-bottom off the mouth of the Tees of evil repute among fishermen and known as Rough Ground. From here boulders of Shap granite have been dredged up, suggesting that this part of the sea bed was the terminal moraine of the Tees glacier.

This far north-western corner of Yorkshire, once part of the old Forest of Teesdale in which there were many deer, is squeezed tightly between Durham and Westmorland, and it is possible to drive over the border and back without being aware of it. The market town of Middleton-in-Teesdale is the meeting-place where a massive bridge spans the river. Unofficially it is the "capital" of Upper Teesdale, officially it is in County Durham. Once a local centre of lead-mining activities, later sustained by the building of a near-by reservoir, now it appears to be "without visible means of support" except as an agricultural market for the neat whitewashed farms which are sprinkled over the fells, although there are those who believe that with the natural wonders of Upper Teesdale so close it could become a tourist centre. "Our greatest export is youngsters," said one man sadly as he pointed to a group of youths and girls preparing to go to their daily work at Barnard Castle.

Beyond Romaldkirk and Cotherstone which in spring are gay with thousands of daffodils—and Cotherstone was once famous for its own special brand of cheese—is Barnard Castle astride the peat-brown river. At least the bridge strides it, but once more the town itself is in Durham. It was named from the castle built by Bernard Baliol in the twelfth century, which is probably why everyone in these parts calls it "Barney". For centuries a Wednesday market has been held here in the broad Horsemarket and Market Place. The market cross, now a traffic roundabout, dates back to 1745. And the castle ruins have for long drawn sightseers to the town because of their association with Sir Walter Scott. The old industries which once maintained the town—stocking knitting and carpet making—have gone, but a new prosperity has come to the place from the army camps outside it and a spate of new industry within. The last carpet factory closed in 1870, but now employment comes from the making of Glaxo and penicillin, concrete and gloves. That is why it draws labour not only from Middleton but from as far away as Darlington. There might even be salmon fishing were not the lower stretches of the Tees so sadly polluted.

A spectacular tourist attraction stands just outside the town. Of all things one least expects to find in this region of moors and rivers is a gigantic and ornate French château which someone described as "like a peacock in a hen run", although this most unworthily denigrates "Barney". Dr. Pevsner has declared that it looks exactly like the Town Hall of a major provincial city in France. The remarkable, if incongruous, Bowes Museum was in effect a belated wedding present from one, John Bowes, the only son of the tenth Earl of Strathmore, to his French wife. The son of the Earl might have expected to become the next Earl, but a long legal dispute ended in the Committee of Privileges denying his claim to the title, although he inherited wealth and several estates in Durham and Yorkshire. He became one of two members of Parliament for South Durham. Yet although he had many northern interests he preferred life in Paris to County Durham and spent much time there. He fell in love with an actress at the Théâtre de Variétés, the Countess of Montalbo, who was an amateur painter and sculptor as well as an actress, and in 1854 they were married in London. Almost at once they began buying art treasures; pictures, porcelain and furniture. John Bowes purchased a French château for his wife, in which to store their treasures, and acquired the considerable art collection of a Spanish count, including an El Greco, some Goyas and pictures representative of many European schools.

From time to time the thought had occurred to John Bowes and his wife that the growing collection might be housed where the public could see it and a site was chosen in the neighbourhood of Calais, as John Bowes always insisted that the inspiration and ideas were his young wife's. So plans were drawn up for the building, and in France the collection would have stayed had not political events in that country suddenly frightened the couple, who felt that the future of France at that time was too unstable to be a repository for so valuable a collection. They returned to John Bowes' home at Streatlam Castle in Durham and he found a new site for his building only a few miles away on the outskirts of Barnard Castle. In 1869 Madame Bowes laid the foundation stone of the museum to be built to the original plans devised for Calais, with living accommodation on the top floor for herself as she anticipated that, being much younger, she would outlive her husband and could spend her widowhood looking after her treasures. Workmen were brought from France, Italy and else-where. Stone was brought from Scotland as well as from near-by quarries. Mr. and Mrs. Bowes went to Paris to arrange the packing of their treasures. Over a hundred packing-cases were despatched to Streatlam Castle to await the completion of the museum. Then, less than five years after laying the foundation stone, Madame Bowes died while in Paris.

John Bowes announced that he would complete the building which at that stage had only the walls up, as a memorial to his wife, and on his death eleven years later left money for the completion of the building and its maintenance. Since then the house has been open to the public. Room after room is filled with the treasures collected by John and Josephine Bowes, furniture, china, ivories, and silver, as well as tapestries, paintings and sculpture. More recently a portion has been set aside as a folk museum illustrative of the arts and crafts of Teesdale, its tool and ways of life. Altogether, despite its incongruity this remarkable building and its collection, now administered by Durham County Council, is a unique feature of the north country.

Less spectacular but gracious in its seclusion is Egglestone Abbey, overlooking the Tees a little south of Barnard Castle, where the birds still sing among the trees as they probably did in the twelfth century when it was founded. Much has vanished, for like all the others this abbey suffered in the Dissolution, but enough remains of the nave and chancel walls of the church to let us people it with the ghosts of the white-robed monks of the Premonstratensian Order who worked and worshipped here. Sir Walter Scott peopled it, too, for he set many of his scenes here. This might almost be called "Scott country", for as a friend of the Morritt family who lived at Rokeby Hall, where the tributary Greta joins the Tees, he stayed here on several visits from 1809 onwards and those who know their Scott will recognize in his romantic poems much of this district, as in the familiar:

> Oh Brignall banks are wild and fair,
>     And Greta woods are green,
> And you may gather garlands there,
>     Would grace a summer queen.

Mortham Tower, on the opposite bank of the Greta, must have attracted him too, for it was originally a pele tower built as a refuge against Scottish raids of an earlier day.

Running almost due west from here is the ancient and historic road through the Pass of Stainmore to Bowes and Brough, where an overflow from the Eden Valley glacier already noted at the head of Teesdale, pushed its way through to Tees mouth. The gap thus left must have been used by the earliest people who ever made the crossing from side to side of England. It was an early trade route in the Bronze and Iron Ages. The Brigantes came this way to oppose the Romans, who in turn used the Pass, setting up forts and camps at Bowes and Brough and leaving their milestones as evidence. After the Roman occupation the Angles came into it from the east, and later, the Vikings used it as a western approach from Ireland. By the roadside on one of the wildest parts of Stainmore is the stump of the ancient Rey Cross, believed to have been erected in A.D. 946 as a boundary stone between the Scottish and English kingdoms.

Sad it is to relate that despite frequent reference to the "Rer Cros in Staynmor", both as a national and an ecclesiastical boundary mark, no one apparently took a great deal of notice of it. The Scots continued to raid around it and beyond for some four hundred years. William the Conqueror laid waste all this land up to the Tees, and the Pass was used for military excursions and alarums over many centuries. The first sign of better times was the establishment of a hostelry known as the Spital on the road not far from Rey Cross. This was used by peaceful wayfaring men and pack-horse trains, pedlar and drovers with their cattle shod with leather shoes for the long journey. Later came the stage-coaches and the cyclist forerunners of our present-day hikers. In due time came the railway almost parallel with the road and the road almost died of disuse. Grass grew where down the centuries men had walked. It was almost impossible to discover even the surface over which the coaches had rolled. In bad winters trains were snowbound and almost overswept by blizzards, but the line was usually kept open. The last stage was the coming of the internal combustion engine. The cars and the lorries and the transporters found their way across the old track. Once more the road over Stainmore Pass came into its own and today with a modern surface and roadside telephones and transport cafés the thunder of traffic is increasing. The story of the Pass is the story of transport.

This is a curiously literary corner of Yorkshire. Along the Tees to the east of Rokeby is the small hamlet of Wycliffe which claims to be the birthplace of John Wycliffe, reformer and translator of the Bible from the Latin Vulgate in the fourteenth century. A similar claim is made by Hipswell near Richmond, some ten miles away. Coverdale in Wensleydale was the birthplace of another translator, Miles Coverdale, who a century after Wycliffe gave us the first complete English translation of the Bible. As well as Scott, Robert Southey was entertained at Rokeby Hall. J. M. W. Turner and J. S. Cotman both painted in the district, and Turner's "Meeting of the Waters"—the "waters" being the Greta and the Tees—is a famous and familiar picture.

Yet it was left to Charles Dickens to create the great literary association of the region, for it was, of course, at Bowes he found his Dotheboys Hall during his stay at Greta Bridge and Barnard Castle in 1838. It was in the January of that year that Dickens, accompanied by Halbot K. Browne, the "Phiz" of his illustrations, travelled by the Glasgow Mail Coach in snow to the north. In a letter to his wife

Dickens described how they "reached a bare place with a house standing alone in the midst of a dreary moor, which the Guard informed us was Greta Bridge". Fortunately Yorkshire hospitality thawed out a rather cold arrival, and a good supper, capital bedrooms and a breakfast which consisted of "toast, cakes, a Yorkshire pie, a piece of beef about the size and much the shape of my portmanteau, tea, coffee, ham and eggs" could enable the travellers to say "we are now going to look about us". They looked to good purpose within the next few days, discovered the school at Bowes which was to become the Dotheboys Hall of *Nicholas Nickleby*, met the schoolmaster who was to become Mr. Wackford Squeers and, in Bowes churchyard, saw the tombstone of a youth which inspired the character of Smike. Not very long ago a friend who had a meal in Bowes was given a bill which, in addition to the proprietor's name, bore the words: DOTHEBOYS HALL, Original proprietor: WACKFORD SQUEERS. It was from a clockmaker in Barnard Castle that Dickens took the title of *Master Humphrey's Clock*.

A few miles further down river is Croft where the Rev. Charles Lutwidge Dodgson, better known as "Lewis Carroll", spent some years of his life. He was born in Cheshire in 1832, but eleven years later his father was appointed Rector of St. Peter's Church at Croft, and from here he went to school at Richmond, a few miles away, and on to Rugby and later Christ Church, Oxford. Even at Croft, we are told, his gift for entertaining children was apparent in the amusement he devised at the Rectory for his seven sisters and three brothers—a model "railway" (then a very new thing), a marionette theatre, and a series of family magazines.

Someone once declared that Yarm was "the only place that was finished when the world was created". He must have been a most loyal native of the place, for only one such could have thought so highly of this curious market town, whose main street straggles along to become the longest market town in Yorkshire, whose ancient market hall is perched in the middle, whose Octobers are disturbed by the liveliest and noisiest fair outside of Hull, and whose activities are overlooked by a railway viaduct which runs high above the rooftops. Perhaps, however, this last is a matter for pride, for it was in a Yarm hotel nearly 150 years ago that the promoters of the Darlington and Stockton line, the first public railway in England, held their inaugural meeting. As there is a plan afoot for brightening up the frontages of the old houses and inns which line the main street—a

Civic Trust plan which the nearby Stokesley has already put through —perhaps the finishing process may not, after all, be complete.

In the short distance between Croft and Yarm the Tees performs remarkable convolutions, now south now north, occasionally appearing to turn back upon itself. After Yarm it straightens itself out on a direct course to the sea, passing through Thornaby and on to Middlesbrough, and becoming decidedly grimy in the process.

One of my prized possessions is a three-part map of Yorkshire, mounted beautifully on linen, and elegantly boxed to look like a bound volume. The North Riding section of this map, which is dated 1817 ("corrected 1827 and 1828") marks Yarm in large type, with rows of black rectangles indicating buildings and a strong coloured double line through it marking the main road. Not far away is Stokesley, in slightly smaller type but still, by its rectangles, a sizeable place. I look hard for Middlesbrough and there it is, represented by three small dots, its name in the tiniest type, with a miserable cart-track of a road to it. Not a dock, not a harbour, not a crane nor a factory in sight. That was Middlesbrough as it was, 140 years ago.

The change must have come very soon after my map was printed for it is on record that in 1829 six enterprising men, all said to be Quakers, bought some 500 acres of land on the south bank of the Tees at one pound an acre for the purpose of developing the coal trade. That was the start of Middlesbrough. Steel soon followed coal. The iron mines of Cleveland were close at hand. The mouth of the Tees offered easy access. The furnaces and cranes, the harbours and docks, the smoke and the grime came with a rush, and the Victorians loved it. Even so good a Yorkshireman as J. S. Fletcher, a novelist and topographer who could paint the rural scene in glowing, lush words and rhapsodize over the hills, was moved to eloquence over the transformation.

"Since then," he wrote in 1908, "Middlesbrough, within a hundred years ago nothing but a dreary flat on the banks of an undredged river, has become a fine town with a hundred thousand inhabitants, scores of miles of streets, a port into which ships of magnitude can enter, and a record of enterprise and hard work of which its people are justly proud. One should see Middlesbrough if only to think of its blast furnaces, its rattle and roar, its ceaseless striving, when one gets to the source of the Tees on the Westmorland borders, and remembers that the water which flows down from the fellsides in such

*The market town of Pickering*

quiet surroundings will ere long sweep past this modern product of foresight and energy on its way to the North Sea."

Perhaps we think differently nowadays.

In those early days of the development of Teesdale, iron ore and shipbuilding played an important part. Today there are only two active shipyards, the metal industries have moved eastwards to become concentrated at the mouth of the river—Teeside produces about one-fifth of the nation's output of steel—the nearby Cleveland orefield is almost worked out and a large proportion of ore is imported. A new industry has, however, arisen which the old Quaker pioneers could not foresee. Middlesbrough is now ringed by vast chemical plants presenting to the observer a strange geometric landscape of metal tubes, shining spheres, squares, cones and weirdly shaped constructions in place of the familiar forms of blast furnaces and rolling mills. Key words now are equally strange: titanium, ethylene glycol, anhydrite. These are produced by odd processes like the cracking of oil and the electrolysis of brine, and the results are conveyed as liquids or gases through giant pipelines across the Tees. A few decades ago the only chemicals known there were the by-products of the iron and steel industries.

All this calls for engineering and ancillary works, for shipping facilities, oil receiving tanks and docks. It also calls for a growing manpower drawn not only from adjacent areas in Yorkshire but also from a wide area in Durham. The population of Teeside has grown rapidly in recent years and although there are areas of depression in the midst of all this prosperity, these flat lands where the mountain-born river flows through the black belt of industry with scarcely a green field to be seen are among the most productive, industrially speaking, in the whole county.

*Whitby, where the Esk joins the sea*

# IV

## THE MEN OF THE MOORS

LOOKING southwards from the vast contorted chemical installations at Wilton near the Tees estuary or from the drab blast furnaces and rolling mills at Skinningrove on the north-east coast of Yorkshire, it is difficult to believe that only a dozen miles away you can be on some of the loneliest highlands of England—the great plateau of the North York Moors. Here you can wander all day and never meet another human being. Here around you are the burial places of antique peoples to whom these moors were home, and strange stone crosses standing like forgotten ghosts. There are something like a thousand square miles of rolling upland in this area of the North York National Park, with its outliers of the Cleveland Hills and the Hambletons.

To know it all intimately would take the best part of a lifetime. It would have to be done on foot, for while there are a few roads across it they are but fine threads in a far-stretching tapestry of hill and valley. From many high places along these moorland roads it is possible to look across this Jurassic landscape into a distance in which you cannot tell where earth ends and sky begins. All around you are steep scarps and plateau-like hills hiding the deep hollows between the "riggs" or ridges moulded and cut by wind and weather out of the limestone, sandstone, shales and clays of which this country is formed. Unlike the western dale country this high land was untouched by the glaciers, although they ground their way round its edges. Its contours vary from the steep rounded "riggs" to high flat tablelands, with odd grit-capped and cone-shaped hills to break their monotony. Here and there are steep escarpments which might be the cliff edges to inland seas. Apart from the Esk, most of the rivers which drain this high land flow south to the Vale of Pickering, forming the series of dales from Ryedale to Newtondale.

There are times in winter when no smile appears on the face of this vast region. Then, swept by fierce north-easterly gales, stabbed by lightning, whipped by hail, it can appear desolate and lifeless.

There are valleys where streaks of snow linger for weeks untouched by the low sun. Scarcely a habitation is visible. Apart from the noise of the elements these are silent moorlands and there is a strange absence of bird life. No curlews, no golden plover, few hawks such as you find on the western hills, and fewer owls, save in the valley woodlands. True, many years ago, I have heard the nightjar churring on summer evenings and larks singing in the summer days, but little else. Gulls seem to spread further and further inland from the sea, but there are few rabbits or, on the hills, hares. It is only on a day of high summer or, better still, autumn, that this dead landscape stirs into life. A golden light spreads over the moorland and something of the sun's own self seems to enter into the texture and composition of the land. The hills glow and no longer appear barren. The heather is touched with flame. And as the light fades into evening and the moorland becomes a golden green and later bronze there is no longer any sense of desolation but rather of intense stillness, as of rare music that sinks into silence.

## The Cleveland Hills

Encircling these moors with a protective arm the Cleveland Hills sweep in a rough semicircle from the coast north-west of Whitby through Guisborough and south to Osmotherley and down almost to Helmsley where across the valley of the Rye the arm continues as the Hambleton Hills. The sandstone waves of this inland sea of hills nowhere rise higher than 1,500 feet on Urra moor. They run in long, airy ridges, separated by hidden valleys and here and there wide moorland stretches. Although trees are fewer here than in much of rural Yorkshire yet there is no sense of bareness in the landscape. These moorlands are famous for their bilberries—whortleberries and blueberries are the local names—which must have been as familiar a summer fruit to those earliest dwellers on these hills and whose burial places are marked by frequent tumuli as they are to picnickers today. Heather lays a dark velvet cloak over the hills in winter, becomes brown in summer, and glows in autumn. Banks of wild thyme colour the rocks and scent the air.

The land reflects the weather and the seasons like a clear mirror. There is an Alpine feeling when the hills are snow-blanketed and appear far loftier than they really are; there is the sense of a fantastic never-never land when the summer mists descend in the green valleys and you are lost to sight and sound; but best of all is the autumn when the green gives way to the purple and gold of the heather and bracken and the hills are transformed into a magical world of light and colour. Scattered over this land are the grey forms of sheep, tame enough to eat out of your hand, beg for food at car doors, and even as at Goathland to wait hopefully at bus-stops for the next load of well-disposed visitors to arrive with more titbits.

The story is told in these parts of a visitor who met a shepherd on the moors and asked approximately how many sheep were allotted to each acre. "Nay," answered the farmer. "Thoo's begun at t'wrong end. Thoo should ask how many acres gan to each sheep."

Much of north Cleveland was once ironstone mining country, but, as we have already noted, the ore is worked out leaving only the scars of the industry. Alum, too, was worked here long ago, but that, too, has gone. Some heavy industry clings to the land between the hills and the sea, and the chemical industry is developing in the region. Redcar, Marske, and Saltburn besides being holiday resorts are also dormitory towns for Teeside. Here and there some fragment of the past remains, as at Upleatham where there is one of the tiniest churches in the country, part of it very old, and the nearby Skelton Castle which has been in turn the home of the Fauconbergs, the Nevilles, the Conyers and the Whartons, great families whose names we meet in other parts of the county. The original castle was erected by Robert de Brus who was given the land by the Conqueror. This galaxy of names inspired Ord, the historian of these parts, to declare magniloquently that "from this little nook of Cleveland sprang mighty monarchs, queens, high chancellors, archbishops, earls, barons, ambassadors and knights".

One eccentric resident of the castle, not included in that catalogue, was a Mrs. Margaret Wharton, who was given the nickname of "Peg Pennyworth" because of her miserly habit of buying everything in the smallest possible quantities. She achieved great wealth and lived to a great age, reputed to be 103.

There are many places on these moorland heights, once you have climbed from the coast, where you have a vast panoramic view of hills and sea which appear to continue without limit. One is from the fine road which comes in from Whitby over the edge of Blackamore to Guisborough. Although it is an old highway, its gradients and its surface were so bad that for centuries it was scarcely used. Today it is a busy motor road bringing heavy traffic through the once quiet town of Guisborough, with its cobbled street, its lovely

ruined priory of which little but the east window shape remains—
and its modern outlook. This was one of the first towns in Yorkshire
to adopt the Civic Trust idea for giving itself a face-lift by a planned
scheme of shop-front improvement. It is a tidy little town far removed from the days when John Wesley protested that there was "so
vehement a stench of stinking fish as was ready to suffocate me". The
Priory was an Augustinian one founded in 1119 by the same Robert
de Brus and a tomb of the de Brus family taken from it is in the
near-by church of St. Nicholas. Guisborough was for a while the
centre of the alum industry for which, in 1606, Sir Thomas Chaloner,
lord of the manor, obtained a monopoly. Later the Crown took over
the rights and more accessible mines were opened along the coast,
where they were worked until early last century.

Guisborough links us westwards with Middlesbrough and the Tees;
you have not to travel far out of this little country town before you
are into the suburbs and turmoil of industry. Turning southwards,
however, is a road which runs down the outer edge of the Cleveland
hills to Great Ayton, Stokesley and Northallerton with the Plain of
York opening out on its right hand all the way. It is an attractive road
even though in recent years it has grown from a quiet byway to an
important traffic artery. Just outside Guisborough it offers to view the
Fujiyama-like cone of Rosebery Topping, once held by the locals to
be "the highest hill i' all Yorkshire". Actually it barely tops the
1,000-foot level, but rising on the edge of the York Plain it is a notable
landmark even though its summit is crumbling away so fast that it
may before long be but a minor hump. This is the starting-point of
a notable ridge walk which continues from Rosebery to Cook's
Monument on the next hill of Easby Moor and then in a giant sweep
all the way down this outer edge of the Clevelands to the Hambletons,
rarely dropping, for more than an occasional hollow, below the
1,000-foot level the whole way.

Cook's Monument commemorates the famous Captain Cook who
spent his boyhood at Great Ayton, at the foot of the hill, and whose
school is still shown to visitors. Local pride, however, was not great
enough to prevent the attractive cottage in which he lived from being
sent to Australia in return for a small monument which stands on its
site; scarcely a satisfactory change in commemoration of one of Yorkshire's most distinguished sons. Still in existence in Great Ayton is a
Quaker School founded over a century ago with extensive grounds
through which runs the river Leven.

A few miles further on is Stokesley, one of the most charming market towns in this half of the county. One could spend much quiet time here in its broad market square bordered by comfortable-looking shops—again "spruced up" under Civic Trust impetus—with a background of dignified houses, the brown waters of the Leven flowing through the town under interesting old bridges, and a plenitude of trees to give it all softness. The peace and quiet of the town is completely broken only once each year at the time of Stokesley Show held every September since 1859. This annual event marks almost the end of the agricultural show season in the county just as the May show at Otley in Wharfedale marks its opening. To Stokesley then comes all the fun of the fair on a gigantic scale, for it flows out of the showground and into almost every street in the town, with stalls and side-shows and loud-speakers and transistors by hundreds. All Cleveland foregathers here on Show day, to look at stock and machinery, to gossip, eat, drink and be merry. And to look at the horses, for this is emphatically horse country

In medieval days there existed in the North of England a race of clean-legged horses, traditionally bay in colour, which had long been cultivated and adapted to the uses of the times—for agricultural and for pack and pillion work. In the horse-breeding district of Cleveland particularly this race of horses was bred in great numbers, and their beauty, action and style received continual attention. It was this type of strong and active horse which was favoured by travelling salesmen, the chapmen, to carry their heavy packs of goods for sale in towns and villages. So the breed became known as "Chapman" or "Cleveland" bays, in these days sadly declining in numbers.

Stokesley is a roundabout from which many roads emerge; north to the Tees; east to Ingleby Greenhow and the wildly romantic Bilsdale, down which runs the oddly named river Seph; and south to Osmotherley on the slopes of the Hambletons and so to Northallerton and Thirsk. On this road is the attractive Tontine Inn, named from the old custom by which a property owned by a founding group descended to the surviving members at every death until it became the possession of the last survivor. At the point where this inn stands a road strikes back to Yarm. Osmotherley itself has a large stone table supported on pillars which appears to have been used for a multitude of communal purposes—a resting-place for corpses on the way to burial, a market stall, and a pulpit from which John Wesley preached.

Peeping over the tree-tops at the foot of the hills near Osmotherley is the tower of Mount Grace Priory, one of the finest examples of an old Carthusian monastery existing anywhere. Built towards the end of the fourteenth century it housed a community whose rule enjoined austerity, isolation and silence. Entering the inner cloister, itself shut off from the outer court, you can see the remains of the little self-contained cells in which the fifteen or more hermit-monks lived as solitaries, meeting their fellows only for matins and vespers and feast days when services were held in the church. Each cell had its garden in which the hermit worked alone. Even his food was provided for him through a right-angled hatch which prevented the inmate from seeing or touching the server. A deep peace hallows the place today, and after periods of neglect, much has been done to restore the grounds to the pleasant order they must once have known, so that it is a pleasant thing to wander among these ruins. Yet always when I have visited it I have been unable to rid myself of the thought of the unnatural peace which must have rested upon this place where men lived and spoke not and tortured themselves—how ingenious and horrible those hatches are—to save their own souls in a complete retreat from the world. Architecturally, compared with other Yorkshire abbeys like Rievaulx and Kirkstall, Mount Grace even in its full glory reflected the austerity and greyness of those within.

Bilsdale lies on the other side of the Hambletons from Osmotherley. Only in recent times has it been threaded by a modern highway linking Stokesley with Helmsley in Ryedale and even now it possesses only a few hamlets and farms. There was an old joke that a Bilsdale man was a foreigner so rarely was he seen out of his dale, but that was before there were buses down the dale. At the top of the dale are the Wainstones, a group of rocks which once had the form of a wagon and horses but are now disintegrating. On the opposite side of the road is Urra Moor, the high point of the Cleveland hills. And if you wander on this high moorland plateau you will find old coal workings and shallow pits used for lime burning and iron smelting, probably by the monks of Rievaulx. The first place of any size—two shops, an inn, and a few pleasant houses—is Chop Yat, as the locals call it, or Chop Gate on the map. One derivation of the odd name is "the gate where trade is done", which rings a little ironically in a dale so far removed from any normal conception of commerce. Streams come in from lesser dales to combine as the river Seph, and the main dale itself loses its original bleakness and becomes luxuriously wooded, with here and there groups of pines which scent the air, and perhaps a few silver birches.

At Spout House, once an ancient thatched and mullioned inn now renamed the Sun, the Bilsdale fox-hounds are kept, the best-known pack in the county. This hunt is said to be one of the oldest in England, having its origins in the pack started by the second Duke of Buckingham when he lived at Helmsley Castle. A few miles further on, the Seph joins the Rye and the country becomes softer with more gentle green as a contrast to steep and purple hills and wooded cliffs. You are prepared for loveliness and it bursts upon you magnificently in the panorama of the Rye valley and the jackdaw-haunted ruins of Rievaulx Abbey, to which we shall return.

## Eskdale

Draining the high moors east of Roseberry Topping the river Esk and its tributaries contrive to provide a contrast to the wide open spaces of the hills by cutting through them a most attractive and secluded dale.

Of all the Yorkshire rivers the Esk is the only one between the Tees and the Humber to flow directly into the North Sea. It has a changeful career from its insignificant beginnings on the high brown Westerdale moors, through a narrow defile near Lealholm, then between wooded slopes and under ancient bridges to Grosmont, where for a century it ran beneath ironworks and furnaces that were forerunners of the industry which moved to the Cleveland coast. In its final stages it becomes a pastoral river with sawmills and flour mills on its banks, eventually to emerge as the river on which Whitby stands, with shipbuilding yards and a busy little harbour and a reputation as a salmon fishery. It was given its name when Esk, like Usk and Ouse, stood for "river". There was no need to define it further for this was the only river known to those who lived on its banks, probably Bronze Age people of one thousand years B.C., whose settlements and burial places have been found on the high moors.

High up near its beginnings is Danby Castle, now a farmhouse, built by the Latimers in the fourteenth century and passing to the great north-country family of the Nevilles, who built a bridge to it across the Esk and adorned it with their coat of arms on the keystone. Alas for human vanity, the bridge fell into disrepair some centuries later, was repaired and restored by a Mr. George Duck, and is now known as Duck Bridge. By an odd chance, another bridge some miles lower down was, according to legend, built by an alderman of Hull name Ferris to mark the place where in his youth he had to cross the river to court a young lady on the other side. When prosperity came to him he built the bridge—which is now known as Beggar's Bridge even though it bears this wealthy benefactor's initials.

On the south side of the dale below Danby there are several smaller dales untouched by motor roads, yet explorable on foot, where the true remoteness of these moors can be most fully appreciated. They take one into the very heart of the moorland country, while the "riggs" or ridges which divide them offer remarkable views of the apparently endless rolling moorlands.

Danby is a reminder that this corner of Yorkshire has in recent times been notable for the number and quality of those who have found special interests in the region and introduced them to a wider audience. For at Danby during over fifty years of last century Canon J. C. Atkinson served as Vicar, coming to it as a "foreigner" from Essex and finding its people, customs and speech curiously fascinating. He gathered it all together in his book *Forty Years in a Moorland Parish* and this is now a Yorkshire classic. Similarly Dr. Frank Elgee, a largely self-educated geologist and naturalist, and his wife made an intensive study of the archaeology of these moors, investigated the tumuli, barrows and every scrap of prehistoric remains and recorded it all in a number of notable volumes like *Early Man in North East Yorkshire*, again classics in their field. I remember, too, meeting at his home in New Wath, near Goathland, the enthusiast F. W. Dowson, an ex-schoolmaster, who had an immense knowledge of the people, customs and folk-lore of these moors. He was responsible for reviving the ancient ceremonial of the "Plough Stots" and local sword dances. He gathered up a considerable collection of old farm implements. And he was delighted to find on land near his own cottage the remains of an early "bloomery" in which early metal workers extracted iron from the ore. Much of all this he recorded in a book on Goathland. Earlier than these was Eskdale's own local poet John Castillo, who died early last century and who was a cut above the average run of country bards. Some of his dialect poems had a remarkable popularity and appear in many dialect anthologies. This part of Yorkshire is well-documented.

There is a pleasant ring about the names of the Eskdale villages Westerdale, Commondale, Castleton, Lealholme and Glaisdale. They match their names in character. Egton Bridge, a wooded hamlet by the river side, and Egton proper lying above it, are particularly attractive, which is why this dale is a popular place with holiday-makers from the north Yorkshire coast. Glimpses of that coast can be seen from the high moors above and we run unmistakably into its outposts at Sleights and Ruswarp. Here are the homes of retired people from all over the county close to tea gardens and river boating. A mile or so further and the Esk becomes tidal, flows into Whitby's busy harbours and out to sea through the gap between the old town and its abbey on one side and the new town and its hotels on the other.

One of the high places with perhaps the finest broad view of this country is Sleights moor, some 900 feet up, from which you can look eastwards over the brown Fylingdale moors to the pearly blue sea, westwards up the wooded Esk valley, and southwards to the deep cleft of Newtondale, a remarkable ravine through the moors down which runs one of the most attractive railway lines in England, now, alas, closed. The track twists and turns like a toy railway with woods running down almost to the carriage windows. On either side are sheer cliffs with occasional glimpses of a river, trickling or frothing, according to the season, down the dale. I once travelled on this line with an elderly man who told me he had heard foxes barking in the woods as the train went by and he had seen many hares in the pocket-handkerchief-sized meadows along the lineside.

From Sleights moor, too, you can see the slopes of Egton High Moor, the oddly isolated cone of Blakey Topping and the course of the Mirk Esk, near which the charming moorland village of Goathland stands. Still further, if you know where to look, is the course of the Roman road coming up from the direction of Pickering in the south, through Cawthorn Camp, an outpost of the legions near Newtondale, and then over Wheeldale moor to Egton.

According to the best authorities a Roman road when completed was a thing to marvel at, and doubtless the natives did marvel then as they do today as our great motor roads spread across the country Some five thousand miles of Roman roads are known to us today in Britain. A first class road, like the Great North Road, was some ten yards wide in actual roadway, and with ditches on either side was nearly thirty yards in width. As the ditches were deep such a road was a barrier as well as a way of travel. Ordinary secondary roads were between twenty and thirty feet wide. The Great North Road itself from London to Newcastle took over thirty years to build, and it was one of a system radiating from the centre of government to the legionary fortresses throughout the country.

This moorland stretch of Roman road, although not comparable with the Great North Road, is known as Wade's Causeway and has been traced for some twenty-five miles across the Vale of Pickering and over the North Yorkshire moors, from the line of another Roman road near Malton. It probably stretches to the coast at Dunsley near Whitby where there was a signal station, although this portion is largely lost. The width of this road was some twenty feet, and although much of it has unfortunately been destroyed by the use of its stones for enclosure walls, by ploughing up, and by wartime use by armoured vehicles, enough has been retained and uncovered on Wheeldale moor to indicate its construction. A recently published survey by the Scarborough Archaeological Society has recorded in detail the finds of coins, querns and scraps of pottery along its length, and has summarized the features of its construction. These are, briefly, a cambered embankment of gravel and subsoil as a foundation layer, upon which was another layer of sandstone slabs with prominent kerbstones, and finally a layer of gravel or small stones as a surface. There is also some evidence of bridges and fords over streams. The survey concludes that the road was built for military purposes about A.D. 80 and probably fell into disuse about the year 120.

An interesting place name on the course of the road is the still existent Julian Park, near Goathland, probably a deer park granted to a local notable by Henry III. But this does not explain the name itself which may have an older association with a Roman entertainment for children in the form of turf mazes, most of them linked with the word Julian. Such a turf maze has been recorded near Goathland. It is a pretty thought that somewhere along the lines of these Roman roads native children, or perhaps the younger Romans, had their games, and that perhaps the original street games of today might have been played on these first Roman "streets".

## Moorland Superstitions

Down the centuries this north-eastern corner of Yorkshire has had a stronger sense of superstition and belief in the uncanny than anywhere else in the county. With the Pendle district in Lancashire this region shared a faith in the potency of witches, in the power of the rowan tree (witch wood) to defy them, and in the significance of the rustling and yelping flight of "t' Gabby-ratches" overhead in the still hours of the night. With these beliefs went a multitude of minor observances, from the messages conveyed by candle grease running down a candle to the growing of house-leeks on the roof to ward off fire.

Walter White wrote in his *A Month in Yorkshire* over ninety years ago:

> "Cleveland, remote from great thoroughfares, was a nursery of superstitions long after the owlish notions died out from other places. Had your grandmother been born here she would have been able to tell you that to wear a ring cut from old, long-buried coffin-lead, would cure the cramp; that the water from the leaden roof of a church sprinkled on the skin, was a specific for sundry diseases—most efficacious if taken from over the chancel. Biscuits baked on Good Friday would keep good all the year but clothes hung out to dry on Good Friday would, when taken down, be found spotted with blood."

He could have extended his list considerably. Indeed, Richard Blakeborough thirty years later compiled a book full of such superstitions, customs and beliefs all gathered from the North Riding and for the most part from Cleveland. Here are some taken from it at random. For whooping cough the best cure came from walking along a road until you found nine frogs, these had to be carried home and made into soup; to break a clock-face was as unlucky as breaking a looking-glass; if a shoe-lace came loose it was necessary to walk nine paces before tying it, otherwise you would tie ill-luck to you for that day. Those came from Bilsdale. On the coast there were many more. Fisher girls would turn their chemises wrong way round if bad weather blew while their men were at sea; if a pig was mentioned while a fisherman was baiting his line he knew he would have bad luck; no fisherwife would wind wool by candlelight as it would be tantamount to winding the husband overboard. At Whitby I was once told that local folk always walked on the outside edge of the piers when going seawards but walked on the inside towards the land.

In the moorland areas the farming community preserved their old customs in the same way that they preserved their independence of character. Cut off from the outer world except for rare occasions, a supernatural world provided explanations for events they could not understand. There were many "Hobs"—which might be either good or evil spirits. A good Hob would help his master bring in the hay or cure an ailing pig. A bad Hob would pester a man so that all went ill. Good or bad, a self-respecting Hob would attach himself to a family and stay with them. Thus the story told in Farndale of a farmer who was so troubled by his Hob that he decided to move to another farm. He loaded his cart with furniture and farm equipment and set off. On the way he met a neighbour who exclaimed, "What's thoo doin' George, flittin'?"

And a voice from the churn called out, "Aye, lad, we're flittin'!"

So the farmer turned his horse and cart round and went back to his farm, knowing that the hobgoblin would always be with him. This may explain why you will so frequently find "Hob" in Cleveland place names.

Witches, too, were known throughout the region and often acquired considerable fame for their prowess as doctors, fortune-tellers, and advisers, no less than for their evil ways. The commonest story, which has many local variants, is of the witch who had a grudge against a particular family. As a result the pigs were always ailing, the horses went lame, and the milk would not churn into butter unless helped by a crooked sixpence. Eventually the farmer decided on desperate measures. While his wife churned wearily he hid himself in an out-building with a gun. Just as dusk came down he saw a hare making its way through the hedge. He fired, the hare rolled over dead, and almost at once the butter came. The next day they heard that an old woman who had a reputation as a witch had died suddenly at dusk the night before. And from that time the farm prospered. Almost within living memory it was as natural to consult a witch about a love affair or a domestic difficulty as to take it to the parson.

The "Gabbleratchet", the "Gytrash" and that spectral animal the "Bargest", were some of the creatures that roamed by night, to the dismay of belated travellers. At Loftus a legendary great "Worm" had its lair, and elsewhere there were dragons. Discussing this once with a local historian, he suggested to me the explanation that in an age when so many of the valleys and hollows of this vast region were almost unvisited and unknown many now extinct animals may have lived on until the time of the earliest human inhabitants, and by a process of folk memory the tradition of the existence of strange creatures was handed down. After all, it was at Kirkdale in the lower foothills to the south of these moors that bones of the elephant, hyena and rhinoceros were discovered a century ago, and Dr. Elgee recorded many unexpected finds in his excavations of the moorland barrows and tumuli.

By now, although the legends and superstitions are remembered and will be told to you without much delving, belief in them is almost wholly gone. The old isolation is now no more and the car and the television aerial, the motor cycle and the bingo poster indicate that civilization has replaced the old hard life on these moors, with its belief in mysterious shapes and spirits, yet with who knows what compensation in spiritual dedication.

## The Vale of Pickering

As you may have gathered, the keynote of the north-east of Yorkshire is colour. There are several lesser chords in the harmony, the wild moorlands, the romantic villages, the abbeys and castles, the pastoral settings and the general air of peace and plenty. But where the limestone of the western dale country is a symphony of greys and greens, and the gritstone of the industrial hills of southern Yorkshire is drabbly brown, and the coal and steel country in parts black, this region from the Plain of York to the coast and from the Wolds to the Tees is picturesquely gay. The rich colours of the soil and the stone and the pantile roofs dominate every corner.

Nowhere is this more evident than in the country which spreads eastwards from the flat and lush Plain of York towards the sea, beneath that tawny plateau of the moors whence rise the streams which flow down a series of almost parallel dales into Ryedale and the Vale of Pickering. This broad valley is overlooked at its start by the Hamble-.ton Hills, which themselves vary in colour from the well-named Black Hambleton to the shining white stone which gives its name to the little village with a long postal address—Sutton-under-the-White-stone-Cliff. To the south are the low, richly wooded Howardian Hills running down to the quiet Derwent valley, and beyond all this, and still further south, is the rolling Wolds country.

The Vale of Pickering is a valley jewelled with colourful villages, lovely great houses, historic castles, picturesque abbeys, and tiny rivers that even many Yorkshiremen do not know—the Seph, the Rye, the Seven and the Dove. You could travel for days among all this richness and find new treasure at every turn. So—where to begin. Perhaps as near the centre of it all as we can by way of compromise, a place of no great importance in itself, the charming old-fashioned village of Pockley off the main road between Helmsley and Pickering, a place of small farmsteads, white thatched cottages, even a thatched post office, with the village street running up into the hills and ending nowhere in particular, the long valley of Riccal Dale on one side and the ancient Kirkdale on the other. That so small a place should appear on a map at all is perhaps surprising, but there behind it is a great expanse of moorland, bronze, purple or dark velvet brown according to the season, to which it has given its name, Pockley Moor. That is typical of all this region, almost unknown wholly delightful little hamlets and villages tucked away in the hills or among the moorlands, giving their name to great stretches of countryside; Spaunton Moor, Egton Moor, Goathland Moor, Dalby Forest, Newton Dale, Farndale.

The waterside meadows of Farndale introduce another colour into the kaleidoscope of the North-east, the golden richness of the daffodils in springtime which brings thousands of visitors during a short spell of a few weeks to gaze upon an incredible show of flowers growing wild along the valley sides. Voluntary wardens guard this treasure while it is in bloom for there was a time when the flowers were taken away not only in handfuls but in sackfuls, almost to the point of their extinction. They have been saved and have returned to their former glory.

A considerable part of this north-east corner of Yorkshire is now patrolled by a full-time warden, assisted by volunteers, since the setting up of the North York Moors National Park, the eastern equivalent of the Yorkshire Dales National Park in the west. And in areas so rich in natural beauty the value of this is self-evident. The threat to the Farndale daffodils in pre-National Park days is only one example. Accumulations of litter on the summits of the western dales fells is another. Yet there is far from whole-hearted acceptance of the Parks either among these moorland valleys or in the dales country.

In many more than one Yorkshire country town I have found the rural district councillors considerably bitter and more than a trifle frustrated, for down the years they have seen their authority steadily whittled away. At present their grievance is against the National Park. Not, that is, against the Park itself nor even against the Park idea, but against a set-up which deprives them of any say in National Park matters even though a large part, or perhaps the whole, of the territory which they are elected to administer is subject to the Park Planning Board as a higher authority. They have no direct representative even on its advisory committees. The greater the powers conferred on the Planning Board the smaller the powers left to the District Councils. And before the Parks it was the local high school, which passed to the County Council, and before that the cottage hospital, which went to the Regional Board. Neither the fire brigade nor the police force is any longer under local control. "All we are left with," one disgruntled rural councillor told me, "is emptying the dustbins and collecting the money to pay the bills of larger authorities."

In time no doubt this feeling of opposition will disappear as the National Parks establish themselves, not as public playgrounds but as areas in which greater use and enjoyment of the land is made possible by preventing its misuse and abuse, and perhaps also by greater local representation on the Planning Boards.

Between the far-spreading tawny moorlands of Cleveland and the darker Hambleton Hills is a delectable land which can offer such pleasant sounding places as Arden on the one side and Rosedale on the other. Between them is a Shakespearian richness of tragedy and romance. The valley of the Rye, from which this district takes its name, is the most westerly of that sequence of dales whose rivers drain the Cleveland Hills, running into and across the Vale of Pickering and all eventually joining the river Rye itself which sweeps in a great arc from north of Black Hambleton to join the Derwent near Malton, collecting the tributary rivers as it goes.

For much of its life the Rye is a dancing river, happy-go-lucky in its twists and turns, often bewitching in its beauty but never moody or sombre like many of the rivers of the western dales. At its beginnings on Whorlton Moor it might as easily have turned north to the Tees or east across Cleveland. Instead, by a sort of feminine waywardness—and I think always of the Rye as an attractive maiden—she turned south to an eventual marriage with the Derwent. Certainly the river has a lonely start on moorlands rarely visited save by gamekeepers, shepherds and those intrepid long-distance stalwarts who do the Lyke Wake Walk, which begins near Mount Grace Priory and ends at Ravenscar on the Yorkshire coast, a break-neck journey of some forty miles over heather, bog and stream done in all weathers.

This Walk, which originated in 1955, is this part of the country's equivalent to the Three Peaks Walk in the west, and attracts a curiously mixed company of entrants from boy scouts to elderly hikers and from soldiers in training to schoolboys, as well as several women.

*The South Bay at Scarborough*

Those who achieve the Walk within twenty-four hours (an extra twelve hours is allowed for every five years of age over sixty-five) become members of the Lyke Wake Club which has as its "club song" the melancholy "Lyke Wake Dirge", one of the oldest songs in the Yorkshire dialect and formerly used at Cleveland funerals. The first verse goes:

> This yah neet, this yah neet,
> Ivvery neet an' all,
> Fire an' fleet an' cannule leet,
> An' Christ tak up thy saul.

There are nine other verses just as dismal!

Next in order eastwards from the Rye valley is the lovely Bilsdale, through which runs the main road from Helmsley to Stokesley and along which a service bus in its mundane way carries its passengers on one of the most delightful routes in Yorkshire. The river of this dale is the oddly named Seph, which runs close to the road. On either side are the moorlands of the Cleveland country. Over these moors came William the Conqueror on his return from laying waste the North Country after the rising at York, and the crossing proved almost as disastrous for him as for Napoleon many centuries later in his notorious retreat from Moscow, and for the same reasons. The journey was made in January 1069 and coincided with a fearful snow-storm. There was no shelter on these bleak open tops. His men were weary with much marching and fighting. Very many of them died before reaching the then hamlet of Helmsley, and the tattered remnants only reached York with difficulty.

Near the point at which the Rye and the Seph meet below Hawnby Moor are the remains of Rievaulx Abbey, built where the dale is a narrow valley of wooded crags. To come upon this from the ornamental terrace which overlooks it—added two hundred years ago—is to have a picture breathtaking in its idyllic loveliness. The Abbey is unforgettable in its grace and serenity. It is dignified even in ruin. Little wonder that Cotman, Girtin, Turner and a host of other artists have come here to paint it.

Records of the Abbey's history are limited but it is known that Walter l'Espec, whose benefactions appear so often in Yorkshire's story, granted this site to the Cistercians in 1131 and that its building was very rapid. One oddity of its erection was that the church had to be set north and south instead of east and west because of the difficulties of the site, and although now, like other Yorkshire abbeys, it appears blessed in its setting, this was described by a monkish chronicler of the time to be "a place of horror and waste solitude".

Much of the recolonization of the waste left by King William in the bitter winter which followed the York rebellion must be attributed to the religious houses like that of Rievaulx set up in the desolated territory. The new monasteries which were introduced into the county after the Conquest made a considerable contribution to local agriculture. Rievaulx Abbey in the time of its third and most famous Abbot Ailred—that is the middle of the twelfth century—had a complement of 140 monks and 500 lay brothers "so that the church swarmed with them, like a hive with bees". That would be a considerable population for this deserted valley even in these times and it must have created a demand for agricultural products over and above what the lay brothers themselves provided as well as a good deal of employment in other ways.

It is on record that great quantities of cheese (then made from ewes' milk) were consumed at Bolton and at Jervaulx Abbeys in the dales, thus starting the making of Wensleydale cheese which is now a factory product. Much of this cheese was made by women outside the monasteries. And as with cheese so with many other commodities that would be needed. "Beef" and "mutton" are words introduced by the Normans and indicate the greater use of animals for food. The old Saxon words "ox", "cow", "calf", "swine", and "sheep" served for the animals while they were being reared by the local hinds. It was the Norman lords and probably the hierarchy of the abbeys who introduced new words like "veal" and "venison" when they appeared on the table. Significantly "bacon" is the exception and this was almost certainly the chief meat of the earliest Yorkshire peasants. Piers Plowman counts it as a blessing for the labourer after the Black Death that his improved status enabled him to scorn "worts (cabbage) a night old" and the accompanying "piece of bacon" and to eat of "fresh flesh or fish fried or baked". There can be little doubt that the monasteries introduced the first ordered daily life to the community, and that the tolling of the monastery bell at fixed times was the outward sign of this order. Indeed, it might be suggested that this bell was the precursor of the factory hooter and siren.

It certainly disturbed the group of monks from Furness Abbey in Lancashire who had been granted land by Roger de Mowbray for their new monastery on the other side of the Rye from Rievaulx at the place now known as Old Byland. Both monasteries could hear the other's bells "which was not fitting and could by no means be endured". They bore it for four years and then the newcomers looked for a fresh site and eventually built their church and monastery some miles further south. It is not so easy to picture Byland Abbey as it was in its glory in the way that we can at Rievaulx. So little remains. Yet the church when it was complete was one of the largest Cistercian churches in the country, more than 330 feet long and with extensive transepts, fine carving, floors of coloured tiles, and spacious cloisters. But it suffered great damage from the Scots when they pursued the vanquished Edward II, after his futile attempt to invade Scotland, for in his retreat he left his stores and treasure at the Abbey, and the Scots made no distinction of secular and sacred in ransacking the place.

Oddly, within a few miles of these ancient abbeys come to ruin, is one of the newest of England's abbey churches, that of Ampleforth. At present it is so new that there has been no mellowing by time of the hard lines and light stone. One is a little startled to come across this blatant newness against the calmer colours of the college buildings around it and the wooded hillside ridge behind. Yet it is undoubtedly impressive in its Romanesque style with pointed arches and with an unusual dome. In St. Benedict's chapel in the south-west corner of the church is the High Altar stone brought from the ruins of Byland. The Catholic College at Ampleforth dates from early last century, and accommodates a total of nearly a thousand, boys, monks and teaching staff. Across the valley, guarding the western entrance to the Vale of Pickering, is Gilling Castle, founded by the same Roger de Mowbray who gave land for the building of Byland Abbey. It passed through many hands, each family adding to its treasures. There was an ignominious end to many of them when they were acquired and removed by Mr. William Hearst, the American press magnate, to his castle in Wales. What were left are now safe as, since 1929, the Castle has been a preparatory School for Ampleforth.

While we are on this fringe of Ryedale we can look at three notable places of a very diverse kind. The first again introduces Roger de Mowbray. This is Newburgh Priory, established by Mowbray some twelve years after he had given the land for Byland, to be used for Augustinian canons. At the dissolution the chaplain to Henry VIII, Anthony Belasye, acquired it and largely rebuilt the property. It descended to a Lord Fauconberg who married Mary, the daughter of

Oliver Cromwell, and in a bricked-up vault on an upper floor is said to be the headless body of her father which she brought there to save it from indignities after the Restoration. As the vault has never been open the truth of the story has never been tested although King Edward VII, when Prince of Wales, urged very strongly that it should be opened while he was staying in the house. His host at the time was Sir George Wombwell, a survivor of the charge of the Light Brigade who had a reputation as an autocrat, and the royal request was refused. The house is still in the possession of the Wombwell family and is surrounded by lawns and pleasant gardens and—until recently—by a bevy of peacocks.

The name of Fauconberg brings us to the village of Coxwold a mile or so away, for this village was owned by them, and a delightful little row of almshouses on one side of the cobbled main street was put up by a member of that family in the seventeenth century. The picturesque street climbs steeply to the church, with the quaint Fauconberg Arms, a popular inn, on one side and outside it an ancient elm which some would have you believe dates to Saxon times. Certainly the village had a Saxon origin made clear by its original name of *Cucvalt*.

In more recent times, however, Coxwold has come to mean the Reverend Laurence Sterne. At the top of the village almost opposite the church is Shandy Hall, the name given to it by the parson-humorist who lived in it for eight years from 1760 while he was incumbent of the parish. This extraordinary man who could preach his sermons, visit his parishioners—though a little haphazard in both—and then turn to the world of Walter Shandy, my Uncle Toby and Corporal Trim, and with a somewhat bawdy wit prove himself the greatest humorist of his age and a man who could make his mark on the future history of the novel, makes him a more interesting character than one would expect to find in a country parish. Coxwold was not his only Yorkshire living. He had been vicar of Sutton and prebendary of York, of which his great-grandfather had been archbishop. But it was in the parlour of this old gabled house with its curious chimneys and creaking floors that he fiddled and ate gargantuan meals and wrote most of *Tristram Shandy* and all of *The Sentimental Journey*.

Our third point of interest in this region is just west of Coxwold in a half-timbered house in the village of Kilburn. You can find the village quite easily as it lies beneath the well-known White Horse, carved out of the hillside a century ago, and now a landmark for many miles around. Kilburn itself is no more than one of many attractive villages in these parts with a stream, a bridge, a church, an inn and a school. But the fame of Kilburn is world-wide because of Robert Thompson, son of the village carpenter, who was sent into the West Riding to learn another trade, but came back to his village after a few years to become one of the finest craftsmen in English oak. A chance piece of work executed for a headmaster of Ampleforth College gave him his first real opportunity and soon work for schools and churches all over the country poured in. He took on local boys to train as apprentices, preferred unspoiled country workers to industrially trained town youths, and refused to commercialize his craft. His only concession to the modern age was a trade-mark, a little hand-carved mouse which he introduced unobtrusively on chair-legs, on bench ends, on bed-heads, even on candlesticks in Westminster Abbey. The mouse signifies "industry in quiet places".

There is a great deal of his work in Ampleforth, at Beverley and Ripon Minsters, at Bridlington Priory Church and the Cathedral at Manchester. There are many prized pieces in homes all over the north of England, for he was as pleased to sell to an enthusiastic individual customer as to a board of governors. His works were always open to visitors. It was feared that his Kilburn workshops might close with his death a few years ago, but fortunately there were enough of those he had trained not only in his craft but the spirit of the craft to ensure that the work and tradition were maintained in and around his old house in the village.

The Rye, after leaving Rievaulx, follows a twisting course through the woods of Duncombe Park, with its classical mansion designed surprisingly by a local architect but showing the influence of Vanbrugh. Several disastrous fires have destroyed parts of the building but restoration has been carried out according to the original plans. It was the home of the Earls of Feversham, but for many years has been a girls' school—probably one of the most beautifully set in the country.

Just beyond the grounds of the Park is one of those delightful country towns which typify this side of Yorkshire. Helmsley has everything; a market square with two memorial crosses, several old but internally modernized country hotels, overlooked by a castle and a church, with river bridges, and woods all round. Few of the houses set about the square have lost their original character and even the former lock-up now proclaims itself "Ye Old Police Station Snack Bar" and has the cell doors within.

Helmsley Castle which overlooks all this is built on a ridge in the valley of the Rye. It is protected by ramparts and ditches across which a helpful Ministry of Works has thrown bridges. Despite the present beauty of its setting it is easy to see how strongly this Castle was planned with a great keep, a tower and curtain walls with a continuous walk round them. An impressive barbican, built to protect the gatehouse, has loopholes through which the long-bowmen could fire. Its original builder in the twelfth century was Walter l'Espec, founder of Rievaulx and Kirkham Abbeys, but much was added later and one of its most attractive features is the range of domestic buildings where it is still possible to see the plaster friezes and ceiling and the oak panelling added by Edward Manners, third Earl of Rutland, who owned the castle for a time in the sixteenth century. One rather sinister aspect is the obvious heightening of the keep and the curtain walls; the change in colour of the stonework provides the evidence. This was probably done as a defence against the Scots at the time of Edward II's defeat which, as we have seen, led to so much damage at Byland Abbey.

Despite its strength, or because of it, Helmsley Castle was involved in a few military conflicts. Its only real test was a three months' siege in 1644 when Sir Jordan Crosland held it against the Parliamentary general, Sir Thomas Fairfax. When eventually it surrendered it was largely dismantled.

From this point the Rye takes a swing south-east, receiving its tributary rivers on the north side and on its south side looking to the Howardian Hills. The main road down the vale from Helmsley to Pickering crosses all these streams in turn, the Riccall from the dale of the same name, the Hodge Beck from Bransdale, the Dove from Farndale, and the Seven from Rosedale. In the beautiful wooded gorge of the Hodge Beck, flowing down Bransdale through the limestone belt which separates Ryedale from the North Yorkshire moors, stands the tiny church known as St. Gregory's Minster, or more popularly Kirkdale Church. It has to be sought, for it is almost obscured by deep woodland and a frame of great yew trees. Its age is unknown but much of the existing building is Saxon and within it are stone relics of still older date. These probably link it with a monastery which existed there centuries before the building of the abbeys of Rievaulx and Fountains. Kirkdale may even have pre-dated the nearby

Lastingham and have been founded by St. Cedd, one of the earliest of missionary priests educated at Lindisfarne sometime in the seventh century.

The dedication to St. Gregory is significant as this was the Pope who sent Augustine's mission to these islands in 597, so that this monastery, whether here or at Lastingham, can claim to be one of the earliest Christian establishments in Yorkshire. It is impossible to look without reverence upon this quiet withdrawn sanctuary, unchanged in its setting down the intervening centuries, where one can make contact with a way of life that existed long before the Norman Conquest. Even more remarkable is the Saxon sundial over the door of the church which records that this building was *restored* when Edward the Confessor was King and Tostig, who played so large a part in later history, was Earl. The actual inscription reads:

Orm Gamal's Son bought St. Gregory's Minster when it was all broken down and fallen and he let it be made anew from the ground to Christ and St. Gregory, in Edward's days, the King, and in Tostig's days, the Earl.

The date of the sundial which bears this inscription, still perfectly readable, is almost certainly 1055, eleven years before events which changed the whole course of our history. In those intervening years the King, whose name is on the sundial, became a weak and ailing man. Tostig linked himself with his kinsmen across the sea. We are left to wonder what happened to Orm, Gamal's son, who up to that time had been a prosperous but devout Saxon landowner in the Ryedale hills. His act of piety was forgotten in the great upheaval which was to come, and which we call the Norman Conquest.

At Pickering comes in Newtondale which links that town to the north with Levisham, Goathland, and Whitby. Almost parallel with the dale—which, as we have seen, runs in a magnificent deep cleft through the moors and offers one of the most beautiful scenic railway routes in the country—is the high moorland road out of Pickering by Saltersgate and the Fylingdales Early Warning Station to descend into Whitby at Sleights, an exhilarating windswept climb compared with the enclosed beauty of the railway route.

Before we arrive at Pickering, however, we must pause on the main road down the vale to look at Kirkby Moorside. Incidentally, there is a continuing dispute over the spelling of this name. The Ordnance Survey insists on the "k"; most of the local folk omit it.

There is certainly a "kirk" there and it is the gateway to a great stretch of moorland running up into Cleveland. This again is a market town, with a broad square, a few remains of a castle and a multitude of red pantiled houses. Its historic interest comes from its association with the Duke of Buckingham whose home for a time was Helmsley Castle. He was a wit and a rake whose star at Court waned when he was arraigned before the House of Lords on a charge brought by the fifteen-year-old Earl of Shrewsbury for the murder of his father and "the public debauchery" of his mother. He lost his position as Master of the Horse and eventually retired to Helmsley. While out hunting on the moors his horse dropped dead under him, which being a superstitious man he regarded as an evil omen. His premonition proved true, for while waiting for a new mount he caught a chill which developed so swiftly that he was unable to return to Helmsley. He was taken to a cottage at Kirkby Moorside, where he died. An entry in the church register under the date April 17th, 1687, records the event. So did tragedy raise its head in this land of Arden.

Today Kirkby Moorside is a flourishing small town, and one of its growing industries is that of building gliders for use at the modern gliding club on the Hambleton Hills.

Farndale with its daffodils lies on the moors above the town. That dale has another legend about a "Hob", a creature of the spirit world who took a liking to a farmer named Gray and helped him, invisibly, with his threshing, and hay-making and shearing, just as he had helped the farmer's family for generations before. His only reward was a jug of cream put out each night which vanished by morning. Alas, the farmer's wife died and he married again, but his new wife would have none of this nonsense. She refused to put out the jug of cream. So the Hob refused to work any more—an early example of strike action—and from that day on bad luck dogged the household. Even the butter wouldn't turn, churn as they would. It seems to be a legend with a moral somewhere!

Near Kirkby Moorside is the ancient Saxon church, St. Gregory's Minster at which we have already glanced and, in the hills beyond, the equally old Lastingham Church. The present church is built over the crypt which was built on the site of a still older church founded by St. Cedd and in which he was buried. The crypt was intended to be the foundation of an abbey to replace Whitby. Abbot Stephen was given permission by the Conqueror to found such an abbey but outlaws drove the abbot and his monks to York where instead they founded the Abbey of St. Mary's. It is a peaceful place in which to spend an hour, with a rough earth floor and illuminated only by a tiny window at one end, a link with a very far-off time. Coming out from its gloom makes the colourful village even more lovely on a bright summer day.

Close to Lastingham is Hutton-le-Hole which comes high in the list of Yorkshire's prettiest villages, with a white-railed village green, several water splashes, and a newly created village museum housed in the old home of the late Wilfred Crosland, an antiquary and historian of these parts. Also near by is the airy village of Appleton-le-Moor, built along a single main street, which won distinction in a recent contest as being the best-kept village in the North Riding.

Just before Pickering is the village which actually tops the list of the prettiest places in Yorkshire, Thornton-le-Dale. This has a picture-postcard setting of streams, thatched cottages, rose-filled gardens and trees. This is the romantic corner of North-east Yorkshire.

Evidence of the Anglian settlement in this part of the country is strikingly apparent in the line of villages whose names end in *ton* along the north side of the Vale of Pickering where the moors descend as warm sunny slopes to the valley: Ebberston, Hutton, Brompton, Sinnington, Snainton, Thornton, Wrelton. Place names with the same termination appear in the Wolds: Weighton, Elloughton, Burton, Riston. And they appear again along the eastern border of the Vale of York at Pocklington and elsewhere. Which all suggests that these early settlers in Yorkshire sought the softer low ground offering good land for cultivation rather than the high rougher land suitable for stock. There are fewer names ending in *ley*, meaning cleared wood-land, indicating perhaps that this was comparatively open country when it was settled.

Pickering, which gives its name to this long and attractive Vale, is one of those surprising places which are "passed through" rather than visited. As the outpost of the Vale rather than its centre, as a place which is within the magnetic field of Scarborough, as the starting-point for the beckoning road over the moors and the equally inviting rail line through Newtondale to Whitby, it has never of itself attracted the tourists and holiday-makers who might be expected to visit it. Yet it has a great deal to offer both scenically and historically. High above it stands the remains of its castle, originally quite small when first built in the twelfth century but enlarged by an outer court in the fourteenth. The site was probably occupied by an Anglo-Saxon fort before the Conquest. A central keep overlooked the outer curtain walls in which were three towers, Devil's Tower, Mill Tower, and the romantically named Rosamonds Tower, so called because the Fair Rosamond, mistress of Henry II, spent some time in it. History crowded its walls for King John frequented it and Richard II was a prisoner there before being taken to his death at Pontefract. During the Civil War the castle was besieged. At one time the Steward of the Duchy of Lancaster, the owner of the castle, used to ride down to the market-place to proclaim the Fair open.

Of even greater fame are the wall-paintings in the parish church. You may have some difficulty in discovering the church, for although it is prominent over the roof-tops it is so hemmed in by houses that it requires some searching to find the stone steps which lead to the large porch. The frescoes covering two walls of the nave were probably painted in the fifteenth century and record events in the lives of the saints, Biblical scenes, allegorical representations of the Seven Corporal Acts of Mercy, the Resurrection and much else. These are not dead and lifeless daubs, but sparkling with colour and vigour. They stimulate the imagination to fancy what thousands of worshippers have thought about them down the centuries. At some time they were covered by plaster and whitewash and remained so until they were entirely forgotten. Indeed memorial tablets were fixed to the outer plaster in ignorance of what was beneath. A century or so ago they were discovered and restored although damaged where the fixing of the tablets had pierced them. They are worth a long day's journey as a remarkable example of religious art. Before leaving the church it is worth remarking the memorial to William Marshall, the rural economist who was one of Pickering's famous sons.

At Pickering we leave the green vale that was once a glacial lake, which began near Ampleforth where the Vale of York glacier was blocked from flowing east along this vale. A similar obstruction operated near Wykeham, close to the point at which the Rye joins the Derwent, to hold it back from the east coast at the Pickering end. So the whole area became a vast lake into which poured all the water from the Cleveland and Hambleton hills and down the Newtondale ravine from a lake in Eskdale further north. The overflow from this lake cut through the Howardian Hills at Kirkham Abbey and this course became the river Derwent, as it has remained since the Ice Age.

V

## THE COAST AND THE WOLDS

In this age of amusement arcades and candy floss, of electric lifts to and from the beach, of speed-boats and water-ski-ing, and of rows of cliff-top boarding houses, floral spas and bathing beauty contests, it is difficult to picture the Yorkshire coast, with its beetling cliffs in the north and its broad crumbling lands in the south, as other than a place for the holiday crowds. Bikini-clad girls, the strollers on marine parades, and family parties building castles in the sand offer no link with those Iron and Bronze Age folk whose flint knives and stone axes are still found in the burial "howes" on the moors within sight of the sea and whose food vessels and cooking pots are gazed at by holiday-makers on wet days in the local museums. Even comparatively more recent events like the coming of the Saxon and Norse invaders, the ravaging by fire and sword of those who withstood them, the landing on this coast of contenders for crowns and power, the sailing from its ports of bold venturers in mere cockle shells of ships to new lands and strange adventures—all this seems remote and shadowy along a coastline dotted with radar masts and overlooked by the great monstrosity of the Early Warning Station on the moors at Fylingdales, a Martian ugliness amid a sea of heather. Those closer, intimate ghosts of the day before yesterday, our Edwardian and Victorian predecessors, with their feather boas and voluminous skirts, their silk hats and dangling gold alberts, who took the waters at our coastal spas, seem almost as far away in reality as the Roman legions which once patrolled this shore line.

I pondered this as I travelled down the Yorkshire coast in the spring of the year when the razorbills and the guillemots and the fulmars were beginning to nest on the high cliffs and the herring gulls were clamorous in their colonies. Oblivious to the activity among the birds, the resorts were all busy on that gigantic clean-up which precedes the holiday season. New coats of paint were going on to old buildings. New signs were being erected. Fresh attractions were being wheeled and hammered and lifted into place. All the fun of the fair was being burnished and polished and made more luridly attractive for the great invasion.

"Aye," said one small man, wrestling with a gigantic ladder. "We always have an eye on tomorrow in these parts. Before one season is done, we're getting ready for the next. Yet, blow me, if tomorrow isn't always catching up on us, as you might say. There's always a mighty rush at the end."

That statement epitomized the spirit of our seaside resorts. They are towns of the future rather than of the past. Their history, though it has its moments, is the least part of them. To this magic pleasure ground come a great many of the families of Yorkshire—and from further afield too—for their annual holiday. The mill workers and the woolmen, the steel workers and the cable-makers, the men of the pits and the tradesmen and the office workers with their wives and families flock here in their thousands. The quiet sleepy little fishing villages and seaside towns of Yorkshire have in the past century awakened to a new fame and glory, and a new ugliness. Old crafts and trades have vanished or have been called upon to give a new allegiance to the crowds which flock to the sands and the fun fairs and the spas. Former lordly mansions are popular hotels or holiday centres.

How it all began can be studied in the observations of William Hutton, a Birmingham antiquary, who a century ago wrote *A Trip to Coatham, a Watering Place in the North Extremity of Yorkshire*. It was a companion volume to similar books on Scarborough and Blackpool from the same pen. When Hutton wrote the seaside habit was in embryo. Inhabitants of the future resorts had no great liking for the annual influx from the towns, they turned an unfavourable eye on visitors because they raised the price of provisions. Of the amusements at Coatham, Hutton wrote:

"These are yet in a confined state; but will advance as the credit of the place advances. The billiard table has not yet made its appearance; the tennis-court is not yet erected; the skittle-alley and the butts are not yet begun; nor has the bowling green showed its face. Quoits are in tune; but this is rather a butcher's game, although an healthful one. The visitants are amazed at present with the sands and the sea in the day, and with cards at night. There is, however, what I should never expect to find, a little modern circulating library for those who are inclined to letters."

Of the residents at these early boarding-houses Hutton gives several racy pictures, and they move him to the conclusion that "the development of human nature is infinite". Here is a character sketch of a "visitant" at a Coatham boarding-house:

"One of our company was a rich banker, a lively companion, though seventy; he would draw up his breeches, stroke down his waistcoat, and shuffling his feet along the floor, in the style of a beau, march up with a smile, and say pretty things to the ladies."

Times have changed, but there is a not unfamiliar touch about this picture of a Yorkshire seaside resort.

Or listen to Tobias Smollett, writing in 1770 about the joys of sea-bathing at Scarborough:

"Betwixt the well and the harbour, the bathing machines are ranged along the beach, with all their proper utensils and attendants. You have never seen one of these machines. Imagine to yourself a small, snug, wooden chamber, fixed on a wheel-carriage, having a door at each end, and, on each side, a little window above, a bench below. The bather ascending into this apartment by wooden steps, shuts himself in, and begins to undress; while the attendant yokes a horse to the end next the sea, and draws the carriage forwards, till the surface of the water is on a level with the floor of the dressing-room; then he moves and fixes the horse to the other end. The person within, being stripped, opens the door to the seaward, where he finds the guide ready, and plunges headlong into the water. After having bathed, he re-ascends into the apartment by the steps which had been shifted for that purpose, and puts on his clothes at leisure, while the carriage is drawn back again on the dry land; so that he has nothing further to do but to open the door and come down as he went up; should he be so weak or ill as to require a servant to put off and on his clothes, there is room enough in the apartment for half-a-dozen people."

The resorts begin almost at Tees mouth with Redcar and Saltburn, the playground of the north-eastern industrial region, not palm-fringed and exotic but down-to-earth holiday places with bingo halls, fish restaurants, fun fairs and broad sands extensive enough to accommodate all the browning bodies of the crowds. They continue at intervals southwards, with great variety in their offerings, to within sight of Spurn point and the mouth of the Humber. Some are no more than caravan sites and holiday camps—on a mightily organized scale. Others provide the whole gamut of seaside attractions from cupola-crowned hotels (now too often in process of conversion to holiday flats) to mussel and winkle stalls. Others again, like Hornsea and Withernsea, are really overgrown seaside villages offering much sand and clean air but few distractions. Their character, I think, derives much from the bays over which they preside; in the north small enclosed rocky havens dominated by great arms like Huntcliff, Kettleness and Ravenscar, in the south the great sweeping arcs of Filey and Bridlington bays where the protecting arms are almost out of sight of each other.

Scarborough's two great bays, divided by the straggling castle on the hill, have on occasion a Mediterranean aspect; magnificent sweeps of white and cream houses, hotels and brightly façaded amusement halls, besprinkled with trees and green parks, and edged with a long marine drive along the base of one bay and a Victorian spa along the other. It claims the proud title of the Queen of Watering Places. On a hot sunlit day when the tide is out and there is no movement in the tiny harbour below the castle, the whole place appears to be set still as stone. There are other times when cold winds over the warm land drop a grey curtain of mist over all this coast. The Queen and her retinue of smaller resorts from Redcar to Withernsea are then lost in a "sea fret" which may continue for days, or may lift within the hour. The persistency of these sea frets had something to do with the abandonment nearly sixty years ago of a grandiose scheme for building a holiday town on the top of the cliff between Robin Hood's Bay and Scarborough. The place, hitherto known as the Peak (or "Peeak" in local speech), was laid out with broad streets and sites for shops. It was given the name Ravenscar when the railway was brought to it. But not more than a few houses and fewer shops materialized before the plan were scrapped. Only the grass-grown kerbs and the name of the station remained as an indication of a once-bright dream.

North Sea storms batter this coastline in the winter months, and every town along it has its own stories of ships lost, heroic rescues and near escapes. I have seen the whole of Scarborough's bay a mass of white foam, with the harbour and its lighthouse almost obliterated by great waves breaking over the harbour wall, the fishing fleet held up for many days at a time, and timber-laden vessels from Scandinavia limping in with shifted cargoes or compelled to drop anchor because of the impossibility of entering the tight harbour mouth. Lower down the coast, at Bridlington, it is a familiar event for the lifeboat to be called out to usher fishing vessels into the safety of the harbour. The tiny blue and white boat seems to bounce from wave-top to wave-top, fussing round the fishing cobles like a sheep-dog rounding up a flock on the moors. A single coble would detach itself from the rest under the watching eye of the lifeboat, would hurry through the pounding seas to the protection of the harbour wall, and then nip in swiftly over the harbour bar to calm waters and safety. Back would go the lifeboat to bring the next sheep into the fold. With all its flock gathered in, the little boat would hasten back to its station down the coast and await its next call, a coaster in difficulties off Flamborough, or a seaman ill on a depot ship some miles out.

Probably the grimmest storm story of this stretch of coast is that of seven members of the Whitby lifeboat crew who on the morning of February 9th, 1861, were near Sandsend looking for hazel sticks for making their crab pots. They were shore bound because an over-night hurricane made fishing impossible, but like all fishermen their eyes were constantly on the high seas breaking round Kettleness and tearing into the bay. Suddenly they saw a Sunderland vessel, the *John and Anne*, drive ashore near the Ness. Let Miss Dora M. Walker (who was herself the skipper of a fishing coble in the 1950s) take up the story as she tells it in her book *Freemen of the Sea*:

> "Borrowing a Sandsend coble, they launched it at once, at considerable risk, and brought off safely all the crew of the *John and Anne*. Seeing the likelihood of other wrecks they then hastened back to Whitby to take their stand by the new lifeboat. None too soon! A collier schooner, *Gamma* of Newcastle, was the next victim. Barely were the same men with the rest of the lifeboat crew back to safety when the *Clara*, a Prussian barque, closely followed by the brig *Utility* and the schooner *Roe*, were driven on the sands.
>
> "Almost it seemed as if some monstrous hand hurled the ships to destruction, and that no sooner was one crew snatched from death than another was flung into the pit. The sweat poured down the men's faces, mingling with the salt and blinding them, as they bent to the oars under the lash of their own mighty determination. A brigantine approaching the harbour was flung broadside into *Collier Hope*. The lifeboat took off the crew. And then the *Merchant*, another schooner, was seen through a haze of searing snow and sleet, her sails in ribbons, driving on to the sands. The seventh ship!
>
> "The men had toiled without food or rest, forcing bodies and nerves beyond the scale of human endurance. No more than sixty yards from the pier a monstrous hand rose to grip them in the form of a mighty wave, and the sea had the victims it had striven for all day, which these men's titanic efforts had denied it. The lifeboat, which had stood so well the frightful

strain inflicted on it, was overturned, and the crew engulfed. The one man wearing the new R.N.L.I. lifebelt, Henry Freeman, escaped the holocaust, and was dragged ashore; the rest perished.

"Their names, engraved on a stone in the old churchyard on the windy East Cliff, are an inspiration, well calculated to 'water the root' of the tree of Service, of which the Lifeboat Institution is so stout a branch. To dwellers by the quayside they have a familiar ring:

"John Storr (Coxwain), William Storr, Robert Harland, John Dixon, Robert Leadley, William Walker, Will Tyreman, George Martin, Matthew Leadley, Chris Collins, John Philpot, and Isaac Dobson."

Along this coastline from Tees to Humber each summer is spent much of the money accumulated during the year in the old and new industries of the towns and cities of the north. The hand of modernity, sometimes in garish form, has our eastern coast in a strong grasp. Yet even so the old and mellowed can sometimes be seen between the fingers. There are moments when, if you can tear yourself away from the crowds and stand lonely and still where the soft rhythmic surge of the tide beats on the sand or where the shingle chatters as the sea rises and falls among it, you can sense a strange eeriness that haunts our coasts, as if something of the past has protruded itself. You forget the shops and the entertainments and the noise, and you realize that this surge of the sea, this sunset glow over the water, this bobbing of boats on the tide, are just as they have been for centuries past. Norsemen, Romans, and all our earliest predecessors knew them —and knew them exactly as we experience them.

Solitary men on watch must have known just this some sixteen centuries ago. Quite early in their occupation of Britain the Romans found it necessary to defend its eastern shores from piratical raids from across the sea. The raiders sailed southwards from the Elbe and the Weser in search of plunder, and to defend the "Saxon shore" a line of forts was established from Portsmouth to the Wash and a fleet was established to maintain a watching patrol. The "Count of the Saxon Shore" was the officer in command of the forts and the fleet. It apparently took some time for the raiders to think of sailing due west from their own lands and to discover an undefended coastline waiting for them. To meet this new threat the Romans extended their coastal defences northwards and created a chain of signal towns between the Tees and the Humber towards the end of the fourth century. A glance at the map of Roman Britain indicates the sites of these at regular intervals; Huntcliff, near the present-day Saltburn;

*York Minster viewed from the walls*

Goldsborough, on Kettleness point; Ravenscar, overlooking Robin Hood's Bay; Scarborough and Filey. South of this point there were probably others since swept away by the sea. From the evidences which remain it would seem that these were watch-towers rather than forts, and from them by a system of fire and smoke signals it would be possible for the forerunners of our coastguards to summon troops from Cataractorium (Catterick), Derventio (Malton) and Eboracum (York). Clearly, when the Roman legions were withdrawn, these partly deserted posts would be the first target of the Saxon invaders and so the evidence shows. At Huntcliff there was a massacre in which the corpses were thrown into a wall. In a corner of the signal tower at Goldsborough the skeleton of a man was found, his skull battered by sword-cuts. Scarborough tower was destroyed by fire.

So long as ever there has been a sea and a coast line between us and the mainland of Europe, and human life to explore it, there must have been communities of people living in the sheltered nooks where Saltburn, Whitby, Scarborough and Robin Hood's Bay now are, winning a livelihood from the sea and ever and anon achieving notice and perhaps fame as history pointed a dramatic and sometimes bloody finger at them. Scarborough is presumed to take its name from the Northman Skarthi, who landed under its burg or Castle Hill. The invading forces under Hardrada and Tostig raided the Kliflond (Cleveland) coast to replenish their supplies before sailing into the Humber and up to York where the English Harold defeated them. Whitby had a monastery in Saxon times. It was burned by the Danes, and rebuilt after the Conquest. It was partially dismantled at the dissolution and the lands acquired by the Cholmley family who built the abbey house. Although the ruined abbey was plundered of its stone for many local purposes down the centuries a better idea of what it originally looked like would have been possible before 1830, when the central tower collapsed. Dignified as it appears to-day, it must have been a noble sight in its full majesty of tower and monastic buildings. Below it, around the mouth of the Esk, Whitby was known as a "fischar" town in Tudor times, it had great prosperity in the days of the Greenland whale fishery; and still later for its odd combination of trades—boat building and jet working.

Further south only Filey seems to have hidden itself from history, possibly because its Brig, that long spur of oolitic rock which juts into the bay and is an adventurous stroll for summer holiday-makers,

*Knaresborough on the Nidd*

can be a formidable barrier to strange ships. Up to a generation or so ago Filey was a quiet fishing town, as it had been for long generations before. It is still among the more peaceful resorts with a vast expanse of sands under its eroding cliffs. So peaceful that you would not even suspect the existence of a mammoth jovial holiday camp a mile or so to the south. From here to Flamborough Head you can walk into history along the tops of a magnificent series of cliffs which can themselves tell a story of long-forgotten seas in which millions of creatures have lived and died and left their shelly remains as chalk, where long-buried fossils can be found, and where evidence of glacial erosion and deposit is often manifest. Along these cliffs sea-birds drift all day like wanton snow-flakes.

At Flamborough you meet history first in a little mild deception. Almost across the headland runs the "Danes' Dike", which has no immediate relation with the Danes, being probably the much older remains of an Iron Age entrenchment across the promontory. Yet the Danes must have known the area later for there is a pleasant little legend that the Constable family, who owned much land here, paid token rent to the King of Denmark each year by firing an arrow bearing a gold coin from the headland into the sea, a rent that was not extravagant as nearly forty per cent of the place names of the East Riding are Scandinavian. Flamborough Head itself is a magnificent lump of chalk as distinctive as the white cliffs of Dover. This chalk probably covered a great deal of Yorkshire at a time when this part of the world was a vast sea. Erosion has moved the cover (which was itself covered with a later layer of clay and sand) everywhere except in the East Riding, and Flamborough is here its most prominent exposure.

Beyond Flamborough to the south the character of the coast changes with almost dramatic suddenness by ceasing to be dramatic. R. D. Blackmore, who wrote the classic *Lorna Doone*, also wrote a lesser known novel *Mary Anerley* with this part of Yorkshire as its setting, and he likened the transformation after rounding the headland to turning the corner of a wall in March and passing from a buffeting, shivering world into a sunny burgeoning garden. The two pictures may be exaggerated but the contrast is valid. In place of high white cliffs we have a coastline of crumbling brown dunes with a vast sweep of beach as far as the eye can see. There is almost a geometrical curve to this extensive bay as though some master mathematician had placed his compass point somewhere in the North Sea and had described a great arc to define the coastline. The bay takes its name from Bridlington, the most southerly of Yorkshire's great seaside resorts.

Bridlington possesses a double attraction in that it has an ancient quay and harbour round which the holiday fun and accommodation has grown up and, a mile inland, an old market town and the remains of an Augustinian Priory, repudiating the noisy glitter of the front. The Priory suffered greatly at the dissolution but though most of the monastic buildings were destroyed, with the exception of the gateway known as the Bayle Gate, built about 1390, the beautiful nave of the Priory was left because it served as the parish church. This has a remarkably fine fourteenth-century porch, a notable clerestory on the south side of the nave, an impressive window in Perpendicular style at the west end and in Decorated style at the east, and a lofty hammerbeam roof. Anyone taking a distant view will notice the unusual dissimilarity of the towers.

To come upon the Priory after a rather dismal suburban walk from the gaieties of the promenade and sea front is to court disappointment. It can seem small, weary and grey, less attractive indeed than some of the little houses which surround it. But venture on and one suddenly sees that beneath the patina of drabness there is something more, a magnificent fragment of what was once one of the richest monasteries in the north, visited by kings, productive of noble clergy, one of whom, John of Bridlington, was made a saint, and still beautiful in its reduced circumstances.

It is worthy of note, bearing in mind some of the sources of monastic wealth in the dales and moorland foundations referred to in earlier chapters, that Bridlington was granted, during the reign of King Stephen, a peculiarly local form of revenue—the right to the goods and chattels of all fugitives and felons coming into the town, together with all the wreckage of the sea cast up "between Flamborough Dyke and Earl's Dyke". The prior and monks had also the right to hold an annual two days' fair and a market every Saturday, which brought in substantial monies. I can remember when the natives of this older part of Bridlington proudly called it Burlington, or more often "Burliton", and some authorities have tried to show justification for this as the original form. Their case, I believe, is a thin one, as in the Conqueror's Domesday Survey it is described as *Bretlinton*, which is as near the present spelling as makes no matter. There was always a pride, too, in belonging to the Old Town rather than to the newer and gaudier holiday resort—a pride that was justified when more of it was red-roofed and rural than today.

Yet even the "new" town round the storm-battered Quay has had its historic moments, most notably when Queen Henrietta Maria landed here on a cold February night in 1643 with arms and aid which she had brought from Holland for her ill-fated husband Charles I. The Dutch ships which brought her had been hotly pursued by Parliamentary naval forces sent from the Tyne to intercept the Queen. The naval vessels arrived too late, and disappointed of their prey the Roundheads bombarded the town, actually hitting the Queen's lodging with cannon balls so that she was compelled to take refuge in a ditch. This "incident" might have had more serious consequences, for the Dutch admiral who had convoyed her from The Hague heard the bombardment and threatened the Parliamentary ships with reprisals, but they decided that discretion was to be preferred to valour and sailed away. Otherwise the incident might have resulted in a war with Holland—and our subsequent history would have been different.

The Queen's own account of the adventure is contained in a letter she wrote to her husband:

> "One of the ships did me the favour to flank my house, which fronted the pier, and before I was out of bed the balls whistled over me, and you may imagine I did not like the music. So, dressed as I could, I went on foot some distance and got shelter in a ditch. Before I could reach it the balls sang merrily over our heads, and a sergeant was killed not 20 paces from me. Under this shelter we remained two hours, the bullets flying over us, and sometimes covering us with earth."

One hundred and fifty years later watchers on this coast witnessed that curious sea battle between the American pirate Paul Jones—whom we commemorate in a dance—and a group of merchant ships escorted by an English naval vessel under Captain Pearson. The pirate's ship was sunk, but not before the naval escort had hauled down its colours. However, as the merchant ships had made their escape in the turmoil the worthy Captain Pearson was rewarded with a knighthood for his work. Even modern Bridlington with all its attractions for holiday-makers from golden sands to speed-boats cannot offer excitements such as this two-hundred-year-old pirate thriller.

From Bridlington southwards the story is of coastal villages which have disappeared into the sea or are in process of doing so. Many

acres of good land and of Yorkshire history have been washed away
by the tides and doubtless more will follow. Just inland are a score
of little villages with delightful churches, village greens and prosperous
farmsteads almost lost amid the largest and most neatly built stacks
you will see anywhere in Yorkshire. They nearly all have good
Scandinavian place names ending in "wick" or "thorpe". Hornsea,
midway in the great arc of the bay, is a typical seaside village mentioned in Domesday Book and which has, according to legend,
already lost one church, as well as houses and even hotels, and may
in time lose more as the sea encroaches. Hornsea Mere, behind the
village, is a delightful stretch of water, the largest fresh-water lake
in the county, beloved of anglers, bird watchers, and those who
"mess about in boats". On its edge is Wassand Hall, the house of
Sir Marmaduke Constable. Its stock of fish long ago provided a continuing source of strife between the Abbots of St. Mary, at York,
and the Abbot of Meaux, near Beverley. One of the great minor
moments of history must have been that mighty contest on its banks
when each Abbot, as a method of solving the argument, hired a
professional champion to fight the matter out. We are told that the
battle lasted all day, but I cannot anywhere discover the outcome save
that it ended without fatal result. Withernsea, still further south, is
another coastal village which, like Hornsea, has a long history, has
ambitions to become a holiday resort, but is so ravaged by the sea that
bold plans seem out of the question. It, too, once had a lake but that
has gone without trace. Instead, it boasts a lighthouse in its main street.

Southwards again the coast curls inwards and ends in the long
spoon-like sandbank of Spurn, whose loneliness is accentuated by its
lighthouse and the immense spaciousness of sea and sky which dwarfs
the narrow promontory. Bird watchers have found the point a
valuable observatory for the study of migrants, and bird traps and
recording apparatus are manned here by volunteers for a considerable
part of the year. Somewhere in the sheltered band of the Spurn sandbank stood a town variously named as Ravenspurn, Ravenser, Ravens-
rode, or as Shakespeare named it, Ravenspurg. It once sent a member
to Parliament, it saw the landing of Henry of Lancaster in 1399 to
make his claim to the throne, it was the place at which Edward IV
landed seventy years later from exile in Holland to overthrow the
Lancastrians at the Battle of Barnet and so end the Wars of the Roses.
Now it is no more and its only tangible memorial is an ancient cross
at nearby Hedon which is said to have stood in its market-place. This

is typical of this part of Yorkshire. Ravenspurn is one of the large number of place names—Auburn, Hartburn, Hyde, Owthorne—which no longer exist, for the sea has swallowed them.

Whether it was the lingering influence of Caedmon, the religious poet of Whitby Abbey, who in the words of a great English critic "laid the first stone of the majestic temple of English poetry", or because this coast has had a romantic history since it was first celebrated in a Scandinavian saga of a thousand years ago, the fact remains that this stretch of country from the Tees to the Humber would appear to have attracted or inspired more poets and writers than any comparable area in the whole north country. Caedmon was, of course, the illiterate cowherd of the seventh century who, as the result of a dream, discovered that he had the gift of poetry in the form of paraphrases of the testaments. The saintly Abbess of Whitby prevailed upon him to enter the monastery and to develop his gifts as "a sweet singer". Seven centuries later a prior of a Carmelitic foundation in Scarborough, Robert Baston, revealed a similar poetic gift and became poet-laureate in the reign of Edward I and later accompanied Edward II at the Battle of Bannockburn. He was captured by the Scots and compelled by Robert Bruce to write poems in praise of Scottish arms, but his verse was so bad that Bruce sent him back to England!

Smollett, whom I have already quoted, wrote of Scarborough when in *Humphrey Clinker* he took Mr. Matthew Bramble to the resort to take tea and watch the dancing at the subscription balls and it was here that Humphrey dragged his drowning master out of the water by the ear. Sheridan adapted a play by Vanbrugh and called it *A Trip to Scarborough*. All of which showed that the place was even then acquiring a reputation as a holiday centre, confirming Defoe's comment that here he found "a great deal of good company drinking the waters". I have mentioned R. D. Blackmore's story of Flamborough, *Mary Anerley*; Mrs. Gaskell wrote of the whale fishers of Whitby in *Sylvia's Lovers*; and an author with a more localized appeal was Mary Linskill, who wrote a series of novels about the moors and the coast.

One of the "might-have-beens" of literary history is linked with a visit Charlotte Brontë paid to Bridlington with her school friend Ellen Nussey of Birstall in 1839. It was in the early part of that year that she had received a proposal of marriage from Ellen's brother, Henry, an evangelical clergyman who was the curate of Burton Agnes, a little village six miles from Bridlington, his rector, the Rev. Charles

Henry Lutwidge, being the uncle of Lewis Carroll. Charlotte declined the proposal, yet I cannot but feel that some sentimental attachment —or it may have been curiosity about the place at which she might have lived as wife of the curate—led her and Ellen Nussey to stay not very far away on her first seaside holiday in the summer of the same year. After a few days they moved into Bridlington itself and stayed near the Quay in a house now demolished. Would *Jane Eyre*, *Shirley* and *Villette* have had different settings or, indeed, have appeared at all if Charlotte had married Henry and moved from Haworth to the east coast? Certainly Charlotte was greatly attracted by this coast. She visited Scarborough ten years later, after the deaths of Branwell and Emily, this time to accompany her remaining sister Anne who was then dying from consumption and for whom sea air was the last frail hope. But Anne died there and was buried in the graveyard of the church on Castle Hill, the only member of the family not to be buried at Haworth. In later years Charlotte returned to the coast on several occasions and stayed again near Bridlington, at Filey, and at Hornsea.

In more recent years the distinguished Sitwell family lived part of their time at Scarborough where their house is now a natural history museum. It was here that Edith Sitwell, the poet, and Sacheverall Sitwell, the essayist and historian, were born, and their memories of the district are reflected in their writings. Storm Jameson, Winifred Holtby, and Leo Walmsley are all well-known novelists who came from this area and who have used it as a background for their writings. There is one East Riding author, however, who seems to me to have been very much neglected yet who gave a picture of Yorkshire life, and particularly of this side of Yorkshire, which is unequalled in its authenticity. That is Edward Charles Booth who died in 1954 at the age of eighty-one. He was one of three brothers, one of whom was a musician, and another a painter. E. C. Booth was a novelist who had absorbed the manners and customs and language of the people of Holderness and set them down in a series of stories written with sympathy and humour. They were stories with uncomplicated plots, told in a leisurely, quiet way, yet they were the means of depicting time and place as they existed in an ampler, richer age. Here is his picture of the market-day bus (horse-drawn, of course) leaving Hunmouth (which is a thin disguise for Hull) for the country and taken from the first pages of *The Cliff End* which he wrote in 1908 when he was thirty-five:

"Tankard's Bus rolls out of Hunmouth every Saturday afternoon, having rolled in from Ullbrig in the dim hours of dawn, wet or fine, brimming over with butter-baskets and early scrubbed faces. It is timed to leave the Market Arms at three o'clock. To make quite sure of a corner seat, you would do well to be sitting in it by four o'clock at the latest. After this the butter-baskets begin to reassemble one by one upon the cushions—some empty, with their white cover-clothes folded into neat squares, or falling in outline over the unfinished piece of pork that had to be set aside for the sale of the last pat; others bulky with the next week's groceries. Fare for the single journey, one shillings; double journey, one-and-six; children, half-price—that is because they give so much less trouble than grown-up people, and never stand on the cushions; small parcels, a penny.

"The getting away of Tankard's Bus from Hunmouth on Saturday afternoons is a stupendous undertaking—only comparable, indeed, to the moving of mountains. Without faith it could not be done . . . slowly, silently, secretly, during unseen moments of the afternoon, the baskets multiply upon the dingy cushions, and in divers distant quarters of Hunmouth Tankard is heard to say with genuine conviction: 'Weeal, wussl' et-ti-be yawkin'!' (Well, we shall have to be yoking.) But it is not till an hour later, when the butter-baskets line the seats in magnificent perspective from the door to the box-end in order of precedence, and Tankard's two horses stand yoked to the shafts by wizard hands, that the great drama of the departure is enacted."

There is enshrined the heart of this eastern side of Yorkshire, beating warm and sound, worn bravely on a homely sleeve, and still I believe unchanged despite the vicissitudes of this modern age.

## Holderness

Holderness is the name given to the triangle of the south-eastern corner of the East Riding; bounded on the west and north by the slopes of the Wolds and to the east and south by the North Sea and the Humber estuary. It is a low-lying plain, made up of clay, silt, and the flood land of the river Hull. Clay is dominant as you can tell from your footwear after walking a short distance in any part of the region. This clay covering is the outward, visible and most recent of that series to which we referred in an earlier chapter as appearing in diminishing seniority from the Pennines to the coast. This land between the Yorkshire Wolds and the sea owes its origin to the material brought here and deposited during the glacial period. It is an extensive carpet of morainic debris—sand, gravel and clay—carried from the Lake District, north Yorkshire and Scandinavia by glaciers and ice sheets. Incidentally, it provides farmers of the area with a remarkable diversity of soils. The chalk Wolds, which contains these lands of Holderness within a roughly-shaped crescent extending from Flamborough through Driffield and Beverley to North Ferriby, were long ago the coastline when Holderness itself was a bay.

This part of Yorkshire is probably visualized most easily as a saucer-shaped depression one edge of which is the North Sea and the other the chalk Wolds. The debris of northern land-ice filled this depression with a series of mounds and marshy hollows. Into it much water drained from the Wolds and the coastal hills and became the river Hull and so ran into the Humber. Most of the marshy hollows of this area have now gone as the result of much reclamation and drainage and Hornsea Mere is the only large survivor, although once upon a time Holderness must have had an appearance not unlike the present form of the Norfolk Broads. The mounds still remain and are locally known as "barfs". They do not rise to much more than sixty feet in height, so that the general aspect of this part of the country is of flat fertile lands.

Yet if this, like so much of our Yorkshire landscape, is the result of geological changes vast ages ago, in one particular that change continues, and at a visible rate. The coastal edge of the saucer is eroding at the remarkable rate of some seven feet a year along a strip of thirty miles long. In consequence this Holderness coastline has an untidy appearance as mottled brown lumps fall away from the low cliff face into the sea. What were once familiar tracks and paths disappear almost overnight. There is some consolation in this for the geologist, for he can confirm or disprove his theories about the structure of Holderness as he sees the land peel away for his information. More important is the complete disappearance of many villages and settlements which were once part of this land. School children in the East Riding accept it as part of their geography lessons to chart the sites of lost villages off the coast. Local poets have long ago used the watery ringing of the bells of lost churches as a stock image. I am told that at intervals Holderness builders benefit from the necessity of moving houses, chalets or caravans further back as the sea moves in. Only an extensive and costly system of sea defences along this entire strip of coast will end the continual process of erosion.

There have been Bronze Age finds in many parts of Holderness as well as evidence of early lake dwellings, and into this land long ago when it was still an undrained swamp must have come some of the earlier invaders of Yorkshire, working down the coast in their shallow craft and turning into the Humber estuary. They left their place names where they settled according to the land of their origin: Holderness itself; Burton, Ganton, Wilton and a hundred other "tons" —the commonest place-name ending—suggest that the Angles soon established themselves, although Grimston and Barmston have a Danish ring about them. The "thorpes" and the "hams" followed, in Fraisthorpe and Lowthorpe, and Fridaythorpe on the Wolds, and in Frodingham and Keyingham. The Danish "by" and "wick" (usually abbreviated in speech if not in spelling to "ick") are common from Atwick to Kilnwick, from Anlaby to Carnaby.

We may suspect that it was from here that originated the dividing terms which were later applied to the whole county, the "trithings", or thirds, from which we get the three Ridings of Yorkshire, and also the old division into smaller "wapentakes", still having some official use. Small boys playing "tig" in these parts are still observing a custom of their predecessors long ago, when to "tig" or touch a weapon was a mark of capture and fealty.

Today this is a land of attractive churches, some like Hedon and Patrington having the glory of cathedrals, but even some village churches displaying a richness of architecture and a flamboyant beauty which compares strongly with the austerity of most churches of the dales. "There's been plenty of money about here to build these," was a visitor's comment, and he spoke truthfully of a time when this was rich cornland supplying a great market elsewhere in Yorkshire. The ease with which, in later years, Hull and its surrounding district could raise vast sums to lend to successive impecunious kings and in its own development, speaks of considerable prosperity in producing and trading, as does the considerable number of windmills once existing in Holderness. Hedon and Paull and other Humberside towns had their harbours and their shipbuilding and their fishermen. Much of this activity moved to Hull later, for, as Leland wrote: "Truth is that when Hull began to flourish Hedden decayed." Yet the wealth was still there and even today this part of Yorkshire has an air of comfortable living.

For the real wealth of this part of Holderness is in the good earth, some of the most fertile in Britain. Oats and barley are the main crops, with oats increasing in popularity as the better feed for stock. Barley-fed beef from this land has a wide renown. Some farms are over 1,000 acres in extent although the average holding is probably about 600 acres. I know of one farmer who on a modest 40 acres had 60 head of cattle, 130 pigs and 18 acres of barley. Such is the fertility of this land. Potatoes are grown, too, and some of these are used locally for the making of potato crisps. Those who do not work on the land usually find employment in Hull. A few miles from Patrington is Sunk Island, once a real, small island but now, with reclaimed land from the Humber, a prosperous part of the mainland nearly 800 acres in extent.

At Winestead, a mile or so north of Patrington, was born in 1621 Andrew Marvell, who has been described by Ivor Brown as "one of the most delicate and discerning poets of that century and indeed of all our centuries". His father was rector of the parish and he sent his son to the Grammar School at Hull and then to Cambridge. Marvell was a Cromwellian and soon became assistant to John Milton, who was Latin secretary to Cromwell. Whether two poets in one office functioned more satisfactorily than two cooks in one kitchen may be doubted. Marvell survived the upheaval of the Restoration, in which so many Cromwellians lost their places, and became an active Member of Parliament for Hull for twenty years. There is a modern touch in his visit to Russia as secretary to a delegation to stimulate trade between the two countries, which included attendance at a banquet in Moscow lasting nine hours. As he was one of the gentlest and most retiring of our lyric poets he probably did not enjoy the occasion. He may have returned in thought during the protracted feasting to the peaceful streams around his birthplace where he could

"Through the hazels thick espy
The hatching throstle's shining eye."

When William Cobbett visited Hull on one of his tours his only criticism of the city was of the gilded equestrian statue of William of Orange who "gave to England the national debt". This, he declared, should be replaced by one of Andrew Marvell. Yorkshire has few reminders of its greatest poet since Caedmon.

The quiet villages of Holderness, the hedges and streams of a gentle landscape, the maze of small forgotten ways dictated in their pattern no doubt long ages ago by the water-subjugated land, the absence of bold aggressive features and an "old-fashioned" air which still clings to this corner of the county contribute to make this an area of considerable yet almost undefinable charm. There is a clean warm odour of placidity broken only by the cold east winds which sweep across these flat lands in the winter.

For their recreation Holderness folk, like those from Hull, turn to Withernsea, their own holiday resort which lies rather flatly against the coast. Here can be found the odd phenomenon of a pier entrance but no pier, as that structure was washed away in a big storm last century less than ten years after it was built, a fate which has befallen most of the piers on this Yorkshire coast. The town also supplies a good deal of the higher education of Holderness in a vast new school catering for over a thousand pupils drawn from a very wide area. A comparatively new industry in the town is a pottery turning out fancy art ware which can be found at most of the holiday resorts along this coast. There are also potteries at Hornsea and at Routh, near Beverley.

Where the gentle slope of the Wolds merge into the Holderness plain are the two market towns of Beverley and Great Driffield. There has long been discussion over the derivation of the name of the first, for although there is little doubt that the "Bever" represents the animal, for the bones of this creature have been unearthed in the district, there is much debate whether the ending stands for a lake or a stream. Either would appear suitable for an area where both abounded. Driffield is simpler for it comes straight from the Anglo-Saxon for "stubble field", which for a town which has always served as the great corn market of the East Riding strikes one as appropriate.

Beverley's chief title to fame is its Minster, an edifice of exquisite beauty and superb dignity. It grew from a church built among the swamps and forest around the river Hull by John, Bishop of Hexham, whose birthplace was not far away. John was soon afterwards made Archbishop of York, but so greatly was he attracted to Beverley that in 718 he resigned the see of York and retired to Beverley where three years later he died. Soon his tomb acquired fame for its power to heal diseases and the ailing made long journeys to be cured at the resting-place of the blessed John of Beverley.

The next great Beverley name is that of Athelstan, King of the English, who in 934 was marching north to drive out the Scots. It is told that on his way he met a band of pilgrims who told him of the remarkable virtues of the place, which induced the King to cross the Humber to Beverley while his army travelled on along the Roman road to York. The King visited the shrine and placed his knife upon the high altar. He was rewarded by a vision of John, who promised him success in his battles. Success came and the King, redeeming a promise to reward the church, liberally endowed it with grants of land, tolls and the right of Sanctuary. The Sanctuary knocker on a door of the church has long disappeared—although there is one at All Saints Church in York and also at Durham Cathedral—but the sites remain of sanctuary crosses which stood at one mile distance from the church on each of the roads out of Beverley. This was the outer limit of the peace of St. John which gave partial safety to a fugitive. Inside the church was the stone Frith-Stool—which still exists—which gave complete protection, even from the King himself.

The miracle-working fame of the tomb spread and in 1037 John of Beverley was canonized and his remains re-interred in a shrine in front of the high altar at which King Athelstan had sought his help. It became a custom for kings to visit the shrine. Edward I, Edward II, Henry IV, Henry V and Henry VI all visited it, nor did its power stop at the sanctuary boundary, for it was said that during the battle of Agincourt the tomb of the Saint sweated drops of holy oil to ensure the English victory.

The building itself was at first probably of wood, to be succeeded by a stone and wood church that suffered from fire and weak foundations. The Minster we can see today was begun about 1225, when the chancel and transepts were built. The church is in fact a glorious textbook of ecclesiastical architecture with every period represented from the thirteenth century to the fifteenth. In addition there are sixteenth-century stalls carved by Ripon woodworkers with later additions almost to our own time. And, strangely, it all harmonizes as if it had been designed by one master hand. It is spacious, it soars, it amazes with its beauty, and it leaves you in a glow as you move from one stimulating vantage point to another. And its attraction is not only in its great proportions—it is bigger than many cathedrals— but in its lesser delights. I was once taken round it by a quiet but enthusiastic verger whose greatest joy was not in the vaulted roofs, the clustered piers, or the tracery of the windows, although I could hear a ring of pride in his voice as he spoke of these, but in the wonderful toy-box figures which adorned every adornable space, from the sculptured stone Biblical figures of the doorways to the griffins and dancing pigs, the woman beating her husband, the man chasing a dog, the flowers, trees, birds, mermaids and dozens of other subjects carved in wood on every miserere seat, on every canopy and stall end. The longest and dullest of sermons marked by any preacher's hour-glass would be as nothing with this art-gallery, menagerie and crazy carver's display to gaze upon.

Beside all this there appear to be acres of stained glass, some remarkable monuments and statues—including those of John of Beverley and King Athelstan—and a noteworthy collection of bells in the towers. Surely this Minster is a verger's delight. He could never be boring in such a treasure house.

Perhaps it is overdoing the glory of one small town that near the North Bar of this medieval centre there should be another richly adorned and truly beautiful church, that of St. Mary, which of itself would confer distinction on any city. It, too, has fine but unusually mixed architectural craftsmanship of the fourteenth and fifteenth centuries, a massive tower and carving and sculpture in abundance. Do you remember the March Hare in *Alice in Wonderland*? Here it is in stone as Lewis Carroll saw it and from which he drew his inspiration when he stayed with friends in the town. Have you heard of the Beverley minstrels, a fraternity of musicians founded in Saxon times? Here they are, five of them, round the capital of a pillar, and all in their original colour. The south transept is supported by some remarkably fine flying buttresses added in Victorian times, one of the few examples of a Victorian church restoration or addition which is wholly successful. Somewhere in this church used to be displayed part of an old ducking-stool, used to cool down unruly women, and the town stocks, which served the same purpose for men. But I have not seen them of late.

In its early days Beverley was a well-defended town, surrounded by a moat and with each of five roads entering the town spanned by a gated Bar. Of these, only the North Bar rebuilt in 1409 remains, and even this is threatened by modern traffic, for the headroom through the gate is little more than ten feet, which means that the double-decker bus service which operates in these parts has vehicles specially designed to pass through the arch. From the Minster the land slopes gently up to the Westwood, one of the pleasant open pastures which surround the town and form a green belt created long before modern town planning. It dates, in fact, from six hundred years ago. These open spaces are still administered by twelve pasture masters elected by the freemen of the borough. The Westwood has both a racecourse and a golf course on it but has still room for grazing stock. The town's borough charter dates back to 1573 and its history to Saxon times. It has flourishing markets which draw support from a considerable area and in its market-place is an ornate but attractive market cross. Unexpectedly in an inland town one comes across a shipyard building trawlers for the Arctic fishing fleet; unexpectedly until you realize that Beverley stands on the river Hull which is a direct link with Humber. Tanning, the making of wire ropes, motor vehicle parts and cattle foods all provide employment which is drawing workers into the town from the much larger city of Hull. All this provides a rich mixture of architectural history and Georgian grace side by side with modern industrial enterprise and the rusticity of a market town. One of its notable citizens was Fred Elwell, a gifted artist of more than local fame.

The little streams which merge to become the river Hull flow round Driffield. Legend once had it that this was the place where Alfred the Great died and was buried but I have never heard this confirmed by authority. There was probably a Moot Hall here long before the Norman invasion, and there is evidence of still earlier occupation in Bronze Age times or before. But in general, history seems to have missed this town and left it to conduct its real business, that of the agricultural centre of a great corn-growing region providing machinery, farm equipment and a market. It also provided the means for transporting the produce, for by an Act passed in 1767 the Driffield canal was opened to link its wharves with the river Hull and so with the Humber. The canal had only a length of about ten miles but early this century it was carrying over 30,000 tons of goods a year.

Sooner or later if you explore Holderness you will be asked "if you have seen the Race?" One of the most curious features of the region are the "gypsey" springs which break out at intervals both of time and space and may flow long enough to form a stream or may vanish again in months or even days. They may or may not appear at the same place twice and although they usually appear after heavy rain on the Wolds, one does not necessarily follow the other. They were known long ago, for a twelfth-century chronicler, William of Newborough, wrote of them:

"These famous waters, commonly called Vipsys, rise out of the ground from a number of springs, not indeed continually, but every other year, and forming no small stream, run through the low grounds into the sea. Their drying up is a good sign, for their running is supposed a never failing presage of famine."

Geologically they are explained as accumulations of water in the chalk of the Wolds which from time to time overspill and by siphon action bubble up to the surface some distance from their origin. Streams and springs appear casually in the Wolds valleys in many places and sometimes have local names. The village of Nafferton probably takes its name from the "naffers" which come to the surface in great numbers thereabouts. Elsewhere they are called "Woe waters" from the belief held down the centuries, as William of Newborough held, that their flowing presaged disaster.

The most famous of them is the "gypsey race" which rises near Wharram-le-Street, on the western side of the Wolds. flows through Kirby-Grindalythe—where an errant spring once forced its way through the floor of a cottage—and on through Helperthorpe and Weaverthorpe to Boythorpe, where it disappears to rise again at Wold Newton. At Burton Fleming it becomes a sizeable stream, so much so that on its appearance local children went out ceremonially to meet it. It continues through Rudston and Boynton and so to Bridlington, where it enters the sea some twenty miles from its starting-place. Almost certainly it was between the high banks of the gypsey race that Queen Henrietta took refuge when the house in which she had sought shelter in Bridlington was bombarded, as we have already recounted. She referred to it slightingly but excusably under the circumstances as a "ditch".

Such a mysterious stream has from the earliest times been regarded as prophetic. When Michael Drayton at the end of the sixteenth century set out to describe the face of England in "Poly-Olbion" he wrote of

> "My Phophetick at Veipsey, I may show,
> That some years is dried up, some years again doth flow;
> But when it breaketh out with an immoderate birth,
> It tells the following year of a penurious dearth."

and both local events and national calamities have, according to local lore, been foretold by the running of the gypsey race; the Great Plague, the fall of a meteor, great storms at sea. You will be assured, and I believe there is evidence for this, that it was flowing strongly in 1914 and again in 1939. There were those who watched the waters closely during the nuclear war threats of 1962.

Holderness, whose story has been largely shaped by the waters which flowed into it, through it and round it, has almost as a matter

KEEP
LEFT

of course a great wealth of legend in which water plays its part, of wishing wells and pin wells, of sacred wells and healing wells, and of wayside wells which once were dressed with flowers each year, as is still done in Derbyshire. The Rev. William Smith, who forty years ago gathered up many of the legends and traditions of the springs and streams of the East Riding, tells the story of Catwick Well which had a ghost, a White Lady who wandered about near it and was accompanied by the cry of a child, although no child was ever seen. Locally it was believed that a young woman had been killed and with her baby had been buried near the well. But the Rev. William Smith suggests an older origin, that Catwick was a Danish village and that invocations were made to Freya, the spirit of the well. This in Christian times became confused with the Virgin and the Holy Child and down the years the ghost was that of "a dual personality— that of the Virgin and her Son, on whom conjointly, and with a certain Christian aspect, the wonder working powers of Freya had, by the people, been bestowed and in whom Freya had virtually been restored. So history repeats itself."

## The Wolds

Driving out of Beverley westwards towards York one enters the higher Wolds country, nowhere reaching 1,000 feet yet by comparison with the Holderness plain mountainous and rugged. From now on it will be green hills, with broad patches of white where the underlying chalk is exposed, with dark strips of woodland running along their tops or clinging precariously to their slopes. Little valleys run up into these hills and are unexpectedly bare of cultivation. Until fairly recent times the Wolds were a great sheep walk and had been from monastic days. Towards the end of the eighteenth century a number of landowners began to transform them into cultivated farms, with sheltering plantations surrounding well-planned compact buildings, very different from the scattered and haphazard farm buildings of other parts of Yorkshire. There is a surprising quality of light and air on these hills and from time to time long views; a glimpse eastwards of Beverley Minster standing up from the plain, or southwards to what appears to be a murky river Humber along which one identifies familiar objects like chimneys or oil storage tanks or the distinctive shapes of buildings.

The colour of the Wolds country changes with the seasons, white

*An early woolcombing machine*

when the fields are bare or under plough, soft green with white, purple, and yellow drifts as the anemones, the violets and the primroses and cowslips appear in the spring, and golden in the summer and autumn when the corn and barley ripen, with the dark copses framing the hills on which grow the campion and bell-flowers. Over all is a sense of remoteness and timelessness which is not jarred by distant puffs of railway smoke, the distant view of concrete towers and chimneys or the smoke-stacks of ships to be seen only on fine clear days. The vastness of this rolling land creates its own sense of proportion.

The open quality of the Wolds makes them particularly susceptible to great snow storms in winter. Villages like Thixendale, Fridaythorpe and Huggate appear in the news for their brief hours of glory under the heading: WOLDS VILLAGES SNOWED UP. Stories are told of heroic journeys by postmen to deliver the mail, or nurses to deliver babies. Children are marooned in schools and roads are blocked for many weeks. Then it all quietly clears, patches acres wide of grey and white appear where cultivation is under way, and soon the whole region is a patchwork of whites and greens of many shades, with the varying browns of the tree strips defining the pattern. And out of the hills run the "gypseys", those curious streams which drain the chalk Wolds and flood Holderness.

Unlike the rest of Yorkshire the Wolds hills bear no names other than those used locally by those who work on them and it is difficult to distinguish one from another. It is the villages which are distinctive, quiet spots like Bishop Burton, on the road from Beverley to Market Weighton, where the village pond has a considerable population of ducks, and where there is a delightful green and an old church on the hill. This village is not only one of the prettiest in the East Riding, it is also one of the tidiest, as an oak seat on the green won in a recent competition bears witness. Market Weighton is a little market town which has probably not changed greatly in size or character since a Norman church was built there, of which the base of the tower still remains. Like a man who has risen in the world not too high or too fast but is content to remain in modest prosperity, this small market centre breathes content despite the traffic which bustles through it from York to Hull.

Nearby is Goodmanham, once the site of a pagan temple destroyed by its own priest Coifi on his conversion to Christianity in the fifth century. Six centuries later a Norman church was built on the same site and of this a good deal remains, including the notable doorway.

Further along the York road is Pocklington, not actually on the main road but within nodding distance as befits a dignified and select market town whose parish church has been called "the Cathedral of the Wolds", which has a grammar school founded as long ago as 1514, and can claim that one of its most distinguished pupils was William Wilberforce. Although there is a surprising number of small industries here, its chief interest is agricultural. York is near enough, however, to pull many of its younger folk to more varied occupations, and there is a tendency for this, like other small towns near by, to become dormitories for the city. A recent acquisition by the town is an attractive old house and grounds, Burnby Hall, which are open to the public.

Pocklington marks the western boundary of the Wolds. On one side are the chalk hills with their grain crops, on the other the sandy lands of the plain with their root crops. Behind it is a curious green valley known as Millington Pastures which draws great numbers of East Riding visitors on fine summer afternoons to park their cars and picnic in the grassy open spaces. This is one of the many dry valleys running down from the Wolds, once excavated by streams but now for the most part waterless. For a region which has a rainfall six or seven inches a year greater than that of the nearby Plain of York it is something of a geological puzzle that active streams are so few and small. Many valleys but few streams seem to be a contradiction. The explanation offered by geologists is that the chalk is exceedingly porous, so that of the rain which falls upon it some evaporates but most of it soon sinks in and continues to percolate through the chalk until it reaches a plane of saturation or water-table below which the chalk cannot take more. At this point it oozes or trickles through the ground and at times bursts through, as we have seen at Nafferton and Wold Newton, where the Gypsey Race begins. Where clay underlies the Wolds springs break out at the point of contact. The present dry valleys were streams during the Ice Age when the chalk was frozen and the rainfall was greater. Since then they have died out and left only the old watercourses.

Not far from Pocklington is Warter, a village attached to the Warter Priory estate. The village street here is probably one of the most photographed places in the East Riding because of its neat row of thatched cottages along one side and the spick-and-span look of

the houses and small greens. Adjoining this estate is Londesborough
Park, an ornate building once owned by the Earls of Burlington and
later by George Hudson, the railway king, at the height of his commercial glory. There is a link here with the Craven country of the
west, for at Londesborough the young Henry Lord Clifford of
Skipton Castle was concealed among the shepherds while his Yorkist
enemies sought him. Later he was taken to Cumberland from where
he returned to Skipton as the Shepherd Lord. The most notable
example of a great estate, however, is Sledmere, the home of the
great Sykes family which did so much by example to stimulate Wolds
agriculture.

If you enter Sledmere from the Bridlington road you will see an
attractive well bearing an inscription:

> "This edifice was erected by Sir Tatton Sykes, Bt., to the memory of his
> father, Sir Christopher Sykes, Bt., who by assiduity and perseverance in
> building, planting and enclosing the Yorkshire Wolds, in the space of thirty
> years, set such an example to other owners of land as had caused what was
> once a blank and barren tract of country to become now one of the most
> productive and best cultivated districts in the county of York."

That sums up part of the debt which this part of Yorkshire owes
to the Sledmere family by which they transformed a vast area into
fertile land.

There were two Sir Tatton Sykes, father and son, and both were
interested in the breeding of bloodstock. The first Sir Tatton, who
died in 1863, laid the foundation of the famous Sledmere Stud and
the second Sir Tatton, who died in 1913, developed it. It was said
that the father believed in quantity and had hundreds of horses in his
paddocks, while the son concentrated on quality. Horses that were
to win notable races went from Sledmere to found other studs in
many parts of the country. The son of the second Sir Tatton was
Sir Mark Sykes who just before the First World War raised The
Yorkshire Waggoners' Reserve of men used to horses from all parts
of the Wolds. This body of drivers became part of the Army Service
Corps when war broke out, and a second memorial in the centre of
the village, designed by Sir Mark and erected after his death at the
Paris Peace Conference, recalls in a series of carved panels in low relief
events in their service. A third memorial to the first Sir Tatton, in
the form of a tall pillar, can be seen on a small hill between Sledmere
and Garton.

Sledmere today retains its old world beauty with its fine park lands, its abundance of trees, and its general air of tidiness. In the park is the beautiful village church, a reminder of another debt the Wolds owe to the father of Sir Mark Sykes, for he spent nearly two million pounds on building churches in the district, Thixendale, Fimber, Kirby Grindalythe, Langtoft and Sherburn are but a few of them. It is said that when this Sir Tatton, a silent, unconventional man, went on foot to see the progress of the churches he was building he would set off wearing layers of coloured waistcoats, with a footman following behind. As he warmed up with walking he would cast off one waistcoat after another, to be picked up by the faithful man-servant. He was a great traveller to other lands and although a great horse breeder was himself no horseman.

In recent years the estate has been considerably curtailed, but the name of Sykes is still widely respected in all this area of the Wolds.

There are many other delights in this scattered undulating country; the tall spire of South Dalton church with a remarkable monument to Sir John Hotham inside the church; a lonely windmill at Skidby, one of the few remaining in a land where there were once so many that (legend has it) one was taken down because there was not wind enough to turn them all; many ancient earthworks scattered over the Wolds as a reminder of dwellers here many thousands of years ago; a gigantic monolith at Rudston whose origin and purpose are still uncertain; and the village ponds which adorn so many of these Wolds communities, unless besmirched as, alas, so many of them are, by use as the repository for local refuse.

Two major architectural gems sparkle in this peaceful scene, one in the north and the other in the south. The northernmost is Burton Agnes Hall on the Bridlington to Driffield road, a lovely Elizabethan house of red brick and stone dressings, with graceful bow windows in the projecting wings framing the recessed central portion of the front. At one time probably all the windows were bow-shaped, but the sash windows introduced in the seventeenth century have not disturbed the harmony, and indeed by contrast may have enhanced it. Viewed from the gatehouse through the topiary of the formal garden the Hall is both gentle and dignified. It welcomes you in a courtly manner as a gracious dowager might. As Celia Fiennes wrote in her diary: "It looks finely in the approach." Against a background of trees it gleams like a lovely flower. As befits so charming a place, war's alarums and excursions have passed by it. Built by Sir Henry

Griffith at the end of the sixteenth century, it passed by marriage to the Boynton family in the middle of the following century and has remained in their possession since, together with the ghost.

Inside is a succession of remarkable rooms; the Great Hall with carving in alabaster stone and wood, an oak-panelled Drawing Room with a gruesome chimney piece, a Dining Room with paintings by Kneller, Gainsborough, Reynolds, Lely and others, and some elaborately furnished State bedrooms. There was on the top floor a Long Gallery from side to side of the house and a haunted room. And thereby hangs the ghost story. Anne, one of the three daughters of Sir Henry Griffith, was greatly attached to the house as she watched it grow, stage by stage, and could not bear to be long away from it. Hurrying back to it one day from the village of Harpham near by she was attacked by outlaws and left dying. Brought into the unfinished house she made her sisters promise that whatever happened her skull must never leave the Hall she loved. If it were ever removed she declared that her restless spirit would make the house uninhabitable.

After her death her body was taken outside the house for burial, but at once the house was disturbed by the banging of doors, groans and crashes, so that her sisters were distraught. The advice of the church was sought and as a result the skull was brought back to the house and calm was restored. The house remained peaceful for many years until a servant girl, who disliked having a skull about and disbelieved the story, threw it out. Then trouble began again; a horse passing by stopped and refused to move, disturbance and uproar swept through the Hall. The frightened maid hurried out and retrieved the cause of the trouble and peace reigned again. That is the legend, and the skull is reputed to be still in the house. It must be one of the earliest examples in England of a poltergeist's manifestations.

Of no less historical interest than the mansion itself is the original old hall, hidden among trees near the church, and built about 1173. Excellently preserved by the Ministry of Works, this has a fine Norman undercroft with cylindrical pillars and a spacious hall above.

The other gem is not in the Wolds country but in the southern part of Holderness. This is the great house of the Constable family at Burton Constable built in the reign of Henry VIII, a much sterner building than Burton Agnes, with fewer external graces. Built of Tudor brick, its west front is some 200 feet long. Appropriate to a family which owned a great deal of the East Riding from Norman times onwards and exercised as immense an influence in the southern district as did the Sykes of Sledmere in the north, the estate is extensive and notable, both for its parklands laid out by Capability Brown and for its once famous herds of wild oxen, fallow and red deer. Inside, the house is a treasure gallery of furniture, paintings, statuary and carving, including some of that delicate workmanship in wood by Grinling Gibbons which appears so fragile and yet has lasted some two hundred and fifty years.

## VI

## YORK AND ITS PLAIN

ONE of the toys of childhood was a series of coloured wooden boxes that fitted one over another with the smallest in the centre. That is how I think of York. It is a town in a town, and the game is not yet finished for in a long time sequence a contemporary town is now ringing the old with a further cover. The historical attraction of York is that with a little effort and a considerable amount of walking it is possible to discern much of the outline and some of the detail of these successive towns. The few square miles in and around its walls contain an embarrassment of historic and architectural riches dating back to the time when this was an imperial site and London was an unknown village beside the Thames. There is scarcely a street or by-lane without some historical association, some link with a name in England's story, or some building still magnetically attractive because of its age and character. Someone has said that there is almost as much of ancient Rome within the walls of York as in Rome itself. I cannot do more here than indicate a few of the treasures and associations which make this a unique city.

First, then, York does not depend upon any nobility of site like Durham and its cathedral, or Richmond and its castle, or Lincoln with its city set on a hill. It occupies a triangular stretch of flat land formed by the junction of the river Fosse with the Ouse. It owes allegiance to none of the three Ridings but has its own special territory known as the Ainsty. For nearly twelve hundred years the city's pattern remained almost unchanged from the plan laid out when it was the capital of the northern provinces of Roman Britain. Even today many of its streets are those of the first fortified town of Eboracum. To walk up the narrow Stonegate from the Mansion House to the south door of York Minster is to travel through history from the early eighteenth century—when the Mansion House was built, several years before London had an official home for its Lord Mayor—along a street which still holds its medieval character, and to come upon a glorious edifice built upon a site where there had been a shrine for at least thirteen hundred years. And every step of such a walk has been along the Via Praetoria, the Praetorian Way, of the first Roman occupation.

Thus we come upon the first of our boxes, the Roman one, built almost symmetrically square with its southern corner in the angle between the two rivers. At first it was little more than a rampart of earth erected by Hadrian early in the second century. In the third century Severus followed Hadrian's line but without actually utilizing the ramparts and built the first stone-walled fortress, with a tower at each corner, a Via Principalis (still there, though known today as High Petergate and Low Petergate) running directly across it, and the Via Praetoria along which we have walked coming in at right angles to it. But not only were there the official streets. Almost certainly the occupants of that first settlement would wander outside its walls, doubtless for a gossip and a change of scene. The paths they made in their perambulations round the outer side of the square are still there, known today as Lendal, Market Street, Lord Mayor's Walk and Gillygate. In time a civil city developed outside the walls, and the way to it can still be followed along present-day streets. In this Roman city two famous emperors died, and Constantine the Great, the first Christian emperor, was proclaimed. Coins bearing the image and superscription of some forty emperors have been found there.

After the Roman withdrawal early in the fifth century the city went through a difficult time and there is much that is still obscure about its history. For a period it was the capital of the Anglian kingdom of Deira, whose king, Edwin, erected a little church of wood where the Minster now stands. Then it was ravaged by the Danes, and the city, then known as Eoforvic, became the capital of a Danish kingdom, its name changing again through Danish pronunciation to Jorvik. Of this dim period of its history little evidence remains, successive occupants probably making use of such of the Roman city as was convenient and unravaged. Eventually in the middle of the tenth century the Danish kingdom of York came to an end and all England became one kingdom.

So we come to the builders of the second city of York. With this already historic place as its focal point, came the first act of that great transformation of our land from an Anglo-Saxon kingdom to an English nation. To appreciate that drama we must recall for a moment some of those scraps of school history we have almost forgotten.

Edward the Confessor died on January 5th, 1066, and was buried the following morning. By afternoon Harold Godwinson, second son of Godwin, Earl of Kent, was elected king by the Witan. The new King was faced by two imminent invasions, one from the united fleets of Tostig and Hardrada, three hundred ships strong, waiting off the Scottish coast, the other from Duke William, of Normandy, whose fleet of eight hundred ships was assembled across the Channel. England's future then as on later occasions depended on the wind. A wind from the north would bring the Norsemen and prevent Williams fleet from sailing. A wind from the south would unleash the forces in France and hold back the waiting fleet off Scotland. It was the north wind which came first, and with it the fleets of Hardrada and Tostig sailed down the coast, attacking and burning Scarborough on the way, and into the Humber as far as Riccall, a mile below the junction of the Ouse and Wharfe. When news reached Harold he acted quickly and with his own force of some three thousand men, and gathering more on his way, he marched north to York and found the invaders encamped seven miles away on the Derwent at Stamford Bridge. He struck swiftly and hard so that the first the enemy knew of his presence was the sparkle of English armour, "like glistening ice" as the chronicler put it. Within the day Hardrada and Tostig were dead, their troops slaughtered or in retreat. Of the three hundred ships which had sailed into the Humber only twenty-four returned.

Three days later Duke William's army landed without a fight at Pevensey, although it took some days for the news to reach Harold at York. The change of wind, which had helped William, kept Harold's fleet bottled up in the Thames. There was no other chance but for him to make a forced march back to the south with the army that had defeated the Norsemen. The journey from York to London was accomplished in five remarkable days, and four days later his remustered army was on its way to the heights above Hastings to meet the new threat. The story of the battle which followed has been told many times and has been pictured in the Bayeux Tapestry. Once again fate played its part. A single battle, perhaps even the twist of fortune which killed Harold by a Norman arrow rather than William by a Saxon axe, decided the fate of England. On Christmas Day 1066 the coronation of the new king took place.

Although it was Archbishop Aldred of York, who crowned the invader Duke William of Normandy King of England in Westminster

Abbey, it was from these lands of Yorkshire that the first real opposition to the new king arose. Although some Yorkshire earls paid nominal homage and swore allegiance others refused it and many who did take the oath changed their minds. There were risings and rebellions against the new counts and barons from France with their strange sounding names when they tried to exert authority in the north. Two years after his coronation William himself had to march north to face a rising by Edwin and Morcar, two of the earls who had reluctantly paid him homage. He established a garrison at York and moved on to suppress other outbreaks. Scarcely had he left the city than a new revolt broke out and back he came in haste with the simple but ruthless remedy of sacking the place, killing great numbers of its inhabitants as an example, and erecting two strong forts on artificial hills—York itself offering no natural hills—with a stronger garrison than before to ensure that there should be no more nonsense. There seems to be little doubt that one of these forts was on the pleasant tree-guarded mound near Skeldergate and known as Baile Hill and the other is the green mount on which Cliffords Tower now stands. Although nothing remains of the original forts, which were hastily built of wood, it is probable that these were the first of the many Norman strongholds and castles in Yorkshire.

Yet this was only shadow boxing by comparison with what was to follow for the better or worse part of twenty years. The rebels called on their kinsfolk the Danes to help them and five hundred Danish ships sailed up the Humber and along the Ouse to York as they had sailed in their own invasions long before. York was recaptured and its garrison killed, but the success was short-lived. Back came William, determined to avenge the victory and to stamp out the rebellion and all who caused it. It was well said of him that "mild he was to those good men who loved God, but severe beyond measure to those who withstood his will". The terrible years of the "Harrying of the North" followed in which towns and villages were wiped out and left as "waste", as they were described nearly twenty years later in the Domesday Survey. Between York and Durham no place of any size was left standing. The dead were unburied and there was no food left for those who remained. Freeman, the historian, described it not merely as plunder but as "simple unmitigated havoc. Houses were everywhere burnt with all that was in them, stores of corn, goods and property of every kind were brought together and destroyed, even living animals seem to have been driven to perish in the universal burning." The countryside was covered by the smoke of burning homes and what in our own time is called a "scorched earth" policy was known all across the north. To ensure that no seed of rebellion should ever ripen, there followed that rash of fortress building whose evidence still stands in our dales and plains as Norman castles, erected first as wooden structures and later rebuilt in stone with great keeps and curtain walls and often a moat as they can be seen today in their sombre ruin at Richmond, at Conisbrough, Middleham and Ponte-fract.

Savage repression of rebellion and the establishment of strong points of control was accompanied by a division of the northern countryside among William's followers as he rewarded them for their share in the Conquest. Alan the Red was given the estates of the rebellious earl Edwin, in north Yorkshire. Ilbert de Lacy received lands in the West Riding and built his stone castle at Pontefract, then called Tateshale. Roger de Busli was granted lands in Nottinghamshire and south York-shire where his castle of Tickhill still remains. The Romilles had the Lordship of Skipton. William de Warenne, the Conqueror's son-in-law, was given Conisbrough.

Just outside the northern angle of the York city wall at the end of Gillygate is the site of one of the gallows used in the suppression of rebels and offenders against the king's peace. Here men were branded, maimed or hanged, not necessarily by William's own orders, for one of his methods of maintaining control was to place the onus of sup-pression upon others, in this case the Dean and Chapter of the Minster, long before the establishment of Judges of Assize and the right of trial. Later, the castle and its adjoining prison were the scene of many hundreds of executions in the troubled years of settlement which followed the Conquest. And as you look upon York Minster you recall that the *Anglo-Saxon Chronicle* said of the Conqueror that "he harried the town and put to shame St. Peter's Minster".

Yet the suppression of rebellion inside the northern territory could not keep out the raiding Scots and security against those from over the Border was as necessary as security within. So more castles went up. It is true that almost all of them began, like that at York, as con-structions of wood on and about a moated mound—the "motte". Yet even so the rate of building would have been notable if they had been telephone kiosks or bus shelters in our own age. According to some authorities, within twenty years of William's enthronement, there were forty-nine castles in Yorkshire. Soon there were not enough barons and nobles to go round as feudal tenants of the king, so the smaller fry came in as sub-tenants, with their ambitions, rivalries and quarrels. Robert, Count of Mortain, for example, who was half-brother to the king, had over two hundred manors scattered widely throughout the county, allotted to him as a reward for his part in the conquest of Britain. The resulting occupation of these manors, the creation of new classes and ranks in the community, the splitting up of estates into new units and their passing by marriage and death into other families, with all the conspiracies, conflict and consequences, repeated in varying degree over the lands of some thirty "tenants-in-chief", with the addition of religious disputes, and the ever-present threat of Scottish raids, created the pattern of Yorkshire's contribution to the nation's history until the days of the Civil War.

The changes brought about in north-country life were, of course, only in the formative stages when the Conqueror died in 1087, but everywhere there were the outward and visible signs of the new order. Not only castles but cathedrals and abbey churches were rising. On the banks of the Thames the citizens of London could watch the new Tower being built. In the north, York was now the second city in England yet as such was a political magnet for the raiding Scots, for if York was captured then the north of England might well become a part of Scotland and the frontier line between the two countries might well move from the Tweed to the Humber. It was to prevent this that William began to build his "new castle" on the Tyne and gave great power to the Percies and the Nevilles whose lands and men would provide a buffer against the Scots. Durham and Carlisle were more than the homes of northern bishops, they were rallying points of resistance where the ecclesiastical powers were almost those of princes. These years of raiding almost certainly account for the number of fortified farmhouses in the north and even for the fortified church towers to be found at Bedale, Spennithorne and else-where in the North Riding.

It was during these years that the existing Walls of York were built, with their posterns and entrance gates—or bars—at Bootham, Micklegate, Goodramgate (known as Monk Bar), and Walmgate. More and more people crowded into it during the following centuries, and overflowed out of it to the surrounding lands. The streets were narrow and although picturesque today probably very dirty then, for as the upper parts of the houses overhung the street little light or air could enter. Churches were built and hospitals to cater for the crowded population, and as the city began to flourish as a trading centre the guilds grew up with their guild-halls where the weavers, tailors, lock-smiths, armourers and other craftsmen and traders met. You can walk into some of these halls and see evidence of the almost religious ritual which arose around the crafts. Little remains, however, of the cloth trade which was once large and important in the city's history; that, as we shall see, went elsewhere.

When, centuries later, Henry VIII suppressed the monasteries he suppressed the guilds too, and as a consequence York lost a good deal of its trading prominence and ecclesiastical importance although it still remained a military centre. Perhaps the lowest point in its fortune came when the Lord Mayor and civic dignitaries knelt in the mud on the city's boundary to present to Henry VIII a monetary bid for clemency after the insurrection of the Pilgrimage of Grace. He re-warded them by establishing the vindictive Council of the North in the lovely King's Manor, formerly the house of the Abbot of St. Mary's Abbey, and which by the strange whirligig of history later became a royal lodging, a Catholic seminary, a ladies' college and a school for the blind. Its final stage is as a part of the new University of York.

As befitted the capital of the north, the city has always basked in royal patronage. I believe that every reigning English monarch has visited the city and it received its first royal charter as long ago as 1122. Richard II gave it another charter in 1396, setting it apart in its own special county, and so proud is York of this honour that on special occasions the sword which Richmond gave to the city is still borne before the Lord Mayor. Not until the close of the Civil War in the seventeenth century when conditions became more stable did the crowded citizens feel it safe enough to venture living far outside the protective walls. Then the city began to expand along the four main roads by which you enter it today. This allowed much tumble-down property inside to be rebuilt or enlarged or replaced—a process which is still continuing centuries later.

The medieval city, although attractive as a museum piece today, cannot have been altogether attractive to live in. In the first place, it was largely built of wood from the nearby Forest of Galtres—so much easier to acquire than stone like that of the Minster, much of which had to be brought from quarries at Tadcaster. The old overhanging, closely packed houses still to be seen in the Shambles must have had many perils—fire, plague, violence, and the general discomfort of lack of air, sanitation, and water supplies. Further, the inhabitants may have been no worse in their ways than in other places but the city by-laws suggest that there was some unpleasantness. Fines were threatened for leaving dunghills in the streets, for allowing pigs to wander, for throwing refuse out of doors, and for butchers depositing offal into the river. Many hospitals were set up, including one for lepers. The squares and open spaces were used for markets and fairs at which the Guilds would present their mystery plays based on Scriptural stories, each Guild providing the play appropriate to their craft—the shipwrights giving Noah and the Ark, the plasterers the Creation, the barbers the baptism of Jesus, and so on. These have been revived in recent years as a summer attraction for visitors.

The tax records of the city towards the end of the seventeenth century give an interesting picture of the social life of the place. One-third of the households were very poor, consisting of widows, orphans, the chronic sick and the unemployables; one-third were reasonably well to do, consisting of small shopkeepers and artisans; and one-third were very rich, consisting of merchants, clergy, attorneys and other professional men. Occupations were very much those of a regional capital, dealing with regional products, and trade imports through the port of Hull. The city also had a fluctuating local trade because of the considerable number of people augmenting the resident population at certain seasons, as when the gentry and their servants came to occupy their town houses for the social season, or when the courts were held and litigants travelled to York. It was also a centre for the early tourist trade and the inns of York were highly esteemed.

A great deal of merchandise passed between York and Hull, its nearest port, but because of growing competition from London, restrictions on the Continent, difficulties of shipping and piracy in the North Sea, the merchant class began to decline. The City Corporation looked after some three hundred to four hundred poor families with a form of poor relief and training in handicrafts to help the younger ones to earn a respectable living, and the wealthy parishes helped the poorer parishes. St. Peter's and Archbishop Holgate's schools provided education, as did many charity and trade schools, and in 1641 and 1648 the Corporation twice petitioned Parliament for a university, a dream that has only now been realized three hundred years later.

As you wander in the streets of York today you can trace one step after another in the transition from the medieval to the day before yesterday. William's College, established in 1461 to house chantry priests, the half-timbered merchants' halls of the trading era, the Mansion House, the Assembly Rooms of later social days, the coaching inns, the Art Gallery, proud of that artist son of York, William Etty, the great chocolate factories now transferred to the suburbs but once in the town streets, the more than a score of churches—all that remain of the forty at the time of the Reformation—much, much more there is, each with its historic story. And so to the railway station.

## The "Railway King"

Railway stations, like humans, have characters. King's Cross and St. Pancras, like other London termini, have an "Here we are, we have arrived" air about them. Stations at seaside towns, however drab they may be of themselves, are the bright portals to a golden future, even if only a day trip. The big new station at Leeds has a brash, no nonsense, look which suggests that its purpose is "Strictly Business". Doncaster touches its cap as the great diesels thunder importantly through on their way north or south. York always suggests that it is the hub of a giant wheel whose spokes radiate to every corner of Britain and that it is a place apart, for no other single station can make such a claim. On your arrival a strong confident voice announces over the loud speakers "This is York", and that's that. There are few trains in the day which do not stop to make a sort of obeisance there. Train spotters of all ages move from platform to platform to capture for their notebooks trains to Scotland, to London, to the eastern counties and to the west of England. Every type of locomotive from the most up-to-date diesels to the tall-funnelled bath-chair-like steamers move in and out of its maze of lines. And, in the museum just outside the station, veterans and pensioners of the line all brightly polished and at ease stand on their abbreviated tracks listening nostalgically to the continuing hubbub of which they were once part.

Yet the present station is not so very old. Just behind it, within the old walls and close to the retired veterans, is the original station now used as offices. This was the station the young Charles Dickens knew when he travelled into Yorkshire to collect the material for his books or later to give his readings. Here he had to leave his railway coach and change to a horse coach to continue his journeys, for then York was the northern terminus of the line. Most probably he

*Queen's Gardens, Hull—once a busy dock*

began the next leg of his journey at the York Tavern or the Black Swan in Coney Street, both early coaching inns of note.

So it was that the next historic stage in the growth of York was heralded by the coming of the railway in the early nineteenth century. And here we must introduce a certain George Hudson, linen draper, Lord Mayor, and eventually—and for a brief time only—a great Yorkshire landowner. In the street known as Goodramgate you can see the shop where he carried on business before he acquired fame as the Railway King. Here he had the idea of making York a centre for the new railway system which was spreading up from the south to the north. He found the idea both exciting and lucrative; he fought and argued and bluffed—the very prototype of the stage version of the Yorkshire self-made man of business. A timely legacy of £30,000 enabled him to take an interest in the York and North Midland Railway which linked the city with Normanton and from that start he built a railway empire which extended over the north country from Edinburgh and Berwick to Newcastle, Darlington and into the East Riding of Yorkshire as well as into the Midlands.

It was in May 1839, when Hudson was Lord Mayor of the city, that his first venture came into being with the opening of the line to South Milford—a modest start, but celebrated with the ringing of the Minster bells, a breakfast at the Mansion House before the inaugural journey, and a dinner and ball at the Guildhall at the day's end. This was attended by George Stephenson with whom Hudson had formed a friendship of mutual interests. From this beginning grew the line to Darlington two years later, and in 1845 the line to Scarborough. From purely local interests Hudson became involved in much larger schemes upon which Gladstone consulted him when the "Railway King" became Member of Parliament for Sunderland.

Although some of Hudson's financial methods were doubtful and his name was besmirched by his actions—so much so that from the great house and lands he acquired with his wealth at Londesbrough in the East Riding he fled abroad in disgrace—he made York a great railway centre. The striking office buildings of the once famous L.N.E.R., the nearby carriage and wagon works, and the busy station are visible evidence of his achievement—a far cry from the little shanty which Dickens knew. Hudson, after all, continued an historic process; from the days of the Romans York has been the hub of a traffic wheel—of legionaries, of chariots, of horsemen, of coaches and of railways.

*The end of Yorkshire—Spurn Point*

With the railway age a new York grew up around the older cities we have seen. Rows of yellow brick houses were built to meet the needs of thousands of railway workers. New industries came to the town or grew up around it—agricultural machinery, printing, chocolate and sweet-making. Considerable markets developed for cattle and the cereal and vegetable products of the Plain of York. These called for new factories, warehouses, offices—and still more homes for the growing population. From a population of some 17,000 at the beginning of the nineteenth century there was a rise to well over 100,000 by the most recent census, and since then the new University has considerably increased it again. The old ecclesiastical importance of the city had long been restored. It is still the military headquarters of the Northern Command. So came the suburbs stretching out into the surrounding countryside, swallowing up little villages like Acomb and Haxby and spreading along the river banks.

The coming of this drab and mundane modern "box" to enclose all the rest has raised a multitude of problems, primarily how to preserve the old while catering for new needs. Narrow streets cannot cope with modern transport, and the city is in danger of being traffic bound. Present-day shop fronts do not accommodate themselves easily into eighteenth-century façades. Modern amenities, from sanitation to electric lighting, have to be fitted into ancient structures and threaded through a maze of medieval and Jacobean architecture. Offices, public buildings, markets, restaurants have to find their place in properties that lean and twist and follow no rules. New industries from chocolate making to the manufacture of optical instruments have grown up round the city, but their workers have to journey to their homes at night and this congests the streets with cars and bicycles by the thousand, for the flatness of York has encouraged the cycle to an extent known in no other town in the north. And every August the ancient race-meeting at York, held on the Knavesmire where felons used to be hanged, adds still further to the problems facing the authorities. A new and as yet barely felt complication is arising with the foundation of the new University, based on Heslington Hall outside the city but certain to add a growing student population, with all its needs and demands. The ancient capital of the North is still alive and vigorous, and there may yet be added a new city to enwrap the old.

## The Minster

Every great city has many aspects and with York you may first be impressed by the entrance into the city through one of its four bars in the creamy white walls, or by the skyline of spires which has something of a Canaletto air about it, or by the sudden transformation from a new brick suburb to the stone of the old town, or even by the incongruity of towering cranes at work on new buildings rising phoenix-like out of the huddle of old streets. But sooner or later you will arrive at the Minster and fleeting impression becomes admiration and awe and wonder at its grandeur and nobility.

Unless you are very important indeed you enter the Minster by the door through the south transept, which looks down Stonegate. And this is perhaps the best and most revealing way for in a few steps you are immediately under the great lantern tower in the very centre of the gigantic building. The tower is supported by four massive columns. In front of you is the famous Five Sisters window, dating from 1200, whose wonderful stained glass was removed for safety during the war years and then carefully replaced. An old legend, which Dickens incorporated into *Nicholas Nickleby*, says that it originated in the work of five sisters who each designed a tapestry from which the windows were copied. The story is picturesque but without foundation in fact. The window is beautiful enough without the story. Looking through the choir screen to your right there is the even more wonderful east window, reputedly the largest single area of stained glass in the world, depicting in magnificent colours scenes from the Old Testament and the Book of Revelations. It is almost impossible to believe that this window was completed as long ago as 1408. Over the transept door by which you have entered is a splendid rose or wheel window, and at the western end of the nave on your left is a great "heart" window of the fourteenth century Decorated period.

How long the original wooden building erected by the Anglian king Edwin remained is uncertain. Successive waves of invaders probably destroyed many buildings on the site by fire but by the time of the Norman conquest there were certainly buildings of stone. William's destruction of the place left few remains, and the first Archbishop after the conquest, Thomas of Bayeux, had to start again. His church lasted just under a century before fire again destroyed it and a new re-building was begun, once again on the same site. Actually you will find here, as at Beverley Minster and elsewhere, most periods of architecture represented, for, as we have seen, there has been a religious building on this site from Saxon times, and some of the earliest work is visible in the crypt. The present building was begun by Archbishop Grey about 1227 with the south transept, and continued for some two hundred and fifty years when the last two western towers were added, following the completion of the great centre tower, which itself took fifty years to build. Those blessed with an abundance of energy may climb nearly three hundred steps to the top of this tower for a magnificent view on a clear day of the Plain of York.

The sheer magnitude of the planning, organization, and building of such a magnificent structure which went on in a world of continuing strife and political upheavals is almost unbelievable. The building shows the handiwork of so many craftsmen each in their own characteristic style; the heavy squat Norman work in the crypt, the delicate Early English work in the transepts, the Decorated nave and chapter house and the tracery of the great windows, the central tower and east window in the fine vertical lines of the Perpendicular period. And everywhere those quirks of sculpture, the human faces, the animals and birds, the carefully modelled leaves and fruit, which must have been works of joy to the individual craftsmen who shaped them. Then, too, there are the great oak chests, the printed books, the rather tawdry (by comparison) marble busts and figures of more recent memorials, the beauty of Evensong as the music floats through the stonework, and the exquisite vistas from this corner and that.

It would require a large volume to detail the treasure of the Minster in stone and stone and glass and manuscript. Indeed many such volumes have been written about them. It is worth while, however, to walk into the Chapter House to look upon the Horn of Ulf, a carved ivory horn given to the Minster in the year A.D. 1030 as a token of the land on which it is built. The donor was no other than King Canute, and the land he gave was the property of Ulf, the owner of the horn, whom he had killed.

At least three previous buildings on this site were, strangely, all destroyed by fire. The present building has twice narrowly escaped burning, once a century and a half ago at the hands of a lunatic and a few years later by a workman's mishap. Unlike Westminster Abbey, whose interest is rather in the dead who are commemorated in it than in its architecture, York Minster is a place of beauty and wonder.

It is a place to be felt as well as seen, and although Yorkshire men and women are not emotionally expressive this is a building of which the county is proud and, even more, which it loves. Seen from a distance its stonework gilded by the evening sun gives it the magic of a glorious mirage. It is the spiritual centre of the county.

## The Central Plain

A vast fertile plain divided by hedges, warm brick cottages and farmsteads with red pantile roofs, gaudy farm machinery, churches, villages, parklands and the occasional big house, prosperous-looking farmers in prosperous-looking cars, here and there a racecourse with its green turf and white rails, aerodromes, jet-planes and perhaps one or two gliders overhead. These at random are some of the details which you can pick out looking westwards from the tower of the Minster or from any one of a dozen vantage points on the Cleveland Hills or from the Hambletons across the Plain of York. Smokily blue in the distance as a background to this detail are the fells which divide the Pennine dales and which stand end on to the Plain. Down those dales come many of the rivers we have met already, and here in the Plain they are gathered up by the Ouse to join the Humber and so flow into the North Sea. Where the Ouse basin forms the palm of the outstretched hand of rivers are the farmers of the vales of Mowbray and York which make up the Plain, growing their crops and raising their cattle in the fertile flat lands.

The Plain of York is the middle territory of Yorkshire, separating the Pennine hills and dales in the west from the Cleveland Hills and the Hambletons in the east, and you cannot fully understand Yorkshire unless you remember this almost flat land which divides the two halves of the county. At its narrowest it is only a dozen or so miles wide, but southwards near York it expands to nearly thirty. Lengthwise it stretches from the Tees some sixty miles to the region round Doncaster. These are the truly "broad acres" of Yorkshire, and those living upon them share the characteristic in their ways and outlook, for the nature of a people is often patterned by what lies beneath its feet. Here they are easy-going, well-living, and in general more prosperous than the hill-farmers on either side of them whom occasionally they will refer to as "dog-and-stick men", meaning that the chief concern of the hill-farmer is sheep. The richness of this land follows from the deposits of boulder clay left by the vast glacier which once filled the Plain and whose moraines provided ridges on which it was possible to cross the swampy lands left behind as it melted. The farm folk you will meet on market days at York, which dominates the northern half of the Plain, or at Ripon or Thirsk or any other of the smaller towns round its edges are friendly people, with a large sense of humour and a strong independence. Yet this independence is not the self-contained isolationism of the hill-farmer. It does not completely smother the idea of co-operation, and it is typical that the largest farming co-operative in the county recently came into being by the merger of a Yorkshire farmers' organization with a West Cumberland farmers' society, with headquarters at York and a turnover of some twenty-five million pounds a year.

Many centuries ago this was described as "a land of plenty, rich in golden corn". To that, contemporary man has added oats and barley, potatoes and beet, and many lesser crops. During the war years it produced sugar beet in vast quantities for the extraction of sweetness in the great factories near York and Selby, and the crop is still important. At Selby, too, as at Hull, are vast mills for the processing of oil-containing seeds from which vegetable fats and oils are extracted and the by-products made into cattle-cake and other animal feeding-stuffs. Everywhere there are fat cattle, Disney-like pigs, and the heavier grassland sheep.

Posterity will have to decide which has been of most importance to Yorkshire, the agricultural development of the Plain or the lustre of its history. For almost every mile is ground of historic importance in the story of the county and of the nation. Many of the great battles of our history books—Stamford Bridge, Boroughbridge, the Battle of Standard, Towton, the Pilgrimage of Grace, Marston Moor—took place within the Plain of York, and almost every town and village can show some link with one or other of them or tell stories about them.

Through the Plain ran the Great North Road and the inn at Scotch Corner is an epitome of the story of our roads over the past centuries. In the days of stage-coaches and when great droves of Scotch cattle were brought this way into England it was a flourishing hostelry, the meeting-place of travellers, the posting house where relays of horses were kept, a place of refreshment for all manner of wayfarers, including couples eloping to Gretna Green. Then came the railway age and the old traffic died, the coaches vanished and wayfarers were few, so that a writer at the beginning of this century would describe the inn as having "a lonely and almost desolate appearance", its chief custom then coming from cyclists. Now the wheel has literally turned full circle, and once more it is a busy and flourishing establishment owing everything to motor traffic which fills its forecourt with parked cars and its public rooms with a new and swifter travelling public.

In the northern half of the Plain of York are Northallerton, Thirsk, Boroughbridge and Ripon, all of them important market centres for considerable areas of this agricultural country, all of them still having an undefinable air of the old coaching days. Northallerton has a solid blustering quality as befits the county town of the North Riding, with a wealth of attractive houses, hospitable inns and a remarkable variety of shops along its broad central street. It has an ancient grammar school, a fifteenth-century almshouse and a notable medieval church. One of the many famous pupils of the grammar school was that Dr. John Radcliffe who was once called upon for medical advice by Queen Anne and, with true Yorkshire forthrightness, told her there was nothing wrong with her—to her dismay.

In the heyday of railways Northallerton was an important junction on the main line to Edinburgh, being about half-way between there and London. Some four hundred trains a day, passenger and goods, passed through the station, and some of them halted there to link with the now closed lines into Wensleydale and into Cleveland. Much of this glory has departed although the expresses still roar through. What it has lost in railway traffic it has not gained in road transport, for the main roads, the A.1 and the A.19 pass on either side of the town, which means that it is still a pleasant place to linger in. On market days you will see more prosperous farmers gathered there than in any other Yorkshire town of its size. Over a thousand cars have been counted there on a good day. And if you are observant you will notice that the hotels, restaurants and eating-houses all provide well-proportioned chairs as seating accommodation rather than the flimsy perches of city establishments—proof, if proof were needed —that local agriculture is broadly based!

There is a two-way traffic between Northallerton and Thirsk, some ten miles to the south, for Thirsk housewives go north for their shopping expeditions and the Northallerton menfolk make a return pilgrimage to the racecourse at Thirsk on the eight racing days of the year. A moralist might muse upon what each takes home.

There are still traces of the Mowbray castle at Thirsk. There is, too, a beautiful fifteenth-century church with fine woodwork and rich glass inside. There is also a notable eighteenth-century Hall with delightful grounds. But the outstanding feature of the town is its market square. This will never cease to be a surprising place, odd-sided, miniature, cobbled with the hardest of stones that make walking a torture, and with a strange and confusing mixture of frontages from the delightful Fleece Hotel proclaiming its link with coaching days to the newest supermarket blatantly proclaiming its cut prices and this week's bargains.

Thirsk has today the most characteristic market place in Yorkshire, with the air of a stage set so that anyone crossing it has the appearance of making an entrance and an exit. For many years its cobbled surface was a favourite parking place for cars and an overnight haven for long-distance lorries, with much roaring of engines, changing of gears, and general garage-like upheaval. The creation of a new by-pass and the provision of parking facilities elsewhere has largely restored its ancient peace to the delight of hoteliers and visitors.

Until a year or so ago the same might have been said of Borough-bridge, an historic town of great roomy hotels, another cobbled market-place, and the *bridge*. This river crossing of the Ure on the Great North Road has been of importance since man first travelled in Yorkshire. Everything from pack-horses to armies have crossed at this point from the West Riding to the North. Horsemen, coaches, cyclists and pedestrians made this little town a resting-place on their journeys, hence the abundance of hostelries. It was truly old-world and picturesque until the motor age. Then the need for overnight halts vanished, the traffic roared by without even a glance at the deserted coaching inns and the quaint courtyards, and Boroughbridge stood for little more than the day-long and night-long rumble of traffic. Until there came the time when even the old road could stand no more; the traffic had overpowered it. A brand-new by-pass arose, broad and unencumbered by hotels and quaintness. And within a short time Boroughbridge had returned to its old ways as a quiet wayside town with only its history as a claim to fame. History, and prehistory. For in fields to the west of the town is a group of three upright stones known as the Devil's Arrows, reminding you a little of contemporary sculpture but in fact tens of thousands of years old, probably the burial chambers of Stone Age man.

One story of the original wooden bridge which spanned the Ure at Boroughbridge goes back to the days of Edward II when a group of noblemen from the Vale of Mowbray joined with Thomas, Earl of Hereford, to oppose the weak king. Like many similar revolts, this one did not succeed and the discomfited rebels were returning north from the Midlands and were on the verge of their own territory when they were intercepted at Boroughbridge by a force of the King's men who opposed their crossing of the only way over the river. In the fighting on the bridge a soldier of the royalist force hid himself in the timbers supporting the bridge and as the Earl of Hereford tried to cross it thrust a long spear through a gap in the beams which "entering under the armour of the earl, so pierced his body and he died on the spot". This so disheartened the rebels that they fled in disorder, one of them, John de Mowbray, being captured and killed within sight of his own castle at Upsall, near Thirsk, in a lane which was afterwards rather grimly called "Chop Head Loaning".

This great Plain contributes much to the agricultural output of Yorkshire—an output surprising to those who think of the county as a region of factories, mills, ironworks and pit heaps. Of the whole acreage of Yorkshire only about ten per cent is industrial, the rest is under crops and grass, rough grazing or forestry. Approximately one-tenth of all the food-producing livestock of England and Wales is reared in the three Ridings. Most of the mixed farming is centred on these Plains of York and Mowbray, while the Dales support the hill sheep and there is another "sheep and barley" area in and around the Wolds. There is a big dairy industry in the urban lands of the West Riding, often with mill chimneys as part of the landscape, and side by side with it goes considerable market gardening to meet the needs of the industrial towns.

Joining the Plain of York, and at right angles to it, comes in the Derwent Valley, with Malton as its centre. This, again, is a mixed farming area, with a good deal of arable land along the river sides.

Malton for most of the travelling public of Yorkshire is a hiatus on the road to somewhere else. Motorists hurrying to Scarborough know it as a fearful and frustrating bottle-neck through which eventually they hope to pass. Train travellers to Whitby knew it as a junction at which you changed into the little push-me pull-you train which carried them across the once marshy land—still known as Marishes—to Pickering and thence up the romantic Newtondale to Goathland and the coast. All this is a pity for the two Maltons—New and Old—are both attractive in a down-to-earth way which might be expected in a district which mixes racing and agriculture, brewing and cricket. There was once a castle here, but its site is vague. There was a Gilbertian Priory, of which the church with its great tower is evidence. And if you read the inscription outside the Cross Keys Hotel in the town you will learn that inside is the crypt of one of a number of hostels once maintained by the Canons of the Priory for pilgrims and travellers—which is the right sort of invitation to any hotel. Malton was the Derventio of Roman times, a station on the road north, so that legionaries too probably thought of it mainly as a place of hospitality.

North-west of Malton a road leads through Hovingham, with its delightful Hall, the Mecca of Yorkshire cricketers, and then through Nunnington into Ryedale. Almost directly westwards another road takes thousands of visitors a year to the Palladian showplace of Castle Howard.

Horace Walpole, visiting Castle Howard some two centuries ago, rhapsodized over its magnificence. He wrote: "Lord Strafford had told me that I should see one of the finest places in Yorkshire, but nobody had informed me that I should at one view see a palace, a town, a fortified city, temples on high places, woods worthy of being each a metropolis of the Druids, vales connected to hills by other woods, the noblest lawn in the world, fenced by half the horizon, and a mausoleum that would tempt one to be buried alive. In short, I have seen gigantic places before but never a sublimer one."

This great house in its 14,000-acre estate is still much as Walpole saw it, although he would never have visualized it as one of the big tourist attractions of the north. Vastness is its chief architectural characteristic and this was what Vanbrugh, its architect, sought to express. It stands magnificently on a plateau on the north side of the river Derwent, between York and Malton, and was built on the site of the old castle of Hinderskelf, largely through the enthusiasm of the third Earl of Carlisle, who began the laying out of the estate in 1702. It has a south front some 323 feet long, a great cupola in the centre, and great solid wings of stone on either side of the main building.

To journey through the halls and corridors of Castle Howard is a memorable experience, but the feeling remains that the house is a museum rather than a private residence. Room after room is packed with art treasure. Precious china—English, Continental and Oriental—line alcoves in the corridors; portraits overflow from one room to another and all the passages between; pictures by Velazquez, Bellini,

Titian, Canaletto, Van Dyck, Lely, Reynolds and Gainsborough catch the eye everywhere; sculptures, bronzes and remarkable antiques are on every landing and in every corner. And when you have exhausted the interior treasures, and yourself, there is a vast parkland round the house, with ornamental waters and more statuary, the mausoleum, a temple, a pyramid, and an enormous obelisk to commemorate the Earl who planned it all.

All this had its own railway station on the York to Malton line, to which at one time thousands of excursionists came to visit the house and grounds. The line is still attractive—although the railway excursionists are now no more—because it runs alongside a lovely stretch of the Derwent where suddenly you come upon the ruins of Kirkham Priory.

According to legend Kirkham Priory had its origin in a tragedy which involved the son of Walter l'Espec who at the beginning of the twelfth century owned much of the land around the Derwent. The son, also named Walter, was out hunting on the river bank when his horse was frightened by a wild boar. The rider was thrown heavily against a stone and died. His father, inconsolable at the loss, sought spiritual advice and to assuage his grief and in memory of his son built and endowed the Priory at Kirkham as well as Rievaulx Abbey and a monastic house in Bedfordshire. This story strikes a familiar note; where have we encountered it before? Away in Wharfedale where a similar legend grew up around Bolton Priory and the young de Romille. It has its counterpart elsewhere, too, and is probably one of those universal legends like that of the Devil building a bridge in exchange for the soul of the first living soul to cross and being tricked when a dog is whistled over, a legend which is known in many places on the continent of Europe as well as in Yorkshire. Little remains now of Kirkham Priory except the finely carved gatehouse and the stones in the turf which indicate something of the original ground plan. Yet it is one of the most peaceful and untroubled places in the county, surrounded by woods, with a placid flower-bordered stream meandering at your feet, and the mellow stonework scattered among the cropped turf.

# VII

## INDUSTRIAL YORKSHIRE

ONE of the most notable productions of the Ordnance Survey is the Map of Roman Britain. On this map the great forts linked by the network of roads are marked in red; tightly spaced across Scotland on the line of Agricola's defensive barrier and across northern England where Hadrian's Wall stretched from Solway to the Tyne, but widely if strategically spaced over the Yorkshire area. Tiny black dots scattered over the map indicate the sites of Roman finds. And it is these black dots that so clearly mark the developments that were to follow down the centuries.

South of Ilkley (Olicana) they are thick upon the ground. There is another cluster between Doncaster (Danum) and Chesterfield, and still another just south of the Humber, and yet a third just south of the Tees. Compare these with a modern map of Yorkshire and the pattern is reasonably clear. Where the black dots appeared are now the great industrial areas containing Leeds, Bradford, Halifax, Sheffield, Barnsley, Teeside and the rest. The working of coal and lead foreshadowed the future. Only round Malton (Derventio) which was chiefly a Roman military centre linked with Cawthorn Camps, four miles north of Pickering, has modern industry failed to appear in any strength. The transformation of one into the other is the story of the making of industrial Yorkshire.

Through the dark page of our history that followed the departure of the Romans there is little that is known for certain of the industrial life of Yorkshire. The newcomers from North Germany, Holland and Scandinavia brought with them their own crafts and skills to mingle with such occupations as the Romans left. Sheep and cattle there were in the valleys, and the wool and hides would be used for clothing. Where the invaders settled they cleared the woods and enclosed the farmsteads. They had common plough lands and common pastures, and many of our small towns and villages, our forms of local government, and our Yorkshire speech in its dialect form grew from this time. There must have been much quarrying of stone for the building of Saxon churches, and the treasures revealed in Anglian burial places suggest some skill in metal work.

Viking intrusions from the west where they had established a king-dom in Dublin and indeed linked it with York must have brought an Irish influence into Yorkshire life in those times, although little indus-trial evidence of it remains. We have already seen how the Norse methods of sheep-farming left its influence in place names in the Pennine dales, and the use of Grizedale suggests pig-keeping. Presum-ably the coal and lead workings of Roman times would still be in use although, curiously, I believe there is no reference to coal in the Domesday Survey, and the appearance of silver coins, of which several hoards have been found, suggest other skills. York retained its impor-tance as a trading centre as well as a local market, despite many raids and periods of destruction, and exports of metal and woollen cloth suggest a continuing industrial life during that period to which the term "the Dark Ages" has been applied.

Between the Norman Conquest and the beginning of the fifteenth century a considerable change occurred in the pattern of Yorkshire. The "scorched earth" policy of William began it when he devastated great areas of the countryside and many communities disappeared for ever. The Scottish raids continued the process to a considerable depth below the Border. The Black Death struck at those villages which had managed to survive or revive from other devastation. But the fiercest change was brought about by the conversion of arable land, with its village communities, into great sheep walks as wool became increasingly valuable not only for home use but for export.

In his book *The Lost Villages of England* Maurice Beresford gives some illuminating examples of this change. Where in the middle of the fourteenth century there were 544 villages listed in official figures for the West Riding, some thirty vanished, often without trace. In North Riding nearly forty disappeared out of 450. And in the East Riding fifty were lost out of 366. Evidences of some of these have been found and extensive digging has recently exposed much of the lost village of Wharram Percy in the East Riding. Mr. Beresford maintains that the demands of the "man-eating sheep" was something that the villages were unable to resist.

As the wool trade and cloth-making ran their course, and increasing demand began to bring imported wool into the country, still another transformation took place. The sheep-grazed moorlands saw the mills arise in the valleys and up the hillsides. The great sheep-runs of the monasteries and great landowners were taken over by the little hill farms, scratching a living from the moors. In time they too found it impossible to continue and today the farms stand derelict looking with sightless eyes upon the mills and the factories around them. The Roman coal workings grew into mining areas. Iron and steel mills sprang up near the coal. And a new Yorkshire appeared.

## On Tenterhooks

The West Riding textile area is a world of its own, a sombre, hilly world whose frontier towns are Leeds, Bradford, Huddersfield and Halifax, and in which there is concentrated one general interest with great diversity of application. Once in that world, where bleak grit-stone moors are interspersed with deep valleys that have dark becks and streams running through them and gaunt chimneys reaching up as if to over-top the moors, you are absorbed in a community which speaks in a strange tongue, not only with a dialect of its own (which, in common with other Yorkshire dialects, is dying as a form of every-day speech) but with a complete vocabulary arising out of its occupation. Beside the main door of any Leeds clothing factory you will see under the heading WANTED a notice asking for "Basters", "Button-holers", "Trouser Hands". Along the sides of long, low buildings in the Shipley district are signs denoting that these are the premises of "Woolcombers" and "Commission Spinners". On the brass plates of Bradford offices are the words "Tops and Noils" and perhaps "Alpaca" and "Vicuna", which carry a curiously romantic air at odds with the background. There are also "Warpers" and "Sizers" and "Top-makers". In Batley and Dewsbury similar signs and notices speak of "Laps and Noils" and "Commission Carbonizing". These all represent particular aspects and processes of the great textile industry whose ancient basis is wool. Inside the factories you will find "Twisters" and "Pressers" and "Cutters", and some of these occupational names have slipped into everyday currency in the outside world. "Spinster" is one and "on tenterhooks" another. "Webster", "Cropper", "Lister" and "Fuller" are a few of many surnames originally derived from the wool industry that can be found abundantly in this area today.

Looking almost between your feet from any of the hill roads which clamber up and down among these textile valleys, almost as the stone walls do in the dale country, it is difficult to realize that the grim factories in the towns below are a more direct link with the remotest days in our history than the stone circles or the castles or the abbey ruins we have already seen. After the primitive skins they stripped from the animals they hunted, wool in some form or other provided our ancestors with their first real clothing, and sheep and shepherds were the basis of our earliest agriculture. It was no idle chance that made the woolsack the symbolic seat of the Chancellor, for this land lived almost entirely by sheep reared by the peasants, by the great land barons, by the monasteries, and supplied its surplus wool for use on the looms of the Continent. "Our island," says G. M. Trevelyan, "produced the best wool in Europe, and for centuries supplied the Flemish and Italian looms with material with which they could not dispense for luxury production, and which they could get nowhere else." Wool production early became the largest manufacturing industry, and was carried on in almost every part of the country.

Using wool sheared from sheap reared on the Sussex downs, on the Cotswold hills, in the eastern fenlands and in the northern dale country, the wool textile industry grew up out of a native product, unlike cotton textiles which were made from raw material imported late into this country. Not until the Middle Ages was there any concentration of the industry into districts, when the words "West of England" became associated with woollen cloths and the little Norfolk village of Worstead gave its name to a particular branch of the industry, and the flannel industry began in Wales and hosiery in the Midlands.

From the fourteenth century onwards, when the weaving of cloth began in the West Riding in substitution for the export of wool to the Continent, the raw wool was brought on the jaggers' ponies to the weaver's house—which was partly living quarters and partly factory. The wool was spread on the house floor in layers, each layer being sprinkled with oil and beaten with sticks, tossed together and reduced to a state of floss. It was then worked into long slivers and spun into fine or coarse threads to become the warp and woof of the weaver's loom. As each piece was made it was again spread on the floor and sprinkled with a fearful mixture of urine and pig's dung, the smell of which pervaded the place, and was beaten and trampled again. This was the process of fulling which preceded the drying on the tenters, the hooked racks where the air no doubt helped to sweeten the material. Afterwards there was a washing process and more drying on the tenters—from which we derive the phrase of "being on tenterhooks". Defoe, in the course of one of his journeys, observed that he saw cloth drying on tenters round almost every house when he came to Halifax. After the final tentering it was stamped by an official—an early example of British standards!—and sent to market.

In a world which takes the mechanization of every process for granted it is not easy to picture the cloth producers of the days when primitive improvization was the only tool. The sorting and cleaning was done by hand; the combing and carding, now done by elaborate machines, was performed by bent wires on crude wooden frames; drawing and spinning the yarn (do you recognize the phrase?) was originally a woman's task with the spinning-wheel and distaff; warping was a tedious hand-labour; and weaving, done by the men on heavy hand-looms, was a day-long and night-long task. They were craftsmen then, skilled to a high degree, rough but capable, with little or no book-learning but shrewd and pungent in their wit, contributing much to that Yorkshire "character" which is so easy to recognize and so hard to define but which still lingers in the small towns and villages of this textile region.

If you wander round Yorkshire textile mills today you will see all these processes continued but in modern mechanical form and by specialized firms—although so elaborate and complicated is the machinery that you may have difficulty in deciding which particular process is going on. Weaving was the first to be mechanized and was almost the first machinery introduced into Yorkshire—unfortunately as it happened, for while the flying shuttle speeded up the process it soon meant that the weavers outpaced the supply of yarn produced by the still primitive spinners. Not until the spinning-jenny introduced what was in effect a power-operated battery of spindles in one frame was the yarn produced in quantity, only in its turn to outpace the speeded-up but still hand-worked looms. The need now was for power-operated looms and this came at the end of the eighteenth century from that Edward Cartwright whose ornate memorial hall stands in the suburbs of Bradford and is an art gallery, museum and cultural centre. Cartwright, oddly enough, was a clergyman, but he had an inventive mind. His first power-loom was erected at Doncaster and the "power" was a bull. But the idea was sound, and it completed the mechanization of the industry.

In the early eighteenth century it looked as if the woollen industry would be shared by Lancashire and Yorkshire. In the Rossendale valley, for example, there was a rising production of cloth, blankets and flannels and the textile industry of the north may have had a very different development had not the advent of power machinery coincided with the entry of cotton imports through Liverpool and Lancaster so that both reached Lancashire at the same time. Cotton was more workable by the new machinery than wool. There were abundant supplies of the new raw material available while home-produced wool was limited. The resulting fabrics were cheaper. So "King Cotton" took over the Lancashire textile industry. And although it was not long before Australian wool came flooding in, it was too late. Now the woollen industry is limited to a few places on the Lancashire side of the Pennines. It is a dominant industry on the Yorkshire side.

It was towards the end of the eighteenth century that the West Riding of Yorkshire, which had always had a share of the industry, began to gain this supremacy partly because those streams in the valleys provided cheap and constant power beyond that of Cartwright's bull, partly that coal was produced close at hand when steam power replaced the water-wheels, and partly because the humidity of the atmosphere was right for spinning. So that the general interest of wool textiles flourished and was in turn diversified within the region. Halifax, Bradford and Keighley were in the main concerned with worsteds. Leeds, Morley and the Colne Valley produced woollens. While Huddersfield in the centre did a fine quality of both. Dewsbury, Batley and Ossett made their own later speciality in shoddy—the use of sorted and cleaned torn-up wool waste and worn garments.

York itself once played a considerable part in the wool and cloth trade—as its old guilds indicate. Exports of these goods were shipped down the Ouse to the ports of Europe and there was a great coming and going of buyers and sellers. But the guilds which had once encouraged enterprise became restrictive. The river began to silt up and big ships could no longer use it. Many of the guilds themselves, like the monasteries, were suppressed by Henry VIII. And by the end of the Civil War the textile importance of York was over. It had moved into the river valleys of the West Riding.

In these days vast quantities of raw wool are imported to meet the needs of the industry but there is still a steady flow from the dale country of Yorkshire. After clipping time on the farms, I have watched the fleeces folded according to an age-old tradition, packed forty or fifty at a time according to the breed of sheep and the weight of the wool into great sheets, and gathered by motor wagon to be sorted at

Bradford. The best grade of fleece nowadays may bring the farmer four shillings and more per pound of wool, although I have talked to many farmers who remember when it was fourpence or less. The wool-sorter works by feel as much as by eye. Surrounded by a number of skeps, he works through the fleeces, distinguishing them by quality with a deftness which comes only from long experience. After this comes the washing and cleaning to get rid of the dirt and the sand and the grease, this last waste product being itself collected by the sewage authorities to become the foundation of many products.

Ask any man in the Bradford trade the difference between woollen and worsted products and he may look at you a little pityingly, but he will go on to explain that it is all a matter of those magic words "tops and noils". In worsted yarns all the fibres of the wool lie parallel to each other, in woollen yarns the individual fibres lie in different directions. After the scoured raw wool has been "carded" (converted into a gossamer-like substance) it is then converted into continuous threads and either spun into woollen yarn or "combed" by a machine which separates the "tops" (or long wool) from the "noils" (the short wool). The "tops" are drawn before being spun into yarn while the "noils" go to the woollen branch of the industry.

When Camden in his travels came to Halifax his imagination got the better of him. He wrote: "Among the mountains themselves, the Calder afterwards leaves on the left Halifax, a very famous town on the slope of a hill extending from west to east. It has not had this name many ages, being before called Horton, as some of the inhabitants relate, adding this tale concerning the change of name. A certain priest, as they call him, had long been in love with a young woman without success, and finding her virtue proof against all his solicitations, his love suddenly changed to madness. The villain cut off her head, which, being afterwards hung upon a yew tree, was reverenced and visited by the common people till it began to corrupt, every person pulling off some twigs of the tree. The tree, stripped of its branches, maintained its reputation for sanctity among the credulous, and the vulgar fancied the little veins spread like hair or threads between the back and body of the yew trees were the maiden's identical hair. A pilgrimage was established from the neighbourhood hither, and such a concourse came that the little village of Horton grew to a large town, and took the name of Hali-fex—Holy Hair." Thus says Camden, but the English Place Name survey declares brutally that there "is no vestige of evidence" for the existence of Horton, and although there is some difficulty in finding another explanation for the place-name Halifax, it suggests as a possible derivation "an area of coarse grass in a nook of land or amongst rocks".

Camden is on safer ground when he says that the town "is famous for the largeness of the parish, having eleven chapels (of which two are parochial ones) and about twelve thousand souls. So that the inhabitants often say this their parish maintains more men than any other kind of animals; whereas, elsewhere in England in the more fruitful places, you will see many thousand sheep and but few people, as if men had given place to sheep or cattle, or had been devoured by them. The industry of the inhabitants here is also surprising, who, possessing a soil which can scarce maintain them at all, much less in a comfortable manner, have carried on such woollen manufacture, first established about seventy years ago, as to raise themselves great fortunes and bear the prize from all the observation that men's industry is often whetted by the barrenness of the soil."

A special aspect of man's industry in Halifax is carpet-weaving, and the name of Crossley is known wherever carpets are bought and sold. It is associated with Halifax in the same way that the name of Mackintosh arises when toffee is mentioned, or the Halifax Building Society (the "largest in the world") in the realm of finance, or Wilfred Pickles as a mark of good humour. And it is another native of the town, Dr. Phyllis Bentley, who has woven the wool industry itself into the stuff of a score of novels.

Most Yorkshire folk know the "Tramp's Litany":

> From Hull, Halifax and Hell,
> Good Lord, deliver us.

but few know why two good and respectable Yorkshire towns should thus be placed in the same category as the infernal regions. In truth it dates back many centuries and is, indeed, a tribute to the towns it at first glance maligns. Hull was known very early in its history as "a town of good government". In the year 1599 an order went forth that each alderman should take an account of all vagabonds, idle persons, sharpers, and beggars in each ward and punish them, severely. They were also to notice and punish absentees from divine service on Sundays. Inevitably the place acquired a "bad name" among the easy-going and the tramps of the time. Similarly they gave Halifax a wide berth because of the notorious Gibbet Law, for necessary precaution where so much cloth was left for days on "tenters", which provided that if a felon was taken with stolen goods to the value of more than thirteen pence in his possession he should be beheaded within three days, a circumstance which was summed up by a local poet in this verse:

> At Halifax the law so sharp doth deale
> That whoso more than thirteen pence doth steale,
> They have a jyn that wondrous quick and well
> Sends thieves all headless into heaven or hell.

There is still a Gibbet Lane with the stone base on which the "engine" performed its grim task so frequently that, if we are to believe the old chroniclers, heads fell as fast there as outside the Bastille in Paris.

Halifax has greater claims to fame than its vigorous treatment of rogues, for it has probably, as Camden suggested, been a centre of the woollen textile industry longer and more completely than any other town in the West Riding. A rather indistinct carving of a pair of cloth shears in the Parish Church porch marks where a cloth-worker was buried as long ago as 1150, and old manorial records mention "fullers" and weavers and dyers in Halifax in the thirteenth century. It has a fine eighteenth-century Piece Hall, now alas used for vegetable stalls, which was one of the most notable cloth markets in the West Riding.

I often wonder what another writer who took his raw material from the world at his door, would have thought of Dr. Bentley. Dickens, who visited Halifax in the course of one of his reading tours, did not like the town, but he had a high opinion of its inhabitants. In a letter he wrote in 1858 he declared:

> Halifax was too small for us. It is as horrible a place as I ever saw. I never saw such an audience though. They were really worth reading to for nothing—though I didn't do exactly that.

Actually he records that he cleared £70 by one night's reading at Halifax, having already made "a clear profit of more than £50" at Harrogate, which he described as "the queerest place, with the strangest people in it". He presented a citizen of Halifax, J. M. Whiteley, with five pages of the original manuscript of *Pickwick Papers*—which were sold for £7,500 seventy years later.

Along the hillsides of the Colne and Calder valleys particularly you can still see the houses which were once both the homes and the workrooms of the weavers and clothiers. Their long rows of windows close under the eaves mark the rooms which once held the looms when the domestic system prevailed. Those who worked in this way were often farmers as well as clothiers, and they mixed the two industries quite happily. They were their own carriers, too, taking the cloth to be sold in the cloth halls which were springing up in all the West Riding towns, leaving their legacy in names like "Cloth Hall Street". The rivers were used for transport too, however difficult it may be to believe it now in their thick grimy state. And many of the now almost unused canals date from this time.

Wool proved a more stable industry than cotton. Journey down any of these outwardly drab textile valleys and you will see still standing many of the great mills which replaced the old domestic industry as machinery and new forms of power came into it. The industry has come down from the hills to be near the rivers which originally provided the power, the canals which provided the means of transport, and later the railways which linked the growing towns. There were grim days in the mechanized textile industry in the first stages of the Industrial Revolution, as in other industries. Women and children worked ungodly hours, and often slept in the mills to save the journey home. The coming of new machines put the older craftsmen like the croppers out of work, at least temporarily, and there were Luddite riots and broken machines and much bloodshed. Charlotte Brontë used these troubles as a background for her novel *Shirley*, and Phyllis Bentley has woven a number of her novels out of the strains and stresses of the growing industry. Later there came slumps caused by wars and tariff struggles and for a time the textile towns became almost a "depressed area" when fortunes were made and lost overnight—although the wool depression was never as dramatic as the cotton slumps on the other side of the border. Yet wool textiles have held a traditional place as one of the country's six greatest exporting industries, the largest of its kind in the world, trading with some 150 countries and nowadays earning nearly £160 millions in foreign currency every year. Sprinkled down the history of the industry are great men like John Foster, Titus Salt, Isaac Holden, Samuel Cunliffe Lister, John Crossley, John Barran and others whose names are still linked with it.

A short bus-ride from the centre of Leeds in what was once the town house of a city worthy is now the headquarters of the Wool Industries Research Association. In the grounds of the house have risen vast laboratories, complete woollen sheds and factories in minia-ture. Here a team of scientists and technicians carry out research—and practical experiment—into every process and ramification of the in-dustry, from the kind of dye used in sheep marking on the fells to the elimination of "shine" in worsted suits, from the discouragement of moths to the tension of every thread in a woven piece, from the technical problems arising in a new process to the putting in of durable creases for men's trousers. This complicated laboratory serves the whole industry which supports it.

Although Halifax has a claim to the longest continuity in the trade outside of the religious house, the infinite variety of the industry now embraces the whole area, with individual valleys and towns having their particular specialities. Even in outline the list is impressive. Bradford is its largest centre and there wool is sorted; tops are combed; yarns are spun; and pieces are woven of infinite variety. There, too, are many merchants, yarn merchants, and piece merchants. Yet primarily, Bradford is a worsted centre and for woollens Huddersfield and the Heavy Woollen District (Dewsbury, Batley and a dozen townships encircling them are known by this comprehensive territorial term) compete with each other. Besides the partly manufactured products, Bradford produces fine coatings, serges and dress goods, the latter being composed of pure wool, wool mixed with cotton, silk, or artificial silk, or of any of these fibres singly or in huge variety of combination. Keighley, its near neighbour, produces similar tissues, while Silsden specializes in artificial silk to so great an extent that it claims with much foundation to be the pioneer home of the artificial silk piece-goods trade, thus foreshadowing later developments in rayon and a multitude of man-made fibres to such an extent that the Univer-sity of Leeds, which has always been "strong" on the textile side, has its special department for such fibres.

Bradford once was a place of tall decorated warehouses, shops and offices, with ornamented gables and commercial-gothic pinnacles. Blackened by grime and streaked by bird droppings—and parts of the city were as popular roosting-places for thousands of starlings and pigeons as Whitby is for gulls—they were not much to look at but they conveyed something of a cosmopolitan air as befitted a cosmo-politan city. In cellar restaurants you could hear a babel of foreign tongues spoken. Textile representatives would drop in from Prague or Berne or Breslau before reporting to their firms and setting out on their travels again.

Apperley Bridge in the Aire Valley is famous for its serges and flannels and Yeadon and Guiseley for women's woollen costume cloths. At Leeds, which is the centre of the wholesale clothing trade, fine worsteds and "low" woollens are made, and Morley is famous for its cotton-warp woollens. When, a few years ago, the demand for that product waned, Morley manufacturers, with commendable enterprise, specialized in the production of low-priced suiting flannels. Situated geographically between Morley and Huddersfield is the Heavy Woollen District, and that large area of scattered woollen mills is not only the home of the rag trade but its products range from low cloths competing with those made at Morley to fine and heavy woollens, Meltons, beavers, velours, tweeds, overcoatings, blankets, rugs, shawls —in fact, all kinds of woollen goods except fine white tennis cloth and billiard cloths—are produced in this district.

At Huddersfield and in the Colne valley are made fine worsted cloths for men's wear and a label indicating that these were made in Huddersfield has had a world-wide reputation down the years. And just as Huddersfield is known the world over for its fine worsteds, so are the two contiguous valleys of the Colne and the Holme known for their tweeds and overcoatings and women's costume cloths. In the Calder valley every kind of product from face cloths to blankets and rugs and, to a lesser extent, cap cloths is made.

The industry, of course, is always changing according to changing needs and new materials. Was it not Carlyle who said that a change of fashion in the wearing apparel of an English gentleman could have its effect on the life of a beaver trapper round the shores of Hudson Bay? So a new synthetic textile can today change a fashion and alter an industry. This in turn will affect the multitude of works which have grown up to supply the textile mills with machinery, dyes and all the ancillary equipment. Similarly the development of new forms of power from wind and water and Cartwright's bull to steam and electricity and perhaps the next step to nuclear energy, creates new patterns in the industry. The old individual skill of the hand-working craftsman has gone. Yet automation in the routine processes may give greater scope in its application. The story of Yorkshire's textile industry is a continuing epic.

## The Blackness of Coal

Hitherto we have had glimpses of English history as it has been made in the open dales, among the fells, on the high moors, and around the castles and great houses of Yorkshire, the picturesque aspect of our history. Shakespeare and lesser dramatists have made use of it, novelists have composed their fictions about it, and in more recent times film and television cameras have captured snippets of it as backgrounds to their imaginings. Yet English history of another sort has been made during the past two or three centuries in that region of the county which is part of Britain's greatest concentration of industrial activity.

If you will draw on the map of northern England an equilateral triangle with its base along a line from Skipton, at the edge of the Dale-country, to Sheffield, at Yorkshire's southernmost point, and its apex at or near Goole, where the Ouse becomes the Humber, you will—within its three sides of roughty fifty miles each—contain nearly all that halo of smoke, most of the collieries with their pit-head gear, and a high proportion of the mill chimneys which to many who know not Yorkshire save by hearsay besmirch the whole of the county. How small a proportion it is of this county of the broad acres, yet how great a contribution this populous region has made to the nation's material power and prosperity!

Even William Cobbett, a man who had a keen eye for the world about him, fell into the common error of regarding Yorkshire as almost solidly black after making one of his "rural rides" into the county in the thirties of last century. He wrote:

> "All the way along from Leeds to Sheffield it is coal and iron and iron and coal. It was dark before we reached Sheffield; so that we saw the iron furnaces in all the horrible splendour of their everlasting blaze. Nothing can be conceived more grand or more terrific than the yellow waves of fire that incessantly issue from the top of these furnaces, some of which are close by the wayside. Nature has placed the beds of iron and the beds of coal along-side of each other, and art has taught man to make one to operate upon the other. . . . As to the land, viewed in the way of agriculture, it really does appear to be very little worth. I have not seen, except at Harewood and Ripley, a stack of wheat since I came into Yorkshire."

This verdict was the more surprising as it was set down nearly a century and a half ago, for although coal and steel were then fast developing industries there were, at that time, very large tracts of what is now manufacturing territory still occupied by great estates with mansions upon them, like the Sitwell house at Renishaw, and the Wentworth, Wharncliffe and Wortley lands around the river Don. There was a time when this was one of the loveliest stretches of our English countryside, with woods and parklands, fine houses and trout-filled rivers. Robin Hood and his merry men often slipped over the border and found it a hiding-place and a hunting-ground when the Sheriff of Nottingham became too persistent. Robin Hood's Well stands on the road between Pontefract and Doncaster. Much of this not occupied by parkland and gardens was agricultural land, although more likely grazed by sheep than raising crops. Hence, no doubt, the absence of those wheat stacks which in Cobbett's eyes were the mark of good agriculture.

The base of the triangle I have drawn lies along the Pennines and into the Peak district of Derbyshire which is only a bus ride away from the centre of Sheffield. It is here that the Pennines show most sharply their influence on the ways of life of Yorkshire on the one side and of Lancashire on the other. They are a watershed not only of our northern rivers but of much of the industrial history of England. Here, as C. E. Montague has said, "English soil is more ancient than anywhere else, and the ways of man's labours more modern." And he might have added "more diverse".

There is, first of all, a difference of climate between one side of the Pennines and the other. This is recognized in the division of the B.B.C.'s daily weather report and in the old, if untrue, assertion that "it is always raining in Manchester"—but not in Leeds or Bradford. The humidity of one side of the mountains compares with the sharp bleakness of the other. The high passes over the tops from Lancashire into Yorkshire are frequently blocked by winter snows at Standedge between Huddersfield and Oldham and at Blackstone Edge between Halifax and Rochdale. Fog may persist almost to the summit on the western side while you drop into clear open valleys on the east. But these passes also mark a difference of temperament and outlook which may go back to the earliest settlement of the north. The Anglo-Saxon invasion swept like a slow tide into the eastern lands and to the foothills of the Pennines, but these invaders, as we have already observed, were not a mountain-accustomed people, unlike the Viking invaders who followed. The western slopes still had links with their Celtic forebears. The Pennines were a barrier to invasion from the east as they had been a dividing bastion when the Roman legions broke and parted to either side when they marched north.

Coal, steel and wool are the industrial foundations of this region.

Wool was the oldest for, as we have seen, sheep had been reared, grazed and tended for their wool on the Pennine slopes since the earliest inhabitants settled on the land. Even now, surprisingly close to the tightly packed brick and stone dwellings of the industrial towns, are tiny farms and holdings from which a man may look out of his barn door to mill chimneys in the valley below. I have seen pictures of these industrial dales painted by a local artist named Tait about 1845 in which there were factory chimneys, mills and railways, but in the foreground are men at work in the fields and cattle grazing in the meadows. At Saddleworth just inside the Yorkshire border the old rural custom of rush-cutting and rush-bearing to provide the church with foot-warmth was carried on into early last century just as it was in the Lake District. Much of the locally grown wool was worked up almost on the spot, and there were many farming-cum-weaving homesteads in these valleys, for cloth-making was a home industry before it moved into the factories.

The discovery of steam power was the start of the revolution which transformed this area from a wool-growing pastoral countryside wringing a hard agricultural living from the gritstone slopes to a thriving if mechanized industrial way of life. The development of steam power increased the demand for coal, which in turn gave further impetus to the use of steam. Those coal deposits which once rested on the tops of our western hills were here, because of the west to east tilt of the land, far below the surface, ready and available for mining. The earliest pits were sunk where the coal seams were nearest the surface, that is in the western sector of our triangle around Leeds and Bradford. Later, as mining methods and machinery improved, deeper pits were sunk following the seams until the greatest depth in Yorkshire is reached at Thorne, on the eastern slope.

Doncaster, Barnsley, Pontefract, Wakefield, as well as the fringes of Leeds and Bradford, are all placed over this Yorkshire coalfield and owe a varying share of their employment immediately to it—and some of their dreariness. You are never long out of sight of a pit-head in the district, and that usually means vast mountainous dirt heaps that overshadow the houses below. These are part of the landscape, along with the pit-head gear, a conglomeration of railway lines and trucks and a collection of unsightly buildings. It must be said that in recent years the streamlining of pit-heads by the National Coal Board and a general cleaning up of "clutter" has made for a tidier appearance, but a pit-head is a pit-head whether in these now bedraggled stretches of the West Riding or among the Scottish hills where they are spreading.

Doncaster always gives me the impression of being caught unawares by all this modern and not too pleasant development, and of looking at it a little askance even though trying to catch up with it—just as many older folk felt about the advent of television; they shook their heads sadly and bought a set. After all Doncaster had been a market town since Roman times, and it remained so down the centuries with a fine collection of grants and charters and fairs. It was so handy for Lincolnshire farmers with their carts and traps, as well as dairy folk from the next-door county of Nottingham. It sold them a special brand of butterscotch for their delight. It was a coaching station on the Great North Road and was later an important railway centre in the days of the Great Northern Railway Company, linking the south with Hull, York and Leeds. And above all, it had its world-famous Race Week with the St. Leger as its crown. Little wonder that black-faced miners in its streets, whippet-races on its fringes and miners' rallies on its open spaces seemed somehow incongruous. I have talked on the same day in Doncaster with a miners' leader in the Union office and later, in a local hostelry, with the proud owner of the winning competitor in sheep-dog trials, with his dog nuzzling my hand.

Between country town and railway and mining centre Doncaster managed a compromise, but by now it has added greatly to its complexity with engineering works, wire rope-making and a score of more modern trades, and is absorbing them all with the same air of surprise, even though it provides garden suburbs for their workers. This keeps it so busy that in the town itself you will rarely hear any reference to the historical treasures on its doorstep; Conisbrough Castle, beloved of Sir Walter Scott, Tickhill Castle, fought over in the Civil War, and the nearby Roche Abbey, one of the loveliest of the Yorkshire Cistercian monasteries.

Probably to many people the name of Barnsley is that most quickly evoked by the mention of "miner", and the relationship between town and industry is here complete. In little more than a century a farming community of a few thousand people grew into a mining town of nearly 50,000. Today it is a county borough of 75,000 inhabitants. True, it has its dismal rows of miners' houses, with few gardens, and not a great deal of imagination in their planning, but it has a fine civic hall, a notable grammar school, and is slowly rebuilding itself and ridding itself of Defoe's term "Black" Barnsley.

When I first heard of Cannon Hall, on the outskirts of Barnsley, I had a mental picture of some strange romantic tower somehow related to Sheffield and its products, perhaps the home of a steel magnate, or a place defended by those ancient cannon which shot great balls of iron into the enemy's midst. But I was mistaken. For Cannon Hall is a beautiful Georgian country house, designed by the famous York architect John Carr, and takes its name from the original owners of the estate, a family called Canun. True, there were some later owners named Spencer, who were active in the local iron industry and spent considerable sums on the rebuilding of the house and who later became Spencer-Stanhopes. One of them mustered the Staincross Volunteers when Napoleon threatened invasion. Today it is in the possession of Barnsley Corporation and is visited by people from all over the world for it is a very attractive example of an English country house set in some seventy acres of parkland and filled with the dignified domestic furniture and pictures possible in a spacious age. To discover this in the midst of what our geography books describe as "the Barnsley coalfield" is another reminder of how easily one can step out of the dirt and drabness of Yorkshire industry into a bit of countryside which has not greatly changed since the Domesday Survey.

It is here we encounter the river Dearne for the first time, rising, like so many other Yorkshire rivers, out of the eastern slopes of the Pennines and probably once as bright and sparkling as the rest but now subdued to its industrial environment. Between the Dearne, the Don and the Aire the great Yorkshire coalfield stretches with outliers, across a territory which might well have become a South Riding had not the very term "Riding" derived from the "thirdings" of its Saxon origins. There are still pockets of ploughlands and rural byways and even when this part of the West Riding seems most drab there is, thanks to place names and all the history for which they stand, romance in the air. Denaby, Tingley, Bawtry, Gunthwaite, Thrybergh, Hooton Pagnell and many more span the course of our English history and tell of successive invasions and settlements. Fishlake, which tells its own story, is hard by the River Don near Thorne. Ferrybridge, Wentworth and Conisborough roll back the centuries and recall days of pageantry and splendour. Doncaster itself was, still further back, the Roman "Danum" and the tramp of the legions was once doubtless as familiar as the rattle of miners' clogs.

Curiously those invasions of "off-cummed 'uns", as Yorkshire folk describe intruders "from away", have continued in this mining area until quite recent times, for as new pits opened they drew colliers from elsewhere to work them. If you talk to men on their way to work by bicycle or bus along any of the roads through the mining villages or in the towns you will discover that they or their predecessors came from Wales, Durham or the Scottish Border. In some cases they still maintain links with their home counties, but in general they have been assimilated into the pit community and as such form an enclave within the Riding with its own traditions and customs, its own forms of speech and phrase, and its own loyalties, as in mining regions everywhere. It is in many ways a closed community with a fiercely independent outlook, and its own pride. What strikes a visitor to Barnsley or Hickleton or Brodsworth or any other of the south Yorkshire mining towns and villages is the decorative effect of brightly-scoured doorsteps and window-sills, the pride taken in allotments, the enthusiasm of the miner for his whippets and pigeons, and the pageantry of the annual miners' union procession with its array of flags and bands. The miners' gala with its orgy of speech-making and general festivities is the great day of the year as was once the county fair.

One of the features of the landscape here is the subsidence which follows the underground working. Every railway traveller on the Midland line from Sheffield to Leeds is aware of the slowing down of the expresses over this section. The subsidence is continuous and drastic. From time to time widening cracks appear in houses, buildings are known to sink by as much as three or four feet in a few years, and ponds appear in hollows in the ground similar to the "flashes" over the Cheshire salt workings. But the mining community have learned to live with it as the price of the prosperity which has come to this district because of its vast underground resources.

It must not be forgotten, however, that there was once a grimmer side to the coal industry in Yorkshire as this bears witness:

"In many of the collieries there is no distinction of sex. The labour is distributed indifferently among both sexes, excepting that it is comparatively rare for the women to hew or get the coals, although there are numerous instances in which they regularly perform even this work. In great numbers of the coalpits in this district the men work in a state of perfect nakedness, and are in this state assisted in their labour by females of all ages, from girls of six years old to women of twenty-one, these females being themselves quite naked down to the waist."

This is from a Commissioner's report on the southern part of the West Riding in the forties of last century. The women and girls were chiefly employed as coal drawers, crawling on hands and feet with a belt round their waists and a chain for pulling their loads passing between their legs. Pit roads are by no means always level and much of the work entailed pulling the loads up steep inclines. In the low portions water was frequently up to the thighs. Children of five were employed in total darkness all day as "trappers", opening and shutting doors they could not see to control ventilation. And hours in 1840, as revealed by the Commissioner, were from sixteen to eighteen a day.

It is possible to lament that the discovery of coal, and all that followed inevitably upon the discovery, has altered the fair face of Yorkshire and given a haggard look to so many of its broad acres. We may deplore the replacement of farm hands, estate workers and rural tradesmen by grim-faced colliers from other parts of the country. Perhaps it is sad that where the pheasant and partridge once called and the bark of the fox was heard, there is now the clatter of shunting coal trains and the whirr of pit wheels. Yet the working of this underlying coal is as much part of Yorkshire as the iron-ore of Cleveland, the arable lands of the East Riding or the sheep-farms of the Dale country. It is an essential part of the portrait.

Altogether the Yorkshire coalfield covers 800 square miles of the West Riding and neighbouring areas and employs some 125,000 people, paying from £100 millions a year in wages and salaries. A century and a half ago the entire output of the coalmines of the United Kingdom was estimated to be ten million tons. The annual output of the Yorkshire coalfield is now well over forty million tons and it is planned to increase this to fifty million tons within the next decade. And side by side with the pits arise the power stations, fed directly from the mines, and providing electricity to the industrial areas through the lines which the great pylons carry over the moors and down the valleys to the mills and factories.

## The Blackness of Steel and Iron

The third section of this trilogy of West Riding industry is to be found further south—strangely aloof from the other two—in the black concentration round Rotherham and Sheffield where the men of iron and steel hold sway. During the early years of the last war it was claimed that the smoke pall over this area would defeat any attempt by enemy bombers to locate their targets, and for a while that seemed true. But the immunity did not last, and Sheffield suffered severely in the air raids. As a result architecturally a new centre has since arisen, the first stage of an imaginative plan for the city, so that the visitor who knew the old Sheffield of a quarter of a century ago would scarcely know the city of today. Yet the smoke pall remains, perhaps reduced because of the greater use of electric power, but a still dominant feature of the region as it has been for several centuries.

A settlement existed at this meeting-place of the five rivers, Rivelin, Loxley, Porter, Don and Sheaf in Anglo-Saxon times, and its name probably derives from "open land near the Sheaf". It had a castle in Norman times, but is not a medieval city like so many in Yorkshire. Yet by the fourteenth century there were smiths and cutlers in the district along the river banks. Chaucer made reference in the *Canterbury Tales* to the "Sheffield thwitel", or knife, which the miller of Trumpington carried "in his hose" and by the reign of Queen Elizabeth the place was known throughout the country for its knives, sickles, shears and similar products. The surrounding hills provided much of the raw ironstone for this early craft. Coal was close at hand and the quarries provided grindstones. So the range of cutlery widened from knives to every sort of implement which required a cutting edge, files and saws and a multitude of intricate tools. Silverware followed, and Old Sheffield Plate acquired an immense reputation, replaced nowadays by electroplating and chromium plating.

The importance of the industry was marked by the creation in 1624 of the Cutlers' Company of Hallamshire which derived from something similar to the domestic system we have already seen in the wool textile industry, when the "Little Master" with his family smithy also had a farm outside. Just as a mark of quality was placed on the tented cloth, so trade-marks were stamped on knives. To control the use of these marks the Cutlers' Company was established with its own guild hall, its Master Cutler and its annual feasts at which in these days statesmen make speeches. Its declared purpose is "the good order and government of makers of knives, sickles, shears, scissors and other cutlery wares", and to this end it is the registered proprietor of the trade-mark "Sheffield".

Side by side with the skill of the cutlery craftsmen has gone the development of the steel industry which evolved the special materials for their craft. This began with a greatly neglected inventor, Benjamin Huntsman, who was born in Lincolnshire in 1704. He was first apprenticed to a clock-maker and set himself up in this trade in Doncaster. In his work he was dissatisfied with the quality of the imported steel springs and sought to improve on them. To do this he moved his business to Sheffield where the clay and the fuel for his clay pots or crucibles were available, and in these he melted scraps of bar steel until, to quote the eminent Samuel Smiles, it had "a clear surface of a dazzling brilliancy like the sun when looked at with the naked eye on a clear day". This crucible steel was then cast into simple shapes for forging. Its virtue was its uniformity and high quality, essential for fine tools. Although Huntsman died a comparatively poor man while others made fortunes from his invention, he had established the place of Sheffield in the British steel industry, and from his labours other metallurgists and chemists have developed the diverse range of steels by adding oddly named elements such as chromium, tungsten, cobalt, titanium and molybdenum.

It is important to remember what distinguishes the specialized steel industry of Sheffield today from the bulk steel manufactured in Middlesbrough, South Wales and Scotland. If it is ships' plates, car bodies, or railway lines you require, you would order them from the bulk steel makers whose works tend to be centred nowadays near the great ports to which their raw materials are brought. But if you need parts for engines, steel cutting tools and stainless equipment then you turn to a Sheffield factory which one authority has described "a small place, a sort of bespoke tailor among the multiples". A third of the firms making steel are in Sheffield, but they only employ a sixth of the total labour force in the industry.

As the demands of the modern age in the matter of metals grow more complicated so Sheffield spreads and intensifies its research, not only in the individual research departments of the great firms but in a co-operative Iron and Steel Research Association laboratory and in departments of its growing university in whose special post-graduate schools for physical metallurgy and mining modern Aladdins are continually finding new uses for old metals.

There are those who will tell you that Sheffield produces a special sort of Yorkshireman of an individual pattern who matches the hard surface of the steel in his character. If this is true then I would add that like the steel he is well-tempered and of sound metal. I will leave others to explain the effect of other trades in the city on that character, for Sheffield also produces snuff, canned foods, printers' type and confectionery. Certain it is that the man of Sheffield is less volatile and less voluble than men of other parts of Yorkshire. You get the impression when walking in the streets or looking round in a café that the majority of its citizens are solemnly meditating some inscrutable problem, not gloomily or morosely, but with a strange intensity. Perhaps that is the effect of steel.

Under her canopy of smoke, the rumble of machinery, the hiss of steam, and the glare of white-hot steel which makes it a dazzling vibrant place, the city has largely built itself anew and has developed a cultural life which might have satisfied John Ruskin, who fondly hoped that Sheffield would become an art centre of the world. It was Ruskin, too, who spoke of the city as "a dark picture in a golden frame", referring to the attractive countryside, with castles and abbeys and green fields around it, and the beauty of Derbyshire on its doorstep.

# VIII

## HULL AND THE HUMBER

It is curious that a county like Yorkshire, with so long a coastline, should have so few ports, and those few so far from the sea. Middlesbrough is several miles from the open sea at Tees mouth. Hull is almost half-way along the river Humber from Spurn Point. And Goole is still further inland along the same river. Whitby, Scarborough and Bridlington had once a passing glory in commerce, but as we have seen they are now holiday resorts and their harbours are little more than local fishing ports. Yet Hull makes up for it all as Britain's third port, measured by its annual Customs value totalling nearly £500 millions. It is the gathering ground of Yorkshire's sea-going trade as the Humber is of Yorkshire's rivers.

Kingston upon Hull—or, as modern usage more economically has it, Hull—is, despite its riverside situation, a salt-sea city where until a few years ago ocean-going ships berthed hard up against the main streets. Its docks came right into the town, or rather the town had grown around them, and although today one of the largest of them has been transformed into a delightful garden-clad square and the newer industrial and residential areas are spreading inland away from the water, a group of busy docks still exists in the midst of the older city. Ships' funnels and the clang of ship-repairers' hammers are still adjacent to office windows and the clicking of typewriters. From the tops of buses you can see the masts of ships arrived from many corners of the world. The Dock Offices and the City Art Gallery are within a stone's throw of each other. And if you are not sure of your direction you soon find that city streets turn into bollarded quays and you will be lost in a maze of congested warehouse-lined alleys where newly unshipped cargoes are being hauled, heaved and hoisted into store. Grey-white seagulls are everywhere—they even whipped up the ornamental goldfish from the ponds in the old Queen's Dock gardens. You may perhaps find yourself acquiring a nautical roll in the seamen's pubs around the pierhead.

Ships and domes are the first and dominant impression of the city itself. What remains of the pre-war Hull—for, like Sheffield, it lost a great deal of its centre from heavy bombing—seems almost entirely to be domed or spired. Before the war a great deal of its architecture was on classical lines, and what has been left of it fits decorously into the new building arising everywhere around the old. Hull is, indeed, a light-hearted and beautiful city compared with the heavier and harder cities of the rest of Yorkshire. There seem to be fountains and flower-beds and green plots at every traffic junction, and sometimes in out-of-the-way corners. Most of the approaches to the city—from the coast, from Holderness and from the Wolds—are tree-lined. And everywhere there is a freshness of atmosphere as if the salt-sea was at the bottom of the road.

The full title of the city tells its story. It was "the king's town" upon the river Hull, at the point where that stream which drains Holderness joins the Humber. Edward I created it as a port as long ago as 1293, and the mouth of the Hull provided berths for ships until nearly five hundred years later when the Queen's Dock was constructed. This was the dock that was filled in and transformed into gardens in the 1930s. Today there are twelve miles of quays, and the docks and tidal water area totals 200 acres. It is a long day's task even to visit the whole reach of the eleven docks along the Humber bank from the St. Andrew's fish dock at one end to the Salt End oil tanks at the other with, in between, grain docks, timber wharves, the Riverside Quay, where perishable cargoes—and passengers—are landed, and the enormous King George Dock, recently extended, where vast transit sheds have been erected to receive goods from ships on one side and load them for distribution on the other, with broad roads everywhere.

Yet Hull is not only a receiving port. It is an ever-open gateway to the world. Yorkshire's products of coal and steel and wool, and a thousand other things besides, pass through these docks to cross the seas to other lands. All the regions we have looked at in this book are linked with the commerce of this port. And the very variety of the cargoes that come in and out of these docks bring strange sights at every turn; curious high straddle trucks like tractors mounted on giant wheels run up and down carrying vast loads of planks between their legs; long chutes stretch across roadways from factories making ice by the ton directly into the holds of trawlers where it is used for storing and preserving fish, and similar chutes suck up grain in hundreds of tons to convey it from the ships to the vast grain silos; a permanent motor-show of cars moves forward from the wharves to ships' decks for export; horse-drawn lorries (an almost forgotten sight elsewhere) transport mountains of bright orange-coloured net bags full of vegetables.

The strangeness is not confined to the docks. As you leave the wharves and the ships you find yourself in Bowl Alley Lane, or the Land of Green Ginger (a very short street), or Blanket Row, or in Whitefriar's or Blackfriar's, or in front of the building of the Brethren of Trinity House, which is an ancient navigation school. All these are links with an older Hull built round the great mansions of wealthy merchant families like the de la Poles who in those days lived and played and cultivated their gardens of green ginger within sight of the ships which made their wealth.

Lying back out of sight of the spires and the domes and the ships of today, along the banks of the river Hull which gave them their start, are the great flour mills, the paint works, the oil-cake factories, the starch and blue works and the confectionery plants of a modern industrial city. And beyond all this are the attractive suburbs stretching along the radial roads of the flat-lands almost to the Wolds. In the midst of the suburbs at Cottingham nestles the growing university, differing from the glass and stone and concrete structures of most newer universities in that its buildings, of warm red brick in garden settings, look like large suburban houses themselves, devoid of academical pretence. They suggest culture as well as learning.

In October each year this solid respectable city goes gay when all the showmen and roundabouts and fair stall-holders of Britain seem to converge into an area of some fourteen acres of land not far from the city centre for a week and a day of merry-go-round. It is the most densely packed fairground in England with every possible variety of entertainment, side-show and mechanical music. Hull Fair has been held since it received its first charter at the end of the thirteenth century. The years have transformed it from a cattle and sheep fair but it has not lost its official status or its popularity in the process. Civic approval of its publicity value for the city runs side by side with an intense local affection for this annual revelry that is handed down from generation to generation. "Hull Fair is not what it was when I was young," says each age in turn, and it may well be said for another six centuries.

Much of the new Hull is expanding into dormitory towns along the north bank of the Humber. There is even some expansion to the south bank. Across the river, when it is not enveloped in a damp haze, you can see the line of Lincolnshire to which a ferry service runs from Hull pier. For long years past there has been talk of a bridge or tunnel to span the river and so save a journey of many miles inland to Goole and back again. But the ferry remains as the only link. The river itself has low shores, many mudbanks and shoals and is not generally picturesque. Even though one remembers it is the great gathering waterway of most of the rivers of Yorkshire it does not, to me, recall high fells, rolling moors, the call of grouse and curlew or little mountain becks. Rather does it suggest the outlet of all those industrial rivers, the Aire, the Calder and the Don which pour their used waters into this grey river just as the products of their towns and cities are distributed through the ports on its bank.

Although this country seems flat and changeless, transformations do occur. Just as Hull was once a great whaling centre and is now a commercial port and the little town of Hedon was an important haven on the river whose harbour is now a grass field, so a once small village like Brough has now a considerable aircraft industry. Goole is still a considerable port, but its importance has declined with the falling off in the demand from abroad for West Riding coal, for the export of which it was built. At one time some three million tons a year were shipped, now it is probably less than half that total. Oddly, Goole is England's most inland port. Fifty miles of muddy river separates it from the sea. Yet memorial tablets in the parish church bear the names of many Goole ships and seamen lost on the high seas. Further inland the town of Howden, with its beautiful Minster, stands rather forlornly as if it had once been busy (as it was) but has now forgotten what it was busy about. Selby, again, with an historic Abbey, a lively market, and a considerable industry in its oil and cake mills, its sugar beet factory and its potato and pea growing farms, appears to recall a past when its river carried a greater traffic and its drab main street (which needs the attention of a Civic Trust) was busy with coaches and horse traffic on the way to and from Hull.

Like so many Yorkshire abbeys, Selby had very humble origins in the middle of the eleventh century as a monastic establishment, but in the next century became one of the most powerful in Europe, with a mitred abbot at its head. The Norman church is still the finest of its kind in the county despite much damage by fire. Incidentally it is the only church I know which contains a memorial to its sexton:

Near this stone lies Archer (John),
Late Sexton (I aver),
Who without tears thirty-four years
Did carcases inter.
But death at last for his works passed
Unto him thus did say,
Leave off thy trade, be not afraid,
But forthwith come away.
Without reply or asking why
The summons he obeyed:
In seventeen hundred and sixty-eight
He resigned his life and spade.

Through all its changes the Humber remains the pulsing artery of Yorkshire without which the county would languish. This is a river which has played a vital part in Yorkshire's history. As the historian of Yorkshire, the late J. S. Fletcher, wrote: "It is not difficult to imagine those early folk of the marshes and the forests stealing down to the edge of the great river by which they dwelt, and looking out across its broad expanse to the greater and unknown waste of waters beyond its mouth. Even of more interest than the thought of their wonder at the vastness of the estuary and the ocean into which it flows, is the thought of the first man who sailed boldly into it out of the North Sea. Who was he and from whence?"

Whatever may be Yorkshire's part in history yet to be written, the Humber will be at once a beginning and an end of the story of the county.

# IX

## YORKSHIRE FOLK

ACCORDING to the Oxford English Dictionary the Domesday Book received its name because, as an old-time writer put it, "it spared no man but judged all men indifferently, as the Lord in that great day will do." So must we try to judge this great county of Yorkshire which is so bewildering in its multiplicity of detail. Behind the hills and the plains, the dales and the rivers, the heavy smoke and harsh sounds of the industrial areas, and the immense variety of the Yorkshire scene, we must look for the soul of the county which is not always obvious on the surface.

In the geographical variations between place and place, in the hilly separation of community from community which is obvious in the mountain dale country but is also present in the industrial dales where one textile town is cut off from its neighbour by steep Pennine spurs, in the barriers which those hills have interposed against "foreigners" down the centuries, in the self-contained conservatism of individual valleys which gives each its own special characteristic, in the preservation of ancient customs—can be found some of the reasons that have helped to create that Yorkshire character which is as distinctive as the countryside itself. The individualism of the Yorkshireman has so far resisted much of the "admass" against which J. B. Priestley, as a spokesman of the county, has so strongly revolted. It is founded on the realism which caused an elderly Yorkshire woman to protest when shown by her granddaughter round a new house complete with all modern amenities: "Nay, lass, there's summat wrong." "What is it, grannie?" "Somebody's bound to have a do with themselves getting a coffin down them stairs." It is founded on that honesty which in the old days of hiring fairs enabled a bargain to be made, and kept, between a farmer and his newly hired horseman or cowman with no more formal agreement than the passing of a "fastening penny" from one to the other. It is founded, too, on that caution which insists that a newcomer to any community should be "summered and wintered and summered again" before being accepted. Mr. Eric Linklater summed it up when he described the stone-built villages of Yorkshire as "the most full-of-character villages in all Britain. They have a four-square solid appearance and the people have the same quality. What they think, they say."

History and tradition, too, have something to do with it, not in any self-conscious "revivals" of ancient custom, but in the acceptance of the old as part of today. The custom of stinting (or allocating sheep rights on common pastures), for example, is still observed in the Dales country. Not long ago I attended a farmers' "herd-letting" in a Craven village at which a shepherd was appointed to watch over the sheep grazing on the near-by fells. These grazing rights, which are sometimes bought and sold separately but which have often "gone with the farm" from time immemorial, are known as "gaits". The owner of so many "gaits" has the right to "walk" and graze that number of sheep on the fell pasture. These sheep he hands over to the care of a shepherd who takes sole responsibility for their well-being. Even the farmer cannot touch his own sheep while they are in the care of the shepherd. The value of the "gaits" in terms of other animals are measured by the "sheep gait". Thus one cow equals four "sheep gaits". One horse is equivalent to eight "sheep gaits". And a mare and her foal are equal to ten "sheep gaits". Thus by a little mental arithmetic each farmer could work out how many of his stock he could put out on the fells to graze and how much he would have to pay the shepherd as his share of the man's wages for the year.

When the matter of "herd-letting" (or shepherd-letting) had been satisfactorily accomplished the meeting turned to decide the dates of "stinting", which in this part of Yorkshire meant the close season on the pastures when the sheep are moved to fresh ground to allow the herbage to grow again. The old calf-bound minute book in which all this was recorded had its first entry dated February 1814, but it is likely that some such ritual had gone on since Saxon times, for the village in which the meeting was held was Austwick, which appeared in the Domesday Survey as *Oustevvic*, derived from the Scandinavian "east dairy-farm". This belief in the antiquity of the custom was strengthened when I discovered that at an earlier period this gathering of farmers used to decide the dates at which hazelnuts could be gathered in the woods, and between what dates stakes for hedging and pea-sticks could be gathered. For this, too, was a feudal right, like that of gathering sticks within reach "by hook or by crook" for fuel, of "pannage", which was the collection of nuts and beech mast for feeding pigs, and of "turbary", which was access to turf for fuel. There are still turbary roads over the hills in parts of Yorkshire.

Church and chapel-going persist in the county not only in the rural areas but in the industrial regions with much of the old fervour that has been lost elsewhere, and out of this has grown that delight in "making music" through choirs and orchestras and communal "sings" which are so much a part of Yorkshire life and which has led to a proliferation of choral societies in each of the Ridings. Oddly, Yorkshire can claim few composers of note and little original music save for a few local tunes like the "Holmfirth Anthem" and that familiar dirge "On Ilkla Moor Baht 'At", but there is strong support for annual events like the singing of *Messiah*—which is a "must" for almost every chapel or group of chapels—and similar oratorios. Even today this traditional music loyalty is untouched by any enthusiasm for "pop" music.

Lastly comes the unextinguishable passion for sport, from horse racing to cricket and from local football to "trotting", which is a feature of most rural sports-meetings. Few cities, towns or villages are without their soccer or rugby team, and the Rugby League game has its home in the county. Thousands of supporters stream each winter Saturday to the big games—and here you will see more traditional cloth caps and mufflers than anywhere else. Minor leagues cover the county and every player is urged on or admonished by his first name or nickname, "Get at 'im, Joe", "Nay, Foxy tha's not laikin' (playing) marbles, think on". Local cricket is still played on the village greens or on pitches where the local sheep act as groundsmen. And it must be admitted that these local "derbys" are often more exciting and full of incident than the county matches, although traditional loyalty still makes it imperative to follow Yorkshire through the ups and downs of the season's matches. Whether the county side still has the "characters" it once had is a debatable point for argument in buses and bars after every match. Hirst and Rhodes are still names reverenced by every cricket lover, but so too are more recent names like Sutcliffe and Hutton and Trueman. Whether we shall hear of new retorts like that directed to a visiting batsman who congratulated a Yorkshire bowler on getting him out first ball—"Good ball that, my man." "Aye I know it was, but it was wasted on thee!"—remains to be seen. There is a goodly store of such cricket lore in every player's bag.

Scattered over the rest of the country and indeed to the far ends of the world are Yorkshire societies who meet to eat native dishes like Yorkshire pudding, York ham and Wensleydale cheese, and to talk about Yorkshire cricket and the virtues of their native county and to reminisce about their days in the Dales or the mill towns or on the coast and their hopes of returning one day to the county's delights. For Yorkshire folk, like Scotsmen, are great travellers and there are few countries and few enterprises in which the county is not represented. Equally, even before these post-war years brought exotic elements from the Mediterranean and the Caribbean lands to work in its mills and factories and public services, there was always a "foreign" element in its industrial parts, and in general Yorkshire has absorbed them with little trouble as it long ago absorbed the Angles, the Saxons, the Jutes, the Danes and the Norsemen to the enrichment of the county as a whole.

And now at the end one realizes how inadequate this portrait of Yorkshire is and how much has been left out. There are still so many stones still lying round waiting to be fitted into the mosaic, so much light and shade still to be portrayed in the image. The painter of a human portrait obtains a truthful likeness by setting down at once more and less than he sees in the subject before him. He cannot paint in every line of hair and curve of skin; the camera can do this more accurately and less satisfactorily. His task is not to convey precise detail but the inner character and quality of his sitter which he does by intuitive inference. What he puts on his canvas suggests more than lines or tones or shapes. His brush strokes portray one effect but indicate another and deeper aspect of the real being. So in topographical portraiture we try to put in both more and less than we see, to convey not only the physical features of the landscape but how those features define the ways of life, the character of the people and the distinctive quality of one area of country against another.

It is the immensity against which we struggle, feeling like Boswell did about another place, that we are "comprehending the whole of human life in all its variety, the contemplation of which is inexhaustible". And this struggle to portray Yorkshire may well continue, in the words of the Hallamshire poet Ebenezer Elliott:

> Till kindred rivers, from the summit grey,
> To distant seas their course in beauty bend,
> And, like the lives of human millions, blend
> Disparted waves in one immensity.

# Index

## A

Airedale, 81, 183
Alum industry, 100
Ampleforth, 115
Appleton le Moor, 121
Appletreewick, 71
Askrigg, 46
Atkinson, Canon J. C., 105
Aysgarth Falls, 47

## B

Bainbridge, 45
Barden, 71
Barnard Castle, 91
Barnoldswick, 82
Barnsley, 186, 187
Beverley, 140
Bilsdale, 103, 113
Bingley Locks, 84
Birkbeck, George, 63
Bolton Castle, 48
Bolton Hall, 49
Bolton Priory, 71
Booth, E. C., 135
Boroughbridge, 167, 168
Boston Spa, 75
Bowes, John, 91
Bowes Museum, 91
Blackmore, R. D., 130
Bradford, 84, 176, 182
Bridlington, 126, 131
Brigflatts, 30
Brimham Rocks, 52
Brontë family, 83, 181
Buckden, 67

Burnsall, 71
Burton Agnes Hall, 149
Burton Constable, 151
Buttertubs, 31
Byland Abbey, 115

## C

Cannon Hall, 188
"Carroll, Lewis", 95, 142
Cartwright, Edward, 176
Castillo, John, 105
Castleford, 86
Castle Howard, 170
Catwick Well Ghost, 145
Cauldron Snout, 89
Cawood, 75
Chippendale, Thomas, 73
Chop Yat, 103
Cliff End, The, 135
Cleveland Hills, 99
Coalfields, 21, 183
Coal Output, 190
Coast, 123
Cobbett, William, 139, 184
Colne Valley, 177, 180
Conisbrough Castle, 156, 187
Costume of Yorkshire, The, 43
Cotterdale, 41
Coverdale, Miles, 94
Cowthorpe Oak, 59
Coxwold, 116
Cricket, 201
Croft, 95
Cromwell, Oliver, 79, 116, 139
Cutlers' Company, 191

### D

Danby, 104
"Danes' Dike", 130
Danish Invasion, 155
Dearne, River, 188
Dentdale, 26
Derwent, River, 122, 169
Dialect, 15, 114
Dickens, Charles, 94, 163, 180
Don, River, 191
Doncaster, 186
Dotheboys Hall, 95
Dove, River, 118
Dowson, R. W., 105
Driffield, 143
Duncombe Park, 117

### E

Earby, 82
*Early Man in North East Yorkshire*, 105
Egglestone Abbey, 93
Elgee, Dr. Frank, 105, 109
Elliott, Ebenezer, 202
Elmet, Kingdom of, 85
Eskdale, 104

### F

Farndale, 111, 120
Fauconberg, Lord, 115
Filey, 129
Fletcher, J. S., 96, 198
Flamborough Head, 130
Folk Dancing, 70
*Forty Years in a Moorland Parish*, 105
Fountains Abbey, 57
*Freemen of the Sea*, 127
Furness Abbey, 114

### G

Garsdale, 23
Gaskell, Mrs., 134
Giggleswick, 76
Gilling Castle, 115

Gisburn, 63, 83
Goathland, 100, 105, 106, 107
Goole, 194, 197
Gordale Scar, 76
Gowthwaite Reservoir, 51
Grassington, 70
Gray, Thomas, 81
Great Ayton, 101
Great North Road, 16, 166
Guisborough, 100
"Gypsey" springs, 143

### H

Halifax, 176, 178
Hardraw Force, 41
Harewood House, 74
Harrogate, 55
Hartley, M., and Ingilby, J., 46
Hawes, 23
Haworth, 83
Hebden Bridge, 87
Hedon, 138
Hellifield, 63, 84
Helmsley, 117
"Herd-letting", 200
High Force, 90
"Hobs", 108, 120
Hodge Beck, 118
Holderness, 136
Holtby, Winifred, 135
Hornsea, 126, 133, 140
Horses and horse-racing, 49, 102
Howardian Hills, 118
Hovingham, 170
Howden, 197
Howitt, William, 27
Huddersfield, 87, 177
Hull, 138, 194
Hull Docks, 195
Hull Fair, 196
Humber, 194
*Humphrey Clinker*, 134
Huntcliff, 128

Huntsman, Benjamin, 191
Hutton, William, 124
Hutton-le-Hole, 121

I

Ilkley, 73
Ingleborough, 19, 20
Iron and Steel Research Association,
    192

J

Jameson, Storm, 135
Jervaulx Abbey, 114
Julian Park, 107

K

Kearton brothers, 33
Keighley, 83, 177, 182
Kettlewell, 68
Kilburn, 116
Kildwick, 83
Kilnsey Crag, 68
Kingsley, Charles, 81
Kingston upon Hull, see Hull
Kirkby Hill Races, 39
Kirkby Malham, 79
Kirkby Moorside, 119
Kirkdale, 109, 118
Kirkham Abbey, 118, 171
Knaresborough, 53
Knitters, 27

L

Land-letting, 67
Lastingham Church, 120
Lead-mining, 34
Leeds, 44, 84, 177, 181
Leyburn, 49
Linskill, Mary, 134
Littondale, 68
Lost villages, 134, 173
Lyke Wake Dirge, 15, 113
Lyke Wake Walk, 112

M

Malhamdale, 75
Malham Cove, 76
Malham Tarn, 77
Malton, 169
Marvell, Andrew, 139
Mary Anerley, 130
Metcalfe family, 47
Middleham, 49, 156
Middlesbrough, 96
Middleton-in-Teesdale, 90
Morecambe Bay, 17
Mortham Tower, 93
Mount Grace Priory, 103
Mowbray, Roger de, 115
Muker, 31, 33

N

National Parks, 111
Newby Hall, 57
Newburgh Priory, 115
Newtondale, 119
Nidderdale, 51
Northallerton, 101, 167
North York Moors, 98

O

Old Byland, 115
Osmotherley, 102
Otley, 73

P

Pack-horse tracks, 61
Pateley Bridge, 52
Pass of Stainmore, 93
Patrington, 138
Peny-ghent, 60
Pickering, town, 121
Pickering, Vale of, 110
Place-names, 44, 66, 78, 121, 138
Plain of York, 165
Pockley, 111
Pocklington, 147

Pontefract, 186
Pontefract Castle, 156
Potholes and caves, 20, 60

R

Railway King (George Hudson), 148,
    160, 161
Raistrick, Dr. A., 31
Ravenscar, 126
Ravenspurn, 133
Rawcliffe, 87
Redcar, 125
Reeth, 35
Rey Cross, 93
Ribblesdale, 59
Riccall, River, 118
Richmond, 35
Rievaulx Abbey, 113
Ripley, 56
Roche Abbey, 187
Rokeby Hall, 93
Romans in Yorkshire, 9, 45, 106, 129,
    152, 172
Roseberry Topping, 104
Rotherham, 190
Rudding Park, 56
Rudston, 9, 149
Ruskin, John, 81
Ryedale, 112, 115, 117

S

Saddleworth, 186
Saltburn, 125, 129
Sawley Abbey, 64, 83
Scarborough, 126, 129, 134
Scott, Sir Walter, 91, 187
Sedberg, 30
Sedgwick, Adam, 29
Selby, 166, 197
Semerwater, 44
Sentimental Journey, The, 116
Seph, River, 103, 113
Settle, 63

Settle–Carlisle railway, 64
Seven, River, 118
Sheffield, 190
Shirley, 181
Shipton, Mother, 53
Sitwell family, 135
Sledmere, 148
Sleights, 106
Smollett, Tobias, 125, 134
South Dalton, 149
Southey, Robert, 27, 94
Spurn, 133
Steel and iron, 190
Sterne, Rev. Laurence, 116
Stokesley, 101, 102
Story of the Pennine Walls, The, 31
Streatlam Castle, 92
Superstitions, 107
Swaledale, 31
Sykes family, 148
Sylvia's Lovers, 134

T

Tadcaster, 75
Teesdale, 89
Thirsk, 102, 167
Thompson, Robert, 117
Thornton-le-Dale, 121
Thorpe, 71
Thorp Arch, 75
Three Peaks, 18, 60
Thwaite, 31, 33
Tickhill Castle, 156, 187
Tontine Inn, 102
Topcliffe-on-Swale, 40
"Tramp's Litany", 179
Trip to Coatham, 124
Tristram Shandy, 116
Turner, J. M. W., 74, 81, 94

U

Upleatham Church, 100
Urra Moor, 99, 103

## W

Wade's Causeway, 107
Wakefield, 26, 186
Walker, Miss Dora M., 127
Walls, building of, 31
Walmsley, Leo, 135
Warter, 147
Wassand Hall, 133
Wensleydale, 41
Wensleydale cheese, 42
Wensley village, 48
Wetherby, 75
Wharfedale, 65
Wharton, Mrs. Margaret, 100
Whitby, 106, 127, 129, 134
White Horse, 117
Wilberforce, William, 147

William the Conqueror's Invasion, 154
Winestead, 139
Withernsea, 126, 140
Wolds villages, 146
Wool Industries Research Association, 181
Wool trade, 174
Wycliffe, John, 94

## Y

Yarm, 95
York, 152
York Minster, 163
York, Plain of, 165
York railways, 161
Yorkshire Character, 198
*Yorkshire Village*, 46